LUCY CALKINS ✦ M. COLLEEN CRUZ

WRITING FICTION: BIG DREAMS, TALL AMBITIONS

This book is dedicated to Beth Neville.

FirstHand
An imprint of Heinemann
A division of Reed Elsevier Inc.
361 Hanover Street
Portsmouth, NH 03801-3912
www.heinemann.com

Offices and agents throughout the world

Photography: Peter Cunningham

Library of Congress Cataloging-in-Publication Data

CIP data on file with the Library of Congress.
ISBN 0-325-00862-0

Printed in the United States of America on acid-free paper
10   09   08   07   06   ML   2   3   4   5

ACKNOWLEDGEMENTS

It was a great joy to work on this book alongside co-author Colleen Cruz. Colleen has taught this unit of study many times more than I, and as the author of the young adult novel Border Crossing and other novels in-progress, she has tremendous resources to draw upon. The book was truly co-authored: we passed it from one of us to the next rather like a ball, with the receiver rereading, rewriting, and then adding on….before calling, "Your turn," and then tossing it back to the other. Sometimes, as we worked on the book or worked on the ideas behind the book in the company of teachers and children, Colleen and I would find ourselves at impasses: novelists across the world write this way, but our children seem to need something else. What a great joy it was to reach these hard parts with Colleen. She is passionate about the work, utterly dedicated to children (and especially to children who need us most), and she is also game for the hard work of thinking through challenges. We both believe the book is better off because we outgrew our own best ideas many times whole in the process of writing.

Sometimes, along the way, we tossed the ball to a third person— Katherine Bomer, and we would like to thank her. Katherine is a close friend of the Project's, a very talented writer, and a teacher who rallies kids to invest themselves with heart and soul in their work. We thank Liz Philips and the students and faculty of PS 321 for being a lab for some of the earliest thinking about ways we can best teach students to write fiction. We thank the 4th grade team at Post Road School in White Plains for their assistance in experimenting with possible modifications to minilessons. We are grateful to the upper grade teachers, staff and students at PS 94, particularly Kirsten Nordstrom, for offering valuable insights. We are also appreciative of Dr. Peter McFarlane and the PS 180 community for their generous support and their willingness to pilot this work in its early stages. We thank especially: Anisha Burke, Carolyn Montalto, Rachel Nall, Amanda Pagan and Jhimy Rodriguez. In the final days, Kathy Doyle, Shannon Rigney and Julia Mooney all contributed to this project, and we thank them.

Colleen and I, together, dedicate this book to someone who is a dear friend: Beth Neville. Beth is the architect of the Project's vast, complex network. She masterminds all of the Project's functions, interlacing the entire structure in ways unfathomable to most of us. Colleen and I are grateful to her.

A note from Colleen Cruz:

As has been the case for many people, Lucy Calkins has been a huge influence on my development as a teacher of literacy. However, almost as important to me, with the completion of this book, I can now say she has influenced my writing life too. Lucy taught me so much about what it means to streamline one's thinking in some spots and flesh it out in others. She taught me the importance of how, just as good fiction builds in an arc, so too should a unit of study. I was consistently amazed at her ability to challenge my hard-won beliefs of how fiction "should" be taught, often leading me to explore unmapped terrain. I am even more appreciative of the way she consistently (and sometimes doggedly) pushed me to challenge her own latest thinking in order for us to come to a consensus. In the end, this book is a decoupage of our work together. The seamlessness of that process is completely Lucy's doing.

WRITING FICTION: BIG DREAMS, TALL AMBITIONS

Welcome to Unit 4

WELCOME TO THE UNIT

WRITING FICTION: BIG DREAMS, TALL AMBITIONS

About This Unit

After students spend a month writing essays, they'll be eager to return to the land of narrative writing, especially if they are finally, at long last, able to write what students want most to write: fiction. By this time, no one will be surprised that the unit begins with learning ways to live like fiction writers, seeing ideas for stories everywhere. At the start of this unit, we let students know that fiction writers get ideas for their stories by paying attention to the moments and issues of their lives. We tell children, "When I was young, I thought fiction writers looked up into the clouds and imagined make-believe stories about castles and puppy dogs. But then I grew up and learned how real fiction writers get their ideas." We let them know that Robert McCloskey got the idea for *Make Way for Ducklings* when he was stopped in Boston traffic while a line of ducks waddled across the street in front of him.

Children collect story ideas in their writer's notebooks, learning to flesh the ideas out a bit so that they contain some of the elements of an effective story. Children learn to take the tiny details and big issues of their lives and speculate on how that could become stories. They might write entries in which they both recount a bit of their lives and then speculate (in writing) on how they could turn this into a story. A child who has recently moved could make up a story about a girl who moved, only this time she could give that girl a companion—a dog? a sister?—the writer wished she'd had. Children can reread their notebooks as well as live their lives collecting possible story ideas. In these entries, children will not actually write their stories; instead they will write plans for how their stories might go.

For a few days, children will collect entries in which they explore ideas that could possibly become fiction stories. As they do so, they will profit from trying story ideas out. A great way for them to do this is by storytelling those ideas to a partner. We teach children some storytelling techniques—for example, the beginning of their stories might sound like the beginning of a famous book or a fairy tale: "Once, not long ago, a little girl named Cissy . . . ." Elevating storytelling a bit helps each youngster bring a storyteller's voice—and an aura of literary language—to his or her own story plans.

Once children have each chosen a seed idea (which will now be called their story idea), it is important for them to develop their ideas. One way fiction writers do this is to develop their main characters, perhaps in notebook entries that never appear in the final story. A fiction writer once said, "Before you can begin writing your story, you need to know your characters so well that you know exactly how much change each one has in her pocket." When children are asked to develop ideas about their characters' traits, most children immediately list external traits, "She has red hair," and so on. We encourage children to also think of a character's internal traits. What is she afraid of? What does she want? The trick is to help children create coherent characters with characteristics that fit together in a way that seems believable. When children use broad generalizations—for example, suggesting the character is a good friend—we ask them to open these terms up, to be much more specific. What are the unique ways in which this character is a good friend? After writers gather entries developing their character, they may dramatize the character, having him perform action in a scene, a fiction writer's word for a Small Moment story.

Finally, it is important to be sure that young fiction writers think especially about a character's wants and needs. Usually a storyline emerges out of the intersection of a character's motivations and the obstacles that get in her way.

As in every unit, we remind children that what they learned once through revision and editing now needs to move forward in the writing process. Not surprisingly, then, the story mountain becomes a tool not for revision but for planning. Children use story mountains to plot their story plans and to revise these, too. We teach children, for example, that sometimes what they expect will be the prelude to their story must actually become back-story so that the actual text can focus on two or three scenes.

When children begin to draft, they rely on their story mountains as road maps. Each item (each dot) on the story mountain is usually designated its own page in a story booklet, and this, plus an emphasis on using skills developed in earlier units and on storytelling rather than summarizing, makes it more likely that children's stories will sound and feel like stories. Since the stories are long, revision needs to begin early; we help students incorporate qualities of good writing as they revise the early sections of their stories. Children incorporate all they learned during the personal narrative units of study into their texts, writing with dialogue and showing rather than summarizing their character's feelings.

We help children see that these story mountains build to a high point and that their main characters struggle harder and harder toward their goals. As they sequence their story, children learn that at the top of their mountain something happens that solves (or begins to solve) the character's problem.

Although the unit is titled Writing Fiction, it is also a unit on rehearsal and revision. Capitalizing on children's zeal for fiction, this unit encourages them to do more of both than they have done before. Although we emphasize the efficiency of revising as we write, once a draft is completed we then emphasize that writers look back on the trail of a story and consider making substantial revisions. Above all, we teach writers to consider the importance of setting in a story. Earlier, when children's dialogue threatened to swamp their story-lines, we taught them to intersperse actions with dialogue, now we highlight the need to ground the entire story (not just the introduction) in a sense of place.

Then, too, children are led to rethink the evolution of their stories. Oftentimes, they approach a fiction story planning for the character to magically receive his or her fondest dream in the form of a solution that flies in out of nowhere like Superman. With help, we show children that in fiction as in life, the solutions we find are generally those that we make, and if there are magic answers to be found, they usually have been there before our eyes all along.

The Plan for the Unit

The "bends in the road" of this unit are these:

- Children collect story ideas, imagining that everyday moments in their lives and entries they gathered previously could be fleshed out to become story ideas. They also gather story ideas by thinking about the stories they wish existed in the world. They select a story idea (as opposed to a seed idea). We channel them towards writing realistic fiction involving just a few characters, and towards stories about characters who resemble the authors, at least in age.

- Once children have selected a story idea, they continue rehearsing for the story they will eventually write. They develop their protagonist, thinking about external and also internal characteristics of that person, trying to create a coherent character. Above all children think about their character's wants and struggles. They may also develop secondary characters.

- Children plot their story on a story mountain, thinking about how to focus on just two or three scenes, narrowing the plotline based on the recognition that this will be a short story not a novel, and tucking some portions of the story into back-story. They revise their plans, taking into account more information about effective stories.

- Children draft and then revise beginnings to their stories, drawing on what they learn from studying published leads.

They write their drafts in story-booklets, with one page of the booklet for each dot on the story mountain. We remind them that front-end revisions are much more efficient than rear-end revisions.

- Children think about how they'll create rising action, making the problems get worse and worse, and continue writing their stories.

- Children revise their writing in significant ways. They reread with various lenses, including looking for "cardboard characters" and thinking about ways to ground their stories in a well-developed setting. Above all, children reconsider the resolution in their stories with encouragement to find the solution within the problem, avoiding the solution that flies in from outside the story.

- Children edit with attention especially to spelling, to making writing sound powerful, and to writing with a variety of sentence types.

GETTING READY

- Anecdote you can tell to describe how fiction writers get their ideas from real life
- Entries from your own writer's notebook that you can use to demonstrate thinking about potential stories
- Several entries from your notebook copied onto chart paper, so children can practice looking for stories
- Several published stories for each child. These will be referenced in Homework. See CD-ROM for suggestions.
- See CD-ROM for resources

IMAGING STORIES FROM ORDINARY MOMENTS

In this session, you'll teach children that writers collect ideas for realistic fictional stories by mining the details of their lives and by rereading their notebooks, spinning likely entries into story ideas.

The long-awaited day has finally arrived. At long last, you'll invite your students to begin writing fiction. This is the genre that most children especially want to write, yet it is one of the more challenging genres that they will experience and you will teach.

Children are born fiction writers. From leaning against the knees of grown-ups, listening to their stories, and absorbing the rhythms of fairy tales, picture books, and novels, they have already learned about pacing and punch lines, about the humor and tragedy of story. They have soaked up the phrasing and structures of story, from the opening invocation "Once upon a time" to the classic signals that something is going to happen—"Suddenly . . . " or "One day . . . ."

In school, children beg to write stories. Sometimes, perhaps out of fear of the runaway stories that go on and on, or out of discomfort over the retold comic book story lines, we've steered them away from this genre. How much wiser to take their energy and passion for fiction, and to channel it with crystal-clear teaching!

Although your children will probably enter this unit expecting it to be altogether different from anything they've experienced, they'll come to see that there is only a thin line between personal narrative writing and realistic fiction. But don't tell them this yet. All year long, they have practiced writing small moments, or scenes; writing with dialogue and action; and crafting tension into their stories. Now they'll join the ranks of short story writers, who know that if they conceive of and revise a plot, develop characters who interact with each other, and follow those characters through trials and tribulations, they can craft short but deeply thoughtful and realistic fictional stories.

In today's minilesson, you'll invite children into the world of fiction writers, showing one way to collect ideas for fictional stories. In the process, you'll help children fall in love with stories.

MINILESSON

Imagining Stories from Ordinary Moments

CONNECTION

Tell a true story about how, during the preceding days, you've savored the children's published work and decided that they're ready for fiction.

"Writers, I took your published essays home last night and sat on my sofa reading them, one after another. One by one, the people in my house called, 'Good night,' turning off most of the lights as they headed to bed, and I sat under a pool of light, reading and enjoying. When I finally finished reading your essays, I realized you have come such a long way as writers! You are ready to write fiction."

Name your teaching point. In this case, tell students that writers get ideas for fiction by paying attention to our lives.

"Today is an important day because we're going to begin collecting ideas for fictional stories in our writer's notebooks, and I want to teach you where writers look to find those ideas. And the most important thing I can teach you is this: We get ideas for fiction, just as we get ideas for personal narratives and essays, by paying attention to the moments and issues in our own lives!"

TEACHING

With an anecdote, tell children that you've come to realize fiction writers get their ideas from real life.

"When I was a little girl, I thought fiction writers looked up into the clouds and *imagined* make-believe stories about castles and puppy dogs."

COACHING

The challenge is to say the expected—to tell children that the texts they just published are beautiful—and yet to do so in ways that are surprising and fresh enough that youngsters don't dismiss our compliments as pap. One solution is to use compelling specifics to name what works in their writing, but we can never do this for every child within the confines of a minilesson. Another solution is to situate compliments into a scene, a narrative, as I have tried to do. I could, alternatively, have described phoning my sister to read aloud bits of their essays, or pinning excerpts from their essays onto my bulletin board. Alternatively, you could use this as an opportunity for children to tell each other about their parents' responses to the essay celebration.

Usually when we tell "I used to think . . . but now I realize" stories, we are trying to persuade kids who identify with the first way of thinking to be brought along to the new thinking.

"But when I grew up, I learned how real fiction writers truly get their ideas. Did you know that E. B. White got the idea for *Charlotte's Web* by lying on a bale of hay in his barn, watching a spider spin her web? The barn animals, the pigs, and the geese were all around, and on the rafters above them all, this little spider delicately wove her tapestry. He probably wrote an entry about that moment in his writer's notebook, and then later, sitting at his desk, he reread his notebook, remembered that moment, and thought, 'I could write a story about that!'"

"Of course, when I say that writers get ideas for writing by paying attention to our own lives, I do not mean that writers just record exactly what happened and call the text fiction. When E. B. White lay on that bale of hay and watched a spider, he did not watch her spell out the words *Some Pig*, and he did not watch her save a runt pig from the butcher."

Suggest that the imagination that matters is one that allows a writer to see story ideas in the grit of everyday life.

"Fiction writers do, however, pay attention to our lives. We cup our hands around tiny true particles of our lives, and we wait. Sometimes, while we wait, the idea for a story grows. And here is my biggest lesson of all. The imagination that *really* matters to fiction writers is this. We—like E. B. White—can find significant stories in something as ordinary as an entry we've written about a spider in the rafters of our barn. We reread an entry or remember that spider—or anything else we have seen or done—and we say, 'Wait a minute. This is giving me an idea for a story . . . Maybe I could write a story about . . . .'"

There are many similar examples. Children may want to know how Patricia MacLachlan got the idea for Cassie Binegar, the story about a little girl who hid under the dinner table, listening to the conversations. Patricia says, "I know that child because I was that child, hiding under the tablecloth in order to watch and listen and become a writer, peering at truths from a safe place." I originally told this story as well as the E. B. White story within this minilesson; you'll find that, like me, you need to resist the impulse to tell everything you know in one minilesson.

Notice that there are lots of ways to create cohesion or unity within a minilesson. In this one, I thread references to imagination, clouds and puppy dogs, E. B. White, and Charlotte's Web throughout the minilesson. That, plus repetition of the teaching point, helps to make the minilesson clear to the students.

Even though Charlotte's Web is not realistic fiction, I use it as an example because it is a story I'm certain my children know (and I suspect your children know this story too!). If you worry that your students could get confused by the aspects of Charlotte's Web which don't fit into the unit's emphasis on realistic fiction, then select another book. You don't want this minilesson to seem as if it is an invitation to write unrealistic stories. You could refer instead to more realistic fiction books such as Cassie Binegar, Fig Pudding, or June Bug—or to a picture book. Be sure to refer to a story that all your students know well.

Implicit in this minilesson is the assumption that children already have some entries to draw upon. These can be entries from much earlier in the year—they needn't have been gathered under the auspices of fiction.

Tell children what to watch for as you demonstrate rereading your notebook for bits that could be seeds for a story.

"Let me show you what I mean. I am going to reread my writer's notebook, looking for an entry that could grow into a whole story. Watch as I read; you'll notice I give each entry a little growing space, a little time to become an idea. I don't just race past entry after entry, saying, 'Nope, nope, nope' as I flick past them."

Looking at a page of my notebook, I read a bit aloud, then looked up, as if savoring what I'd written. Then I read on. This time when I looked up, I pointed at the entry excitedly. "Here's an entry about when we moved to a new town. I wrote it at the start of the year! Before we moved into that new house, I had all these ideas about how everything would look in the new place and I imagined that moving would open new worlds. I could make a whole story out of just this entry, because my hopes for the move were so high, and after we were in the new house, it echoed with awful loneliness. If I write this as a story, I think I will give my character something that helps—a friend, a pet, a cause—anything to ease her aching heart."

ACTIVE ENGAGEMENT
Set children up to practice mining entries for story ideas. Recruit children to help you find more story ideas in your own entries.

"Can you help me continue rereading my notebook and thinking of possible story ideas? On this chart paper, I copied a few more of the entries I've written. Would you and your partner reread them? Remember to reread them slowly, like writers always do when they're looking for story ideas, giving each one a chance to grow. Try to read with a writer's imagination, seeing possibilities in what at first might look pretty ordinary."

> I've been noticing that the neighbor's dog barks and runs at me whenever the boys who live there are in the front yard. When the boys aren't outside, their dog just sits on the porch and stares at me.

> When I was young, no one taught girls how to bat or catch the ball. I was always picked last for teams, and then the captain would put me way out in the outfield. I felt so lonely, and I knew they put me out there because if I had an important role, I would probably make the team lose. Maybe that's when I started to

Today's minilesson presents the concept that we get ideas for fiction from the moments and issues of our lives, then the minilesson channels writers to reread their notebooks, expecting to find ideas that could be developed into stories. The concepts I'm teaching in this minilesson are more complex and multifaceted than those that I conveyed at the start of the year. In this session, I am building on what children already know about writing and writer's notebooks.

Notice that although I haven't yet talked about the fact that characters struggle and change in stories, the examples I cite do already involve characters who change. That is, when I share an idea I have for a fictional story, that idea is fleshed out enough that it contains the broad contours of a story. A story always contains the three Ds: desire plus danger creates drama. My story ideas are good models, though I haven't yet talked about what those models contain.

I could have asked children to reread their own notebooks during the minilesson, looking for story ideas, but I often have children work with a case-in-point that I set up for them. There are several reasons for this. First, I can deliberately steer kids in ways that'll make it likely they'll succeed. For example, the entries I give children to work with in this minilesson contain tension, and therefore children should have success turning them into story ideas. Then, too, if I had asked children to look in their own notebooks for possible story ideas, this would probably take more than three minutes, and I want to keep my minilessons short so they don't cut into children's writing time. Also, children will be looking for story ideas in their own notebooks as the main work once they disperse from the meeting area—I don't want them to complete that work now and be at loose ends during work time. On the other hand, if the children needed extra scaffolding, I might have asked them to start finding story ideas in their own notebooks, as this could have gotten them halfway toward doing the work they'll soon do alone.

become a writer. I had a lot of time to daydream,
standing way out there in the grass with nothing to do
and no one to talk to.

"Turn and talk with your partner. Together, see if you could imagine growing one of
these into a story." I listened in on the conversations.

Help one child demonstrate how she mined your entries for possible story ideas.

After two minutes, I convened the group. "Marissa, I'm excited by the story you
imagined. You took the entry about the girl playing softball and grew it into a possible story
idea. Will you share the story idea with us?"

Marissa said, "I picked the softball one because the same thing happens to me. Maybe
the girl could get catching lessons and one day catch the ball and win the game!"

Joshua, Marissa's partner, chimed in: "Don't stop there. She could teach all the other
girls how to catch and bat!"

"Wow! I love that your story is reversing the discrimination that led me to write the
entry in the first place. That's the way that we, as writers, take the true stuff of our lives, even
if it's hard or sad, and *imagine* that things could go differently."

LINK
**Repeat the teaching point, celebrating that fiction writers find story ideas in the
moments and issues of their lives. Send children off to do this.**

"Writers, I have always known that fiction writers need imagination to write. But I used
to think that most fiction writers found ideas by looking up into the clouds and imagining
stories about castles or puppy dogs. What you have shown me today is that fiction writers *do*
have imaginations. We look into everyday moments of our lives—into moments as ordinary
as watching a spider make a web or a girl in the outfield—and we see possibilities."

"Today and for the rest of your lives, whenever you want to write fiction, reread your
writer's notebook with a fiction writer's eyes. Remember to reread and then wait, and
imagine. It's easy to just flick away the idea of a story about a spider, thinking, 'That's not
important.' Don't do that. Have the imagination to say, 'Wait. There might be a story here.'
And when you get a story idea, mark it with a sticky note, and then write a new entry based
on your original entry, putting the idea it sparks onto your page."

*These are the entries from my notebook, written on chart
paper. You'll want to use your own. You may notice that each
of my entries is very different. One is an observation; the other
has more of a narrative feel. I try to be sure my examples open
up possibilities for kids.*

*When children talk to their partners and I listen in, I get a
chance to decide which child's suggestion will be especially
helpful to the class. It's not an accident that Marissa has
imagined a very realistic story, one which features a child who
is her age and which revolves around an everyday life issue.*

*When we are teaching anything, we are teaching values. Be
conscious of the messages that are tucked into your teaching
and make sure you are empowering your children to imagine
alternatives.*

*In the link, I generally revisit the teaching point. Here I also repeat
a few tiny details from the very start of my minilesson. Writers of
all sorts often find that one powerful way to end a text is to
return to some of the details with which we began the text.*

*Because this is the first minilesson in a new unit, I want children
to be inspired. I want them to believe, as I do, that there is
something majestic about finding significance in the small
moments of our lives and writing these as stories. I also want to
spell out very concrete, doable strategies they can use today.*

WRITING AND CONFERRING

Using Your Imagination to See Promise and Power in Children's Work

In today's minilesson, I have told children that writers need the imagination to look into everyday moments and see possibilities. I have urged young writers to resist flicking away the little bits of life—observations of a spider making her web—and to instead get used to saying, "Wait. There may be a story here."

Of course, this advice is even more important for *teachers* than for writers. Our students will bring us entries and story ideas. We need the imagination to look at what they bring us, and to see that these entries could become something grand. Even if we can't quite see what the writer values in his or her entry, it is important to remember that almost any topic can become a spectacular piece of writing. E. B. White, after all, wrote an essay on warts! The secret to finding something of value in all writing is to slow down, to listen to what the writer is saying, and to be moved by the details of the subject. Teachers, therefore, would be wise to be pushovers. "What a topic!" we say. "This is going to be some story! You definitely need to write the details because this is amazing stuff."

> MID-WORKSHOP TEACHING POINT *Using Notebooks to Plan Possible Stories*   "Writers, can I stop you? I love the energy in this room. It feels like a fiction factory here! Marco just asked a really important question. He asked, 'How do fiction writers put ideas for stories on the page? Is it a list?' He wasn't sure which words we actually write. So I thought it might help if I shared what I wrote in my notebook when I thought about turning my entry about moving to a new place into a story." Opening my notebook, I read:
>
> Maybe I could write a story about moving because that was a huge part of my life. I want the story to be for older kids, so I could make the main character be about 12. Yes! Cause friends really matter to kids of that age. This girl (boy?) finally finds the perfect best friend, and then she has to move to a whole different state where they call middle school "junior high," and the kids seem tough. Maybe she starts acting tough too, even before she moves away.
>
> *continued on next page*

Beccah, for example, reread an entry she had written back in November, describing her observations one day during recess. She noticed the faded yellow paint lines that marked the playground boundaries, two third-grade boys who tempted nearby pigeons with cracker crumbs, the way one recess monitor clasped her hands firmly behind her whenever she walked around the playground, and the way one fifth-grade girl rolled her eyes once the girl she had been talking to turned away. At first, Beccah couldn't figure out why she was drawn to this entry; she thought she had just collected a series of random observations.

"Hi, Beccah," I said, "I noticed you keep flipping back to this page and reading this entry. There must be something rich there that you can write about."

"I don't know," she mumbled, shrugging and sighing. "I like the way I wrote these descriptions, but I don't know if there's a story idea here."

"Hmm," I said, crouching beside her to read her entry along with her. "Well you certainly did write vivid descriptions! Your observations come to life right off the page. And remember that one way we can find ideas in stories is to think about what moves us. Something here, other than your descriptions, must have moved you enough to make you keep coming back to this entry. Maybe that's where the story idea lies."

Beccah reread her entry, twisting her lips in thought. After a few seconds, she sat straight up, pointed to a line in her entry, and announced, "Well, I thought the way that girl rolled her eyes was funny."

"I wonder why she did that?" I mused.

"I know! I thought they were friends. So maybe I could write about some girls who pretend to be friends, but really don't like each other."

"Why don't they like each other?"

I could tell Beccah had latched on to something because she began rattling off a list of possibilities: "Maybe they used to be friends, but one copied the other's homework and got her in trouble. Or maybe one of them didn't invite the other to her birthday party. Or, I know! Maybe someone else was making fun of the first one and the other one thought it was funny, so now they're not friends anymore."

"This would make a great story, Beccah. I can't wait to find out how it develops," I replied. Before I could finish that sentence, though, Beccah had already taken up her pen again. She turned to a fresh page in her notebook and started writing out her story idea.

> continued from previous page
>
> "Do you see how I began with some of the 'true stuff' from my entry about when I moved as a child, but then I started to imagine layers that would turn it into a juicy fiction story? And do you see how I am not actually writing *the story* in my notebook now; instead I'm thinking, planning, on the page? I even asked myself questions in the entry, questions like whether the character should be a boy or a girl."
>
> "Would you reread your notebook, take an entry you particularly like, and try to write that as story idea in a similar way? Make your entry sound as if you are thinking on the page. Write with phrases such as *I'm thinking I might* or *later I could tell about*. And write five or six sentences about that one story idea. Then, of course, skip a line, and do similar work for another story idea. You'll probably do this for about five story ideas today."

Some students, like Beccah, will become enthusiastic about the opportunity to write fiction and they'll be eager to get started. As we coach these students, it is reasonable to keep in mind some broad parameters for the stories we expect children will end up writing. Our expectation is they will write short stories, not novels. In very short stories, writers can usually handle only two main scenes. This means that if the story involves a sequence of nine major events, before the writer even sets to work, he or she will probably need to zoom in on the two or possibly three events that can then be conveyed in detail. Usually, one of these main actions (scenes) will represent a point of conflict or a turning point or a moment of change. Then, too, when writing a short story, authors usually decide to develop two (and conceivably three) characters in detail, rather than simply mentioning a whole host of people. If the child imagines a story about a girl and her parents, you may suggest that actually the story could focus on just one parent.

Keep in mind that when children write fiction, they turn first to the models that exist in their immediate, daily environment. So you might notice that their characters and plotlines resemble those they find in comic books, video games, television sitcoms and melodramas. These texts are not inherently bad, but their plotlines are difficult to write well without many years of practice.

As you listen to and read these early attempts toward story ideas, try to return to lessons from the units on personal narrative and essay writing. Remind children that over and over again, they've grown grand and beautiful ideas simply from attending to the details of their lives.

Steer children firmly toward generating ideas for realistic fiction and toward writing about subjects on which the child is an authority. Recently, a third grade teacher said to one child, "You need to know your character well, so I'd suggest you write about someone who is roughly your own age." The child said, "But I instant-message my twenty-five-year-old cousin all the time so I know all about being twenty-five." The teacher responded, "No, you know all about being nine and IM-ing someone who is twenty-five and that's different!" Celebrate also the power of making the ordinary extraordinary. Young people need to know that powerful drama exists in the details of growing up; there are stories hiding in their memories of finding a best friend, losing a beloved pet, or making a birthday gift.

Elexa

Elexa is a 11 year old girl that wants to be the head cheer leader, but her best friend Lexie also wants to, so will she do it in the cost of her friendship. She has notieed that the boy that was following her around [Max] is now following Lexie, what will happen next

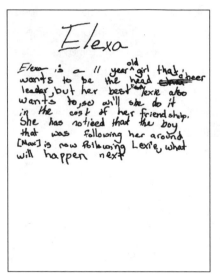

Fig. I-1 Deveonna's story idea

Story: Harrison's parents are getting divorced, his mom is dating a construction worker who only talks about jack hammers. his dad is in England. In the midst of all this, Harrison is starring in a play that is the school's biggest event. Can Harrison juggle it all?

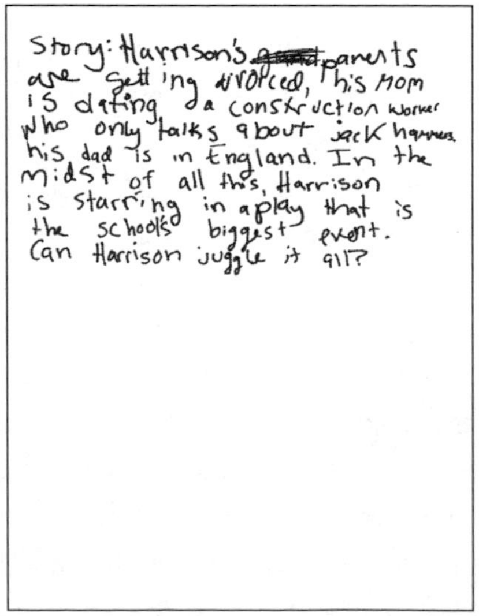

Fig. I-2 Ari's story idea

SHARE

Mining for Gold: Finding Nuggets of Stories

Offer some examples of the kinds of stories children are finding in their notebook entries. Read a story idea entry or two.

"Writers, I love seeing your notebooks filled with sticky notes that say, 'Here's a good story idea!' And I love, even more, seeing that you've each developed *old* entries into *new* story ideas by thinking on the page about what you could write about!"

"Remember Naomi Nye's poem 'Valentine for Ernest Mann,' in which she suggested that poems hide? Well, Lisa has found four places where she thinks *stories* hide. One is an entry about sitting in the park watching a bird scare another bird away from some crackers on the ground. Another is an entry about that big fight at recess a few weeks ago—remember? And this is an entry about getting Rollerblades™ for her birthday. What Lisa has already done—and what each of you needs to do—is this: Reread the story ideas you have written and star the ones that you especially like."

"Sofiya reread entries from the start of the year and several of them gave her ideas for stories she could write. She put a sticky note on an entry she wrote early in the year about the day the Nature Center woman brought a snake to our classroom. She'd been so scared to touch that snake! So she took her fear and gave it to a character. Listen to her story idea." *[Fig. I-3]*

Titles:

Elizabeth Touched a Snake!

Should I Touch the Snake or Not?

Elizabeth was a small first-grade girl. She lived with her parents. Elizabeth is afraid of snakes. The reason is because she was once bitten by a snake herself. Not even once, a few times.

Then one day her class went on a trip.

Once home, Elizabeth told her parents all about the trip. The animals, the lady, the outside lunch they had, and how Ronald got stung by a bee. She saved the best for last. When Elizabeth talked about the snake she said everything. How the snake felt, how it stared at her, its skin, everything! After she said everything about the snake, her parents asked her if she was still afraid of them. She said yes, but tame ones are okay.

Notice here that I have purposely named drastically different topics: receiving a birthday gift and seeing a fight on the playground. You will want to fill the room with a wide variety of topics that offer alternatives to themes from the latest hit movies or video games—ideas that are already in the air since they are in popular culture. We can help students find stories in places where they might never have thought to look.

> Titles:
> Elizabeth Touched a Snake!
> Should I Touch the Snake or Not?
>
> Elizabeth was a small first grade
> girl. She lived with her parents. Elizabeth
> is afraid of snakes. The reason is
> because she was once bitten by a
> snake herself. Not even once, a few
> times.
> Then one day her class went on
> a trip.
>
> Once home, Elizabeth told her parents
> all about the trip. The animals, the
> lady, the outside lunch they had,
> and how Ronald got stung by a bee.
> She saved the best for last. When
> Elizabeth talked about the snake she
> said everything. How the snake felt, how
> it stared at her, its skin, everything!
> After she said everything about
> the snake her parents asked her
> she was still afraid of them. she said
> yes, but tame ones are okay

Fig. I-3 Sofiya turns a personal narrative entry into a story idea.

"Sofiya also noticed that in an entry from the start of the year, she'd mentioned a stuffed animal that was especially important to her, a German shepherd named Esther. She started thinking about maybe writing a story about that stuffed animal. So she wrote an entry about Esther." *[Fig. I-4]*

> I have a lot of stuffed animals. My most, most favorite is the German shepard dog. I named her Esther, after myself. Esther is my middle and Hebrew name. When I used to play with her, I thought of Esther as a heroine. She was very brave.
>
> Whenever I look at Esther, I get courage. To me, she's a real dog. Once, when I was falling asleep, it felt like I was falling. It was the second or third time that I had that feeling. I took Esther, held her close, and fell asleep.
>
> Since the day that I had to sleep with Esther, I didn't have the falling feeling anymore. I knew the reason: Esther had given me courage.

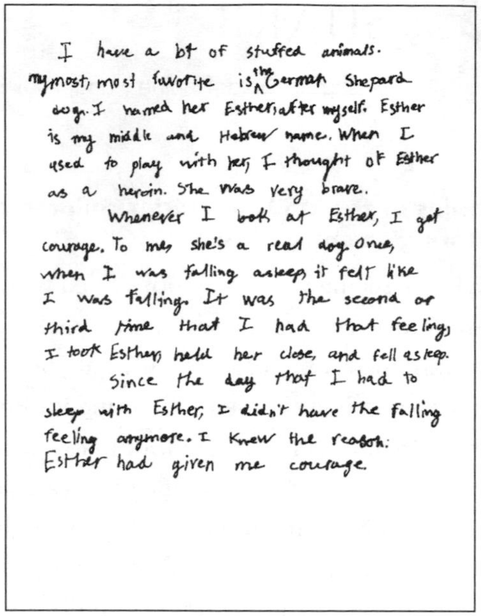
I have a lot of stuffed animals. my most, most favorite is the German Shepard dog. I named her Esther, after myself. Esther is my middle and Hebrew name. When I used to play with her, I thought of Esther as a heroin. She was very brave.
Whenever I look at Esther, I get courage. To me, she's a real dog. Once, when I was falling asleep it felt like I was falling. It was the second or third time that I had that feeling, I took Esther, held her close, and fell asleep.
Since the day that I had to sleep with Esther, I didn't have the falling feeling anymore. I knew the reason: Esther had given me courage.

Fig. I-4 Sofiya's entry

"And finally, she put sticky notes on entries about her gymnastics work because it gave her the idea she could write a story about a girl who enters a gymnastics tournament." *[Fig. I-5]*

> Every week I go to gymnastics. I go twice a week; for two hours each day. My coach's name is Mila. She's Russian and I feel extremely comfortable with her. I've been going there for four years; this is my fifth.
>
> On the days that I go to gymnastics, I do my homework extra fast. My two-hour lesson begins at six, so I have to be ready by five o'clock. I have less than two hours to do my homework, eat lunch, change, and pack.

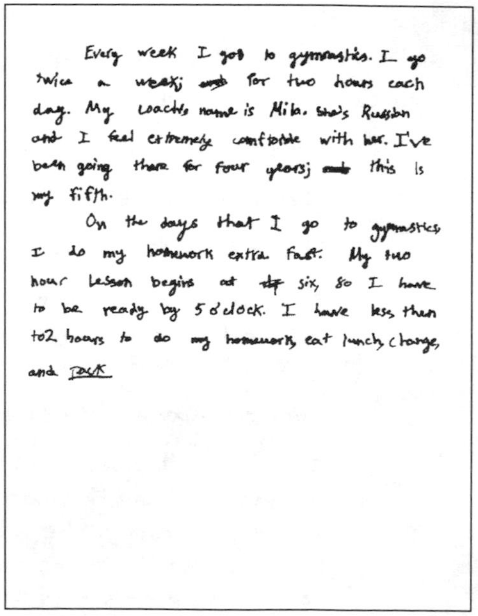
Every week I got to gymnastics. I go twice a week; for two hours each day. My coach's name is Mila. She's Russian and I feel extremely comftorble with her. I've been going there for four years; this is my fifth.
On the days that I go to gymnastics I do my homework extra fast. My two hour lesson begins at six, so I have to be ready by 5 o'clock. I have less than to2 hours to do my homework, eat lunch, change, and pack.

Fig. I-5 Sofiya's entry

Encourage children to listen to each other's story ideas with excitement and appreciation.

"So now, when Sofiya meets with her partner, she'll read this story idea (and others) aloud and she and her partner will talk together. And I hope that her partner will be appreciative and excited about Sofiya's idea—story ideas will flow more quickly in this room if the whole place is washed in a spirit of enthusiasm and appreciation. Let's all meet with our partners, then, and remember to be appreciative, responsive listeners."

Immersing Ourselves in the Sort of Text We Hope to Write You already know that when a writer wants to make a particular kind of text, we read texts that resemble the text we want to write. You are already reading fiction. My question is this: Is the book you are already reading a great model of what you'll be writing?

I ask this question because my hunch is that you may find *parts* of your novel that take your breath away, and make you think, "Ohh! If I could only write like that!" Mark those places. For example, I think there are chapters in *Because of Winn-Dixie* (a book we've not only read but practically memorized!) that resemble the fiction stories we're aiming to write. So tonight, look at the chapter-book you are in the midst of reading and notice sections of it which could be great models for your own fiction writing—and mark those sections, reread those sections, jot observations on those sections.

But mostly, you need to remember you will not be writing a novel. You won't be writing a three-hundred-page book! You will instead write a short story. So it is important for you to read short stories and picture books throughout this month. For homework tonight, would you choose one of the short stories which I've enclosed? Study it, and look at two things especially. First, let the short story help you answer the question: How do these kinds of texts tend to go? Write about that in your notebook. And second, would you think about how the story you read may have grown from the writer's life? What story idea might the writer have recorded in *her* writer's notebook? Then look at the story ideas you wrote in school today, and revise one of them in the wake of what you have just read.

TAILORING YOUR TEACHING

If you'd like to use an alternative opening to this minilesson . . . you could read aloud Marc Brown's very short picture book, *Arthur Writes a Story*. In this book the main character—Arthur—turns a bit of his life into a story. But then, Arthur feels pressured to instead write a splashy, imaginative, wild tale. In the end, he returns to the story that was grounded in his life, thereby conveying a lesson that could be an important one for your children.

If children are experiencing this lesson for a second or third year . . . after acknowledging that children already have strategies for generating ideas for stories, you may want to invite children to revisit published fiction they know well, speculating on the life work that led to those texts. Remind children that books don't come from Barnes and Noble; books instead come from writers. Say, "I wonder what this author collected in her notebook that allowed her to grow this story idea." Speculate, "I wonder whether she got this idea when she was sitting at her desk, or if it came to her when she was grocery shopping, or parking at the

You need to send home two short stories. See the Bibliography on the CD-ROM for suggestions.

Early in the year, you'll recall that the homework mostly asked children to live writerly lives. The homework enriched children's experiences, but it wasn't an essential part of a unit of study. By this time in the year, I expect that your children will make time for writing homework and therefore some of the homework is critical to the unit.

mall?" Then help your children think about how they can live the sort of lives that will help them generate ideas for stories. Ask them to think about how they will use their writers' notebooks differently, now that they are generating ideas for fiction. Convene the class around a discussion of homework. Now that they are writing fiction stories, maybe they want to write their own assignment ideas for homework? Use this unit as an invitation to help students author writerly lives.

If children are experiencing this lesson for a second or third year . . . be sure to acknowledge that children already have strategies for finding the stories that hide in the nooks and crannies of their lives. To talk in a new way about the process of finding story ideas in one's own life, you may want to remind children that just as a seamstress can look at a bolt of cloth and imagine it becoming a vest or a gown, a fiction writer can look at the raw material of life and think, "What kind of story might I make out of this?" Our response to such a question draws on all we know about stories. For example, because we know characters in stories have motivations that energize the story, we look at bits of life and think, "If I were to turn this into a story, who might the main character be? What might this person want? Hope for? Struggle with?"

COLLABORATING WITH COLLEAGUES

My sons and I have always loved September because it is a time for new beginnings. We make a very big deal out of the shopping trip to buy school supplies. We deliberate over a new form of datebook or a set of plastic drawers; each purchase contains all our resolve to do more, to be better, to outgrow ourselves, to reach new heights.

I hope that the start of a new unit of study contains a similar magic for you and your colleagues. Let a new unit feel like a New Year's celebration, and mark the occasion not just with an aura of celebration, but also with opportunities for reflection, looking backward as well as forward. Above all, I encourage you to take the great risk of talking about your own collaborations with each other. Have you and your colleagues found ways to support each other as you teach writing? Perhaps before embarking on this very ambitious unit of study, you could talk about the nature of your collaborations, and address issues that are sure to be there.

Roland Barth, author of *Improving Schools from Within*, points out that in every school, there are "unmentionables"—topics that are talked about in the parking lot or the bathroom or at home with one's spouse or partner, but that are not addressed in the light of day. These are the elephants in the room. Everyone knows they are there, and everyone pretends not to see them. Barth suggests that the more unmentionables one finds in a school, the more toxic that school is for those who live there. And in most schools, the greatest unmentionables of all are the relationships that exist among teachers. Talk about your relationships with each other.

What aspects of your collaboration have gone well and deserve to be built upon? What aspects of your collaboration need to be repaired?

It is easy, as teachers, to devote ourselves entirely to the challenge of helping our children learn well, but the truth is that the most important way to nurture our children's learning is to nurture our own learning. And this means talking candidly with colleagues.

I've been lucky enough to work with a leadership coach who gave me some advice regarding these "clearing the air" meetings. She suggested my colleagues and I begin such a session by agreeing upon an agenda, one that includes some time for frank conversation about what has and hasn't gone well. She suggests the time be limited—perhaps ten or twenty minutes for that conversation. Then, she advises, the conversation needs to turn toward these questions: What do we as a group want for our time together in the end? What positive steps forward can we take right now toward these goals?

As a result of this conversation, you and your colleagues may decide that reconstituting the group would be helpful. Sometimes a study group can tap into a fresh energy source by assembling a different combination of people. If you've been studying with grade-level colleagues, you might consider creating a cross-grade study group. On the other hand, you may decide the grade-level group would be more efficient if it subdivides into partnerships. Or perhaps you haven't actually been meeting, and you resolve to start doing so now.

You may want to imagine ways to give yourselves more time for more and deeper collaboration. In many schools, it is not terribly difficult for children from one grade level to have an extended playground time at the start or end of one particular day each week. For example, on Wednesday mornings, third graders might stay on the playground for an extra half-hour; if their teachers agree to come half an hour early on Wednesday, and to also meet while children are in extended recess, those two half-hours could combine to provide a nice block of time each week. Similarly, in some schools, the music teacher might be willing to convene all children at a particular grade level for an hour-long chorus period, again creating time for a study group.

Then, too, most study groups become infinitely more powerful if the group occasionally has a very long stretch of time together. Perhaps your principal would be willing to forgo the faculty meeting one month, allowing that time to be devoted to study groups? Perhaps teachers could be paid per session to convene on a Saturday? I've found that in every school, there are ways to tweak the schedule so that a group of teachers can gather together as a study group. The challenge is to be imaginative and resourceful.

The other thing I want you to remember is that the culture of a school is amenable to change—and a single teacher can make an unbelievable difference. Teachers often say to me, "In my school, everyone keeps to themselves. We don't plan together—my school isn't like that." Teachers say this as if the professional culture of a school is set in stone and as if their decisions and actions have no bearing on that culture. This is far from true!

Take it upon yourself to be an active agent. Rally yourself to have big hopes, and to make those dreams come true. The questions I suggested earlier aren't just for the other guy—they are for you!

- What do you want the learning culture in your school to be like? What are your best hopes for your school?

- What positive steps could you take today toward making those hopes into realities?

- What's getting in the way of you taking those steps and how can you address those issues?

This unit is titled *Writing Fiction: Big Dreams, Tall Ambitions* because the challenge of writing fiction can rally children's energies, tapping an unbelievable source of power. Let the unit do the same for you and your colleagues.

IMAGINING STORIES WE WISH EXISTED IN THE WORLD

Today's session will help your students take the risk of writing stories that are deeply significant and personal. This can be a challenge. When we first invite children to write fictional stories, it can be as if we've opened Pandora's box. Suddenly, from all corners of the room, one finds children planning to write stories about people who win the lottery, fly into outer space, escape from kidnappers, and star on Broadway.

You'll try to bring children back to earth by emphasizing that they are writing realistic fiction and by spotlighting stories which revolve around everyday life events. But your goal is not only to encourage children to write stories about the hopes and heartbreaks of everyday life, your goal is also to show children that fiction can be a way to explore and to write about the truest and deepest parts of ourselves. Although you do not address this directly, there is no question that today's session helps children to write stories which are often more personal and more real than those they wrote during Raising the Quality of Narrative Writing *unit of study. Fiction can give children a cloak of invisibility, allowing them to travel fearlessly into areas of vulnerability.*

Specifically, you will teach children that fiction writers sometimes get ideas for stories by thinking about the stories we wish existed in the world. You can tuck in tips about how writers go from an image to a story idea, imbue ordinary details with significance, and live with notebooks always open, ready to record everything that catches our attention.

IN THIS SESSION, YOU'LL TELL STUDENTS THAT WHEN THEY SIT DOWN TO WRITE FICTION, THEY MIGHT GET IDEAS FOR STORIES BY IMAGINING THE BOOKS THEY WISH EXISTED IN THE WORLD. YOU CAN ALSO TEACH THEM THAT FICTION WRITERS GET IDEAS FOR STORIES BY THINKING ABOUT ISSUES IN OUR LIVES.

GETTING READY

- Example of a student who found a story idea from her own life
- Your own story idea for a book you wish existed
- Chart paper with the start of a list: How to Find Ideas for Fiction
- Your own writer's notebook or other demonstration text to use during conferring
- *The Three Billy Goats Gruff* or other fairy tale students know well
- See CD-ROM for resources

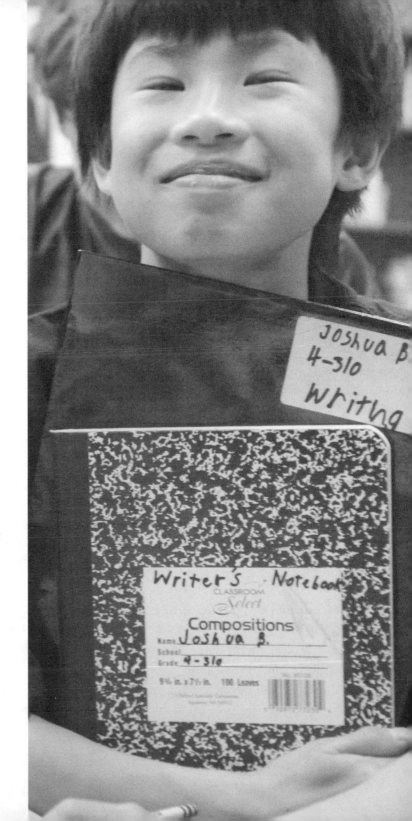

MINILESSON

Imagining Stories We Wish Existed in the World

CONNECTION

Tell a story about a child who grasped that writers often find story ideas in the details of our lives.

"During the previous share session, I heard you all telling each other story ideas that sounded like they could be written into real library books, sitting on our shelves. And this morning, as you came in, many of you told me that when you read a short story last night, the text gave you ideas for stories that *you* could write."

"At home last night, Rashann wrote a story idea that was sparked by an entry in which she'd written about just sitting on her porch, watching a squirrel crack and eat a nut. The squirrel was sitting inside a place where two branches formed a *V*; it sat right in the bottom of the *V*, all cozy and safe. Rashann watched the squirrel travel all over the tree until it found just that special, protected spot, and when she reread the story idea, she realized she could write a story about a kid watching that squirrel, a kid who doesn't have a home and is also trying to find a cozy spot, a safe spot, like the space at the bottom of a *V*. Rashann thought maybe the story would start with the girl watching that squirrel search for a nook. Inspired, the girl decides to find *herself* a similarly safe spot."

"Do you notice that Rashann's story idea began with her looking at something so tiny and ordinary? Her work reminds me of the lesson we learned yesterday when we saw that E. B. White got the idea for *Charlotte's Web* from something as ordinary as a spider, at work on her web."

Name your teaching point. In this case, teach children that writers also get ideas for fiction by thinking of books we wish existed in the world.

"Today, I want to teach you that writers collect ideas for stories not only by finding bits of life or entries that could grow into whole stories, but also by paying attention to the stories *we wish existed* in the world. Sometimes we get ideas for stories by thinking, 'How can I write a story for people like me, so we can see ourselves in books?'"

COACHING

This minilesson lays out the great work one child has done. The child's work illustrates the previous session's teaching, but describing what Rashann did also makes this one child famous to others, and this is terribly important. Many people go through life feeling invisible; by telling just this tiny story about Rashann's writing, Colleen gives Rashann a voice and shares a model of good work with the class. By likening her to E. B. White, Colleen elevates Rashann as a writer.

Over and over, you'll see that when Colleen and I tell children about a story idea, the idea is fleshed out. In this example, the story idea encompasses several scenes, and it conveys the main character's desires and struggles. Notice that the plot line in the story idea we share is not a long one. The children will write short stories not novels!

For many children, today's minilesson, about finding stories they wish they could read, involves revealing some of those injustices—revealing, perhaps, that there are too few stories of females acting powerfully in the world, or too few stories with immigrant children as main characters.

TEACHING

Point out that we each hope to find ourselves in the pages of books.

"Many times when any one of us looks through the library shelves for a book, we are looking to find ourselves in a story. I may find myself wanting a book about a kid like me who is afraid of the dark, or a book about a kid who is usually the last one picked for sports because she's not any good at them or a kid whose mother said, 'Every night before bed, you have to tip your head down and brush your hair one hundred strokes.'"

"Maybe one of you searches library shelves for a kid who lives with his grandma or a kid who likes to draw cartoon cats and dreams of having a cartoon strip in the Sunday paper. If you want to find yourself in a book on the library shelves and no book seems to tell the story that you want told, then you might decide it is important to put your truth onto the page in your own story."

Demonstrate by creating a story idea out of your longing to see books you'd like to read—in this case, books that contain people like you.

"Let me show you how I use this strategy to come up with a story idea," Colleen said. "First of all, I'm thinking about the books I want to read. For one thing, I wish there were more books about people like me who are half Mexican, kids whose fathers are Mexican and whose mothers aren't. *And* who are afraid of the dark. So in my notebook, I'll write down my story idea. I don't just write the big outline of my story—girl with Mexican dad and American mom. I want to put the stuff about a Mexican father together with true little details, like the part about being afraid of the dark and wanting a night-light. Those had been separate items on my list—the girl who is half Mexican, the girl who is afraid of the night—but in a story plan, I often combine things that were once separate. Watch."

Then Colleen wrote,

> A girl who is half Mexican lives with both her parents, but she thinks her father works too much. She wishes her father were around more because when he's home, she isn't so afraid of the dark. But his job keeps him far away so the girl usually sleeps with the light on to make her feel less alone in the night.

Notice the contribution that details make to this minilesson. The details act like pictures, and a picture is worth a thousand words. Notice, too, that when we want to speak or write with specifics, this generally means that we use more words. Children are apt to describe characters with generic terms, saying, for example, "the girl who loves soccer." How much more effective it is to use more words, as Colleen has done.

It is worth noticing that this is a unit on fiction, and the message is that we can develop ideas for fictional stories if we try to put the truth on the page. Donald Murray once helped me to write fiction by suggesting I write the Truth with a capital T, but not necessarily the exactly true story. "Change things around so that you convey the Truth of your experience," he said to me.

Naomi Nye, the poet and novelist, once said that a teacher told her when she was in school that "the things that cause you friction are the things from which you might make art." Notice that Colleen isn't shying away from the things that cause her friction.

In an earlier book in this series, I mentioned that I imagine the first few minilessons from all of the books constituting a giant course in keeping writer's notebooks. Earlier in the year, the entries your children wrote in their notebooks probably tended to be personal narratives, and most were written out in full. During the essay unit, the entries your children collected may have been observations, lists of questions or musings. During that unit, they also used the notebook as a place to draft and revise outlines boxes and bullets. Colleen and I are now hoping to let children know that writers also use notebooks as a place to mull over possible story ideas.

Debrief. Point out that you also invented a character who has desires and difficulties.

"Do you see, writers, that when writing my story idea, I didn't just say, 'I wish there were books on kids who are half Mexican'? I actually jotted a few sentences about how such a story might go. And specifically, I thought about what the character might want, and what she might struggle for. Characters in all stories have big longings."

"What I want to tell you is this: When you are collecting ideas for stories in your writer's notebook, you get ideas not only from rereading old entries, but you also get ideas for stories from thinking about books *you wish existed* in the world. Today you can use either of these ways to grow story ideas."

ACTIVE ENGAGEMENT
Set children up to try turning a wish for a certain kind of book into a story idea.

"So let's try it. Pretend that you think to yourself, 'I wish there were books about kids like me who aren't that good at sports.' Remember that to make that wish into a story idea, you need to invent some details. You can do so by asking questions of your story idea. Why isn't the kid in the story good at sports? Which sports? What has happened lately which shows these struggles?"

Ask children to turn and talk about the character traits and the struggles the character in the exemplar-story might encounter.

"Tell your partner how you could turn this into a story idea. Remember, think about the character, his or her character traits, the character's very particular struggle, about what he or she wants, and about what the character does."

In any unit of study, it is important to decide on the qualities of good writing that you want to highlight, and then you need to be sure that you refer to those qualities at many junctions in the unit. Colleen and I want children to understand story structure, and for this reason when she shows how she's devised a story idea by thinking of the books she wishes existed in the world, Colleen mentions a tip which for today is a subordinate one—the fact that her character has motivations and struggles. This will be the focus of a later minilesson.

The main point here is to help children come up with story ideas by thinking, "What stories do I wish existed in the world?" But Colleen also devotes some teaching to a subordinate tip she tucks into her main idea. She tells children that writers embellish their ideas with details. She then goes further and shows children a sequence of questions that will help them do this. These questions are carefully chosen—notice the sequence, because the questions, asked in this order, scaffold children to do some good work. First the questions channel a writer to think about the character's traits and related struggles, then the questions move writers to consider how these struggles play out in an event.

In example after example throughout this book, you'll see that story ideas contain some tension; they contain a predicament. When I was a kid and wrote fiction, my stories had magic carpets—but no tension. Hopefully, your children will sense that "a boy becomes a billionaire" is not yet the stuff out of which one makes stories.

After children talked, Colleen recruited Ramon to share. "I'd write: 'A kid comes to school at the start of fourth grade and everyone else has gotten taller. He is a shrimp, so he is no good at basketball any more. He doesn't get called on to play.'"

"I love the way you gave your character certain characteristics: He's a fourth grader who isn't as tall as the others, he used to be a great basketball player but now that height gets in the way, kids call him a shrimp. Those details really make your story start to grab me!"

LINK
Send writers off after reminding them of their growing repertoire of strategies for finding fiction ideas.

"So writers, we pretended we wished there were more stories about kids who aren't good at sports, and then imagined a character in such a book. When you are living your life as a fiction writer, you won't write about the character *I* lay out—you'll invent your own characters. As we saw yesterday, Sofiya's character may be a girl who enters a gymnastics tournament, or a child who gathers up enough courage to touch a snake. Whatever idea she pursues, Sofiya will need to think about her character's traits, and about her character's hopes and struggles. For now, you'll continue collecting story ideas. You can use any of the strategies we've learned, or others that you invent, to do this. Let's start listing these strategies in a chart," I said, gesturing to the list I had started on chart paper.

How to Find Ideas for Fiction

- Observe the world or reread entries. Mine your notebook for story ideas.
- Ask, "What books do I wish existed in the world?" Let this question lead you to invent a character with traits, struggles, actions.

"The blue table can get started . . . now the red table . . . ."

It's the second semester of the year; by now the class community is really strong. The combination of the fact that the class has lived through a lot together and that now they're writing fiction and can hide a bit under its cloak means that writing workshop will be a time when children write about huge issues in their lives. We aim to make them feel safe enough to do so.

Because you gave a hypothetical starting point, this is just an exercise. You don't expect children to write about the character from the day's minilesson, but instead to invent their own characters. There will probably be a few children, however, who decide that the story idea you have given to them could become their very own idea, and that's okay.

By now you are anticipating that in the early sessions of any unit, we'll offer children a repertoire of strategies for gathering entries that pertain to the work, and genre, of that unit.

You will find that your children are raring to go. Many of them will collect two or three ideas and they'll decide one of those ideas is perfect, and before you can say 'Jack Rabbit,' they'll have written four pages of the story. Prepare yourself for this, and galvanize yourself to deliver the news that those four pages are one draft of one possible story idea. Insist that children postpone closure, and that they continue to generate story ideas and (if they insist) story-beginnings. You will want an opportunity to teach them more before their stories are set in stone.

WRITING AND CONFERRING

Using an Exemplar Text to Respond to Predictable Problems

When you confer and lead small groups, you will probably notice that many students have long lists of undeveloped story ideas. Children won't be sure whether they are expected to write actual stories in their notebooks, or whether you are asking for lists of story ideas—and actually, you are hoping for something in between. You'll want to teach kids to stay a little longer with each idea, fleshing it out a bit. You might carry with you the first story idea you wrote in your notebook. For example, Colleen had started with this:

> Girl is afraid of the dark

Then Colleen revised her initial cryptic note to say a bit more.

> The girl is afraid of the dark. She knows she is being silly but sometimes she thinks she sees things, like monsters, in bed. She gets scared enough that she has started sleeping with the light on. Sometimes in the middle of the night, she crawls into bed with Mom. Her birthday is coming up. She wants to have a sleep over party but she is worried the other girls will make fun of her because she is afraid of the dark.

Colleen will probably want to carry both versions with her. Similarly, I could carry my story idea around with me—the idea about the girl who moved.

When conferring, it helps to carry your own exemplar text around with you so that if you decide to use the teaching method of demonstration or the "explain and show an example" method, you'll have the materials to do so. But don't let the fact that you have materials under your arm propel you into using them. As always, begin your conferences by asking, "What are you working on as a writer?" and by trying to understand what the writer has already done and is trying to do.

It will help if, before this unit begins, you and your colleagues try to predict the conferences you'll probably need to conduct early in this unit. As I mentioned earlier, you can expect that you'll often need to help children say more when they write about their story ideas. You may also:

MID-WORKSHOP TEACHING POINT   *Sharing Struggles with Characters*   "Writers, can I have your eyes? I want to teach you one more strategy for collecting ideas for fictional stories: You can write stories in which the character wrestles with issues that are important to you. I once knew a young writer named Donald who had a big issue with 'fitting in.' In his school, cool kids all had a certain haircut. Donald wanted to be popular but he didn't have the money to go to the 'cool' barbershop. So he tried to cut his own hair, but it looked ridiculous, and kids made fun of him. He didn't just ignore that this was happening to him; Donald wrote a story about a kid who struggled with and overcame a similar issue. The kids in his story didn't have haircut troubles, but they had similar struggles."

"This was Donald's story plan":

> I'm going to write a story about a kid who tries really hard to fit in, but the more he tries, the worse it gets. Maybe he will do something bad like he steals sneakers to be like everyone else. Then he gets caught by a secret camera. Now he's in trouble with the manager, with his mom, with his principal. Maybe he gets really sick and all the people who were mad at him feel bad about it. Nah—that's dumb. Maybe he DOES something that everyone thinks is cool and makes people look at him differently. Not sure.

continued on next page

- Help students postpone closure, and to entertain the prospect of a wider range of story ideas. Some students will generate a story idea and immediately start writing that story from start to finish. Teach them that writers force ourselves to imagine more possibilities before making a commitment to one story idea. And once a child does settle on a particular story idea, the child needs to spend a lot of time rehearsing before he or she begins a draft. I think of this unit on fiction as a unit also on rehearsal and revision.

- Remind students that they know a lot about how stories generally "go," and specifically, remind them that story ideas usually originate from a character who has motivations and faces a predicament. If a child imagines a story in which an unnamed guy lives through ten daredevil activities, you'll want to explicitly teach the importance of developing a very particular character. You'll also want to show children that a character's traits and motivations lead that character to encounter struggles, and in this way a story hangs together.

- Steer children to grow story ideas from the particulars of their own lives. It is inevitable that some will want to write adult stories, and you'll want to channel them toward dramas they know from the inside.

- Anticipate that children will imagine their stories as containing a necklace-full of events. Teach them that they are writing short stories, and this generally means they'll be writing two or perhaps three Small Moment stories.

continued from previous page

"Do you see how Donald took the same issue that *he* was dealing with—trying to fit in with kids at school—and he started thinking about a story where the character wrestles in a different way with the exact same issue? Donald was incredibly brave to write about an issue that is hard in his own life." I said this because, in a subtle way, I hope to encourage children to write from the heart. "When Donald read the story idea to his class, they got really quiet; I realized that the issue wasn't important just in Donald's life, it was important to most kids in the class. It really helped them when Donald had the courage to name the issue."

"I am telling you this because I know some of you will want to think about the issues that are big in your lives or in the world. You might write an issue on the top of the page and then see if you can spin some story ideas that could possibly allow you to address the issue. We can add this strategy to our list:"

How to Find Ideas for Fiction

- Observe the world or reread entries. Mine your notebook for story ideas.

- Ask, "What books do I wish existed in the world?" Let this question lead you to invent a character with traits, struggles, actions.

- Think about an issue that is important to you and create a character who struggles with that issue.

Although it is helpful to plan for and anticipate conferences, if you find yourself giving mostly preplanned, almost canned conferences, then you probably need to listen more intently and to expect children to surprise you, to take you to new places. That is, it's helpful to expect that when you confer with children, they will stir up new ideas in you. As you draw a chair alongside a child and ask, "What are you working on as a writer?" expect that the child's response will be instructive to you.

SHARE

Storytelling

Glory in children's stories and suggest they deserve to hear each other's stories. Demonstrate storytelling by retelling a familiar tale, extrapolating pointers.

"Writers, I am so lucky because I have been able to move among you, listening in on your story ideas. So many of your stories are giving me goose bumps! You all deserve the chance I have to hear each other's stories. Right now, before you share, I'm going to give you a quick lesson in being storytellers. Then before you tell your stories to each other, we'll practice storytelling by telling just the beginning of *The Three Billy Goats Gruff.*"

"After that I am going to ask some of you to tell the story of one of *your* story ideas. Are you ready for some hints on being a storyteller?"

"First, begin the story by sweeping the listeners with your eyes as if saying, 'Welcome, draw close, for I have a story to tell.'"

"Second, tell the start of the story in such a way that it sounds like a famous book or a fairy tale; start it with a phrase like, 'Once, long ago' or 'One day, a little girl . . . ' or something else that sounds like a real story."

"Third, as you tell the story, be sure your mind is picturing whatever you are telling. If your mind isn't painting pictures, how will you choose the words that can help your listeners paint pictures as they hear the story?"

"I'll try storytelling first, using *The Three Billy Goats Gruff.* I'll try to follow all those tips. Then partner 1, I am going to ask *you* to storytell the same story (but in your own way) to your partner. Here goes."

> Once, long ago, there were three billy goats Gruff. They lived on one side of a stream, and everyday they would look across the stream to a lush field of grass. There was a bridge across the stream, but the three billy goats Gruff knew they were never to cross that bridge, for a mighty troll lived there.
>
> One day, however, the three goats were so hungry they decided to cross the bridge so they could eat the sweet lush grass on the far side. First the littlest goat started across the bridge. Trip, trap . . .

Colleen and I have found that in some classrooms, the children do not know The Three Billy Goats Gruff. *Obviously this reference works only if the text is familiar to kids.*

It may seem abrupt to suddenly channel students to go from generating lots of story ideas to storytelling one. We've brought storytelling into this very early session because we want the magic of literary language and the storyteller's persona and voice to help children generate and select between story ideas. But it is true that children are still generating lots of story ideas.

The hints here are ones I learned more than a decade ago when I studied with Mem Fox, author of Koala Lou. I teach these tips to children now because I think that by following these bits of advice, children will take the opportunity to storytell more seriously. I hope these tips elevate the storytelling and allow it to make a bigger contribution to children's work.

Practice telling the fairy tale you select so that you can tell it very well. As you tell the story, alter the pace of your voice, and remember the power of a pause. Appreciate crescendo—the hurrying of time and intensity. When you reach a section of the story that is especially significant, slow down, and tell these events in smaller steps. And when you reach the ending, slow your voice almost to a halt. Your timing will have terrific implications for the emotional power of the story.

Notice the literary language: The goats "knew they were never to cross that bridge for a mighty troll lived there." I'm using story language on purpose.

Set children up to retell with a partner the story you've just modeled, and then to storytell one of their own story ideas.

"Okay, partner 1, try telling the same Billy Goats Gruff story to partner 2. It doesn't matter if you remember the details of the story—you can change it as you go. But tell this story like you are a professional storyteller and this is the most amazing story in the world. Go nice and slow, create a storytelling aura."

After a few minutes I interrupted. "Writers, can I stop you? Using the same storyteller voice, will partner 1 take one of your own story ideas, any one of them, and tell your partner that story. Remember to start it in a way which signals, 'I'm telling a story!', perhaps with a phrase like, 'Once, long ago' or 'One rainy, gray day . . . .'"

The language of a book is different from the language of conversation. When we tell a story that begins, "Once, long ago, there were three . . . " or "There was once a little girl who . . . ," we are speaking in the cadence of story. Children need to be so immersed in story language that it is in their bones.

HOMEWORK *Collecting Story Ideas* Tomorrow, writers, you are going to be choosing a story idea. This means that for homework tonight, it is really important that you do two things. First, reread a published short story you've read before, but this time, read it like a writer. Ask, "How does this story go?" Turn it inside out in your mind and notice how it's put together. Is one section of it essentially a Small Moment story? What else is there other than that? A second Small Moment story? A third? What glues these scenes (as fiction writers call the Small Moment stories) together? Write a page about what you notice when you look at the story with a writer's eyes.

And second, take some time to develop another story idea. You could use strategies we've already explored, or you could do this: story watch. Have you heard of bird watching? You know how some people tramp through meadows with binoculars around their necks, at the ready for a whir of color? "I see it," they say, after finding a scarlet tanager. Writers live in a similar way, but we're watching and listening for story ideas. Remember we learned earlier that Robert McCloskey was driving through Boston when he came to a long line of traffic. He looked ahead to see what was causing the problem and saw a line of ducks quacking across the street. Presto! The story idea for *Make Way for Ducklings* was hatched!

Tonight is your last chance to be sure you have a story idea, so in addition to reading like a writer, live like a writer.

In Wordstruck, *Robert MacNeil writes about the importance of hearing and saying and coming to know the cadence of literary language. He writes: "Words and word patterns accumulate in layers, and as the layers thicken they govern all use and appreciation of language thenceforth. Like magic, the patterns of melody, rhythms, and quality of voice become templates . . . and the patterns laid down in our memories create expectations and hungers for fulfillment again." He goes on to say, "It was the sound of English that moved me as much as the sense, perhaps more" (p. 185).*

Teach students to carry their writers' notebooks with them on the bus or subway ride home, to sit with their notebooks open in the lunchroom and at their kitchen tables as life buzzes around them. Teach them to capture conversations, the minidramas, and the subtle nuances of character and environment for all this can be material for writing. Teach them, too, that fiction writers read newspapers and watch the news on TV, noticing ways in which the world feels unfair for some people. All this is grist for the mill.

If you'd like to give children more time to generate ideas for possible stories . . . you may want to teach them that writers live wide-awake lives, recognizing that if they look closely and listen well, they'll find ideas in the details of their lives. Cynthia Voight once saw some children sitting in a station wagon outside a mall, watching the door of the mall with a strained look on their faces—and the idea for her *Homecoming* series was born. In her memoir, *One Writer's Beginnings*, Eudora Welty wrote, "Long before I wrote stories, I listened for stories. Listening for them is something more acute than listening to them." You may want to teach children that one way to listen for stories is to visit the people in their lives, and ask them to talk about whatever they know best. Within their talk, children may find story ideas.

If you notice children want to write extravagant tales of marriages, battles, winning the lottery and so forth . . . teach them that writers usually look for stories that hide within the areas they know best. Melville traveled on a whale ship, and his story ideas reflect this! Mark Twain traveled on the Mississippi River on steamboats, and again, his novels reflect his experiences. Charlotte Brontë was a governess—and not surprisingly, her most famous character had the same career. Invite children to find stories within the terrain they know well.

If your students often find inspiration from your writing experiences . . . begin this unit by telling the story of your childhood experiences writing fiction. Your experiences might not match mine, of course. I turned the playroom into an office for myself, bought reams of paper, and began my story. Every day I added on. It became longer and longer and longer. I wasn't sure how to end it. It became so long that no one (myself included) ever read it. Now I realize that two things would have made the world of difference. I needed to take the time to plan my story before writing it. And I needed an image of what it was that I wanted to write.

COLLABORATING WITH COLLEAGUES

Just as writers begin a draft by planning, so, too, you and your colleagues will want to begin your collaboration by planning. Now that you've reconstituted your study group, spend a bit of time planning the work you'll do together this month.

You'll definitely want to be writing your own fictional stories. The idea of sitting down and writing a story is overwhelming and scary for most of us, but you'll see that this unit of study takes you along in a step-by-step fashion. Give yourselves the minilessons.

In your study group or at home in the evenings, be the student as well as the teacher, working on your own writing. You'll see that the story you write can thread its way through most of this unit. You'll want your writing to be an effective model for your children, so if you feel insecure about this, closely follow the story model we provide.

The learning that you do will be especially important in this unit because your children will probably need five weeks instead of four for this study. This means you and your colleagues will definitely need to write your own minilessons. The research you do about fiction writing, combined with your own work as a fiction writer will help immeasurably. But of course, you'll learn the most by watching what your children do as writers.

It's very important to read stories that resemble those you and your children will write. The chapter books that you read aloud can serve as models for particular techniques that fiction writers use, but there are big differences between novels and short stories. In fact, many of the problems

children run into when they write fiction derive from the fact that they're modeling their writing after novels, not short stories. No one can write a strong novel in three pages!

There are lots of professional books that can inspire and inform you and your colleagues if you want to learn more about teaching children to write fiction. I recommend two books by educators: *After the End*, by Barry Lane and the fiction chapter from *Time for Meaning*, by Randy Bomer. I also recommend a number of books for adults who want to write fiction: *The Art of Fiction*, by John Gardner; *Writing Fiction*, by Janet Burroway; *The Plot Thickens*, by Noah Lukeman; and *Creating Fiction*, an anthology edited by Julie Checkoway. As you read, look for material you can include in the minilessons that you will write.

You'll also want to learn from fiction by becoming someone who watches for and listens for stories. In a staff development afternoon at a school, Don Graves gathered the teachers into the school library. Dividing them in teams of three, Graves gave each team an envelope. One team's envelope contained a note that said, "Mr. Blakely works in the furnace room. You'll find he has amazing stories about foster children. Find him and hear his stories." In another team's envelope, they found, "Mrs. Huber works in the cafeteria. Her granddaughter is a never-ending source of stories. Go and hear them!" Consider, for a moment, the people with whom you work every day. How could you hear their stories? Pull close, listen well. You'll soon find that there are stories everywhere.

IN THIS SESSION, STUDENTS LEARN
THAT, LIKE ALL WRITERS, FICTION
WRITERS NEED TO CHOOSE A SEED
IDEA (A STORY IDEA) AND THEN
BEGIN TO DEVELOP CHARACTERS BY
CREATING THEIR EXTERNAL AND
INTERNAL TRAITS.

GETTING READY

- How to Find Ideas for Fiction chart from preceding lesson
- Your own character and story line that you will use to model throughout the unit
- Start of a Developing My Character T-chart on chart paper, with two columns: Outside (external features) and Inside (internal features)
- Advice for Developing a Character chart on chart paper
- See CD-ROM for resources

DEVELOPING BELIEVABLE CHARACTERS

Today's lesson is a critical one. You'll teach children that once writers get some ideas for how a story might go, we resist the temptation to begin drafting the story and instead we rehearse for it. Often children think that the writer's job during rehearsal is to come up with a topic, a subject. But when writing fiction, we need more than just the topic, we need to create the story world, we need to know our characters. We need to know them with intensity—well enough that we can live inside their skin and see through their eyes.

Children often think that the central element of a story is plot, and they enter a fiction unit expecting that the story of a father and a son hiking will revolve around all that happens to them (perhaps they meet a grizzly bear, get caught in a rock slide, fall into a cavern, are bitten by a rattlesnake). However, the truth is that the better story will revolve not around what happens to the father and son, but rather, what happens between the father and the son, or within them.

You'll see that we suggest children begin with fairly easy work—but the level of difficulty will escalate quickly. So, although you'll begin by teaching children that fiction writers rehearse by fleshing out their characters—detailing their external features—you'll soon point out that these external features need to reflect and describe the internal features.

Throughout this work, you will teach children that fiction writers write not only drafts of a story, but also plans. Fiction writers use pen and paper to mull over possible directions, to gather and sort information, to plan. More specifically, children will learn that rehearsal is also a time for revision! By thinking through a story idea in some detail, writers progress through a whole sequence of possible ideas—even before we actually begin our first drafts.

In this session, youngsters choose their seed idea—their story idea—and begin developing that idea by developing their characters. This will involve thinking about their internal attributes—their likes, dislikes, thoughts, and feelings—as well as their external attributes, such as physical characteristics, age, and habits.

MINILESSON

Developing Believable Characters

CONNECTION

Chronicle the learning journey the class has been on in this unit to date. Emphasize that children have learned the ingredients of a good story.

"For the past few days, you've been living like fiction writers, seeing ideas for stories everywhere. You've been writing entries in which you think on the page about your story ideas. I read through your notebooks during gym yesterday and what I saw blew me away."

"Listen carefully to what I noticed because it is important. Although our minilessons have been about the strategies fiction writers often use to come up with story ideas (and the chart How to Find Ideas for Fiction, lists those ideas), you guys are so alert as learners that on your own you have gleaned a whole lot about the ingredients that go into a good story idea."

"Looking over your notebooks, I could tell that when we started this unit, you thought a good story idea might be one like this."

A girl climbs a mountain by herself and she's proud.

"And I could tell that now, many of you realize that a story idea needs to include some more specifics about the character and the story, so it might go like this."

A 9-year-old girl has had a knee injury and will never be able to bend her knee. At first she gives up on life but then something happens to change this and she decides to not give up anymore. To prove herself she sets out to climb the mountain that overlooks her house. She doesn't get to the top but she proves herself in a different way and learns something, I am not sure the specifics.

COACHING

Children are choosing their seed ideas very early in this unit because once they've chosen their story ideas, they still need to devote lots of time to rehearsal.

Colleen has a few options right now. Because today's lesson will channel children to settle on one of their story ideas, she can contextualize this session by referring to the sessions in earlier units when children chose their seed ideas, reminding them of what they already know about this phase of the writing process and then highlighting ways in which this phase will be a bit different now that they are writing fiction. Similarly, she can reference the Monitoring My Writing Process chart from previous units, reminding children that always, they begin writing by gathering ideas and then, before long they pause to make a selection. A third option is that she can summarize the previous session's work, aiming to either consolidate what students have learned so that it becomes more memorable for them or aiming to put a new slant on their prior learning. Then, too, another option is that she can simply share observations about her students' work. She decided to summarize previous learning and to do so in ways she hopes make that previous work more memorable and accessible.

The truth is that children probably have not made this much progress yet! This second version of a story idea is considerably better than those most children will be writing, but no harm is done in overstating how much they've learned.

Tell writers that today they'll select a story idea.

"Today, each of you will reread all your entries and select one seed idea to develop into a publishable story (in this unit, we'll call it your *story idea*)."

Name your teaching point. In this instance, you'll teach children that after fiction writers have chosen a story idea, they rehearse by writing — by thinking on the page — about their character.

"I am going to teach you that fiction writers don't just go from choosing a story idea to writing a draft. Instead a fiction writer *lives with* a story idea for a time. Specifically, I will teach you the thinking-on-the-page strategies that fiction writers use to live with our characters and to rehearse for our drafts."

"You will see that these strategies focus less on planning what will happen in our stories and more on bringing to life the people who will make things happen. A fiction writer once said, 'Before you can begin writing your story, you need to know your characters so well that you know exactly how much change each one has in his or her pocket.'"

TEACHING
Set the children up for your teaching by quickly summarizing your process of selecting a story idea.

"I mentioned earlier that we'll need to reread all our story ideas and select one to develop into a publishable story. Honestly, I think the truth is that usually there is one idea that chooses *us*. Usually I find that, in the end, one idea stays with me, and haunts me enough that it feels inevitable that I must write about it."

Notice that this sentence—today you will reread your entries and select (a story idea)—is not a teaching point. This is an assignment, not a lesson! Sometimes, as in this instance, we will want to tell writers to do something, and of course we can tell them so within a minilesson. But it's important to keep in mind that telling writers to do something can't substitute for teaching them a strategy or a skill.

It is often tempting to keep the teaching point vague, saying something like, "Today I'll teach you a strategy for writing good leads." Then, in the teaching component of a minilesson, we can name the strategy. However, I've found that when we force ourselves to be more explicit in the teaching point, then we are less likely to fool ourselves in the Teaching component into thinking that simply naming the strategy amounts to teaching it. Notice today's teaching point is specific and contains several sentences.

People hunger for information. Whenever possible, Colleen and I try to weave little facts, quotes, stories, and tips into our minilessons. We want children to feel as if the moments when they gather close for a minilesson are heady times. We want them to come to a minilesson expecting to learn, learn, learn. We certainly couldn't, six months into the year, pretend that children's minds could be on fire if we simply "taught" them to reread and select a seed idea—that would be old hat by now!

In a moment, Colleen will introduce a story that ends up weaving through this entire book, becoming the class' story, my story, and perhaps your story too. Ideally you'll substitute your own class' story, but the story that weaves through this book is one that can belong to many of us.

"This morning on my way to school, I realized that I had already decided to write about that girl who is afraid of the dark and wants to buy a night-light. So I put sticky notes on the pages related to that entry, and now I am going to begin developing that seed idea, that story idea."

"Notice that I don't start by thinking about what *will happen* in the story. I rein myself in, I hold myself back from doing that, and try instead to get to know my character."

When you want children to listen well to your teaching, it helps to embed your points into little vignettes such as Colleen does here when she retells the story of how she came to this realization.

Demonstrate that you develop your story idea by listing external and internal features of your main character.

"I already know she's part Mexican, so I add that to the external side of my chart. I need to give her a name that goes with the fact that she's Mexican. I'm thinking whether there's anything else about my character that could help me find a good name . . . I definitely know she's afraid of the dark." Colleen added that to the internal side of the chart. "Oh! I'll name her *Luz* 'cause that means 'light.'"

There are lots of reasons to rein children in so that they don't bolt ahead into writing a draft before they develop their characters. One reason for postponing the draft is that the work on character development will enrich the eventual draft. But another reason to ask children to work on developing their characters before they launch into a draft is that this gives us a bit more time to confer, making it more likely that children get off to as strong a start as possible.

Developing My Character

Outside (external features)	Inside (internal features)
Part Mexican	Afraid of the dark
Luz	

Shifting from the role of author to that of teacher, Colleen addressed her children directly. "Did you see that I don't just come up with any ol' random characteristics for my character? I try to put together a person in such a way that the parts of who she is fit together, they cohere, into a person who begins to come to life."

Watch the way in which Colleen weaves between demonstrating and debriefing, embedding writing tips or pointers into her debriefing. Notice, also, that although she gives a lot of pointers, her written work is lean. Within a minilesson that aims to be just ten minutes long, Colleen can't rattle on and on about her character. Everything she says here is chosen because it helps illustrate a larger principle Colleen wants to teach.

Returning to the role of author, Colleen looked at her chart and mused, "What else? I want Luz to be a bit like me—if this chart were about me, not Luz, I think that in the internal column, I'd write that I'm sensitive. I think I want Luz to be sensitive too, and sort of artistic." Colleen added this to her chart.

By explaining how she constructs her character, Colleen is sharing with children some essential fiction writing truths: characters need to be believable. They need to be real and often this means they have parts of us in them. It isn't surprising or accidental that Luz is sensitive like Colleen, or that she's part Mexican or a bit artistic. Colleen is drawing on important aspects of herself—both internal and external—because she knows that doing so will allow her to create a convincing character.

Think aloud to highlight the fact that the external and internal traits need to cohere.

Colleen reread all of what she had written. "Let's see, does being sensitive and being artistic fit with everything I know about Luz? When her father is gone, she is afraid of the dark. She's sensitive. Sensitivity often goes hand in hand with imagination and creativity. I can imagine Luz conjuring up all sorts of inventive, frightening thoughts about the dark. I can also picture her creating interesting artwork. So yes. Those go together."

Notice the way Colleen emphasizes that the traits she gives to her character need to fit together in a logical fashion. This is an emphasis we added after seeing children throw random traits together with abandon ("my character likes peach ice cream, her favorite color is purple, she walks funny," and so on). The fact that Colleen models the process of developing a coherent character does not insure that students will follow this example!

Debrief. Highlight that you first decide on the main goals for your character and let these guide what the character develops into.

Shifting again to the role of teacher, Colleen said, "Do you see that when I am creating a character, I begin with whatever I know? I knew I wanted my character to be a bit like me. You may know that you want your character to resemble someone else in your life, or that you want your character to go from being tough to being gentle. Start with whatever you know you want for your character."

"I hope you also noticed that I often pause to reread everything I have created, asking, 'Do these different things make sense within one person? Do they fit together in a believable way? Are the traits here for a reason?' I reread to test whether the character I've created thus far stands up to the test of believability."

When you debrief, you have another chance to incorporate tips into your demonstration. So be sure that when you retell what you have just demonstrated, you do so in a manner which highlights whatever it is you want children to take from your demonstration. In this minilesson, Colleen's point is a very sophisticated one. She could have made this easier for kids had she left fewer options open, perhaps suggesting that many of the children, like her, may want their main character to resemble themselves.

Alternatively, you could ask children to extrapolate their own tips for creating a character from what they saw you do, perhaps listing across their fingers the steps they saw you take that they could also take. If you do this, however, avoid trying to extract your points from them through a series of leading questions!

Show children a chart of advice for developing character and model how you might use it.

"I'm going to do one last thing that I want you to notice. I am going to look at that word *sensitive* and say exactly what it means. Lots of people can be sensitive, but what exactly does it mean for Luz? Um . . . let's see . . . I think for Luz this means she really cares about people. She is really kind."

"But as I write this, I am still keeping in mind that question, 'Does the character seem believable?' I'm worried that I just made Luz too good to be true. If she is human, she can't be all-caring, all-kind. She needs to be more complicated."

Advice for Developing a Character

- Start with whatever you've decided matters to you about your character. Is he or she like you? Like someone you know?

- Put together a character so that all the parts fit together into a coherent person.

- Reread often, asking, "Do these different things make sense within one person? Do they fit together in a believable way? Are these traits here for a reason?"

- Open up any broad, general descriptors—words like sensitive—and ask, "What exactly does this word, this trait, mean for this particular character?"

- If a character seems too good to be true, make the character more complex and more human by asking, "What is the downside of this trait? How does this characteristic help and hurt the character?"

Anne Lamot says that "Plot grows out of character. If you focus on who the people in your story are . . . something is bound to happen." Children are often tempted to skip the step of developing their characters. They may think of stories as sheer plot and want to jump right into the action. It's important to encourage them to slow down, to stay with their characters long enough to know them inside and out. Some fiction writers believe that characters begin to make their own decisions, even lead writers where they want to go. For this to happen, though, a writer needs to know her characters well.

Colleen is wise to examine what she means by "sensitive" because this will get children to think more deeply about the choices they make when naming their characters' traits. Children are often apt to throw around trite words like "mean" and "happy" without giving too much thought to what those words mean. By teaching them to think about the words they choose, we're encouraging them to be as precise as possible about who their characters are—to challenge clichés, and to get at the truth.

You could add something like, "Writers know that interesting, fleshed-out characters are at the heart of good fiction, but we often create wooden, two-dimensional characters when we're first writing. When I find myself doing this, I try to remember that the best characters are like real people; they're a mix of good and bad. Sometimes they even have contradictory traits: they're gentle yet tough, kind and cruel, self-assured but doubtful. Think about Harry in the story, "Papa's Parrot," who gets furious at his father's bird, calls it "stupid" and attacks it with peppermints. Harry is really cruel. At the same time, he sobs for his father because he understands that the parrot's words, "Where's Harry? Miss him" are just an echo of what his father has been saying. And because we relate to that mixture of anger and hurt, we forgive Harry his cruelty, sympathize with him, and grow from his complexities."

"I am going to think some more about Luz being sensitive and about her caring about people. I am thinking about why she cares for people and about how there needs to be a downside to this."

"Okay. I think Luz is really thin-skinned. Things get to her easily. Like the dark gets to her, and her father being away gets to her. People's judgments get to her too. Her feelings get hurt easily. This is why she is careful of other people. She assumes other people are thin-skinned like she is. I'll add these things to the internal side of my Developing My Character chart."

ACTIVE ENGAGEMENT
Set children up to join you in creating the main character in your story.

"So now it's your turn to try. Let's think about this character, Luz. For now, will you and your partner try to add some things to the other side of the chart—the external side? (By the way, I often develop the internal side first, and then make sure the external reflects the internal.) As you work, remember these things we've learned so far about developing characters," Colleen said, and pointed to the Advice for Developing a Character chart.

"Also, as you talk through things you might add about the external side of Luz—her hobbies, her looks, her ways of acting in the world, her friends or family, her experiences at school—remember that you are going to talk about external features that *fit with the internal ones*. So begin by rereading what we've already written, and then turn and tell your partner how the things we've already written affect your ideas about the external side of Luz." The room erupted into talk.

Intervene to lift the level of what children are saying by reminding them to use pointers from the chart.

After three minutes, Colleen interrupted. "Writers, can I have your eyes?" Then she said, "Please pause to reread the chart of Advice for Developing a Character and then use that advice to revise what you are saying about Luz's external features." Again, the room erupted into talk.

This bit of character development is sophisticated, and you may decide to postpone it for another year. But on the other hand, it is important work because we do want children to think about people, including characters in books, in complex ways. So this minilesson will be echoed in the reading curriculum. If children try to reduce characters in their novels to clichés, we say, "Most characters are not so simple." I used to point out to children that even J. R. Ewing loves his mother, but the reference doesn't mean much to the children in our classrooms today! Probably it'd be more effective to say, "Even a good guy like Harry Potter doesn't have good thoughts all the time!"

The story begins as Colleen's story but it will become a story that belongs to the entire class.

Colleen wisely steers students toward the often short-changed aspect of a character's internal nature. Young people can easily list external, physical features, and love doing it: tall, baggy clothes, dark brown hair, and so on. But we fall in love with characters not for what they look like, but for who they are— how they feel about things, their particular perspectives on the world—so the more time spent learning how to flesh out the character's interior life, the better. Still, there may be some children who begin creating their characters by elaborating on the external features. When you confer with these children, ask questions that will help them link physical and external qualities to internal states. For instance, if a character is tall for her age, ask the child how the character feels about this.

If we want a particular pointer (or a particular chart) to influence how children go about their work, we need to thread it through our conversations.

Elicit suggestions for character development from a few partnerships and add these to the list of external and internal features.

Colleen soon requested the children's attention, asking Paige to report back on what she and her partner had said. "We thought about how Luz is part Mexican so we said she has light-brown skin and then we thought she has a ponytail with long brown hair. We thought casual clothes would go with that and with her being sort of artistic. This is probably stupid but we made a sketch of some dangly earrings we thought she wore; she made them herself." Colleen added Paige and Francesca's suggestions to the chart.

Developing My Character: Luz

Outside (external features)	Inside (internal features)
Part Mexican	Afraid of the dark
Luz	Artistic
Light-brown skin	Cares for people
Long brown hair in ponytail	Thin-skinned
Casual clothes	
Self-made dangly earrings	

"Sketching her earrings is not in the least stupid. In fact, it is really smart to know your character well enough that you can sketch her dangly earrings. Do you know what color beads she used in the earrings? I bet you could tell me why that is her favorite color. Remember, you need to know your characters well enough to know how much change they have in their pockets!" Then Colleen added, "I'm beginning to think that Luz needs to become shared property and that this story is being co-written by all of us!"

Celebrate your children's imaginings about characters. It takes time for characters to unfold, for us to know them. When children find themselves thinking of tiny details about a character without quite knowing why these are so right, they're writing intuitively, creatively. They're allowing themselves to really see their characters. This is fiction writing at its best! You can help them understand the details they choose later. For now, let them enjoy the creative process.

Keep in mind that just because a writer knows the color of a character's earrings and knows even why this color is special to the character, this information will probably not show up in the actual story! And bear in mind, too, that your children learn as much from the writing that does not end up in their publications as from the writing that does. You are, after all, hoping to develop great writers, not simply great writing. So nothing is wasted!

When Colleen says, "Do you know what color beads she uses in her dangly earrings?" and suggests she's sure the children know why that color is so important to the character, she is nudging them to go further, to dig deeper—but doing so in a supportive manner. What a wonderful way to extend these children's efforts!

LINK

Rally members of the class to choose their story idea and begin charting external and internal characteristics of a character. Remind children that fiction writers do this always.

"You've got some big work to do during the writing workshop today. You'll begin by thinking whether one of your seed ideas, one of your *story* ideas, has chosen you. If nothing seems inevitable, if nothing feels like it can't be ignored, you may want to spend a bit more time collecting story ideas, going back to generating ideas. Either way, you need to end today feeling committed to one story idea. And once you have your story idea, you can begin getting to know your character."

"To think about what your character is like on the inside and the outside, you may want to use a two-column chart like the one we made together. I've got forms in the writing center. When you go to your writing spot, you can tape one of these forms into your notebook. Or you may prefer to just divide a page of your notebook into two columns. Or you can alternate paragraphs, with some paragraphs telling the internal side of your characters and others the external. You are in charge, of course."

"From this day on, I hope that whenever you write fiction, you remember that instead of launching right into a draft or focusing only on planning the plot line of a story, you always rein yourself in, taking the time to develop your character."

Listening to this, you may think, "Geez, I bet none of my kids feel as if a story idea has chosen them!" I encourage you to act as if your kids are zealously committed to their stories. Act as if they love writing. You'll surprise yourself by finding the drama becomes real life. As you've heard me say before, the literacy researcher, Jerry Harste, once said, "I see teaching as creating, in the classroom, the kind of world we believe in and then inviting our children to role play their way into becoming the readers and writers we hope they'll become." Over and over again, you'll see that in our minilessons, we speak to children as if we know they're passionately involved in their writing. We hope that our assumptions become realities.

The truth is that this minilesson channels children in a very direct way. So it helps to highlight that, within the constraints of this directive, children still have some choices.

Pause to marvel at the amount of instruction you fit into today's teaching!

WRITING AND CONFERRING

Anticipating the Help Children Will Need Developing Their Characters

As you confer with individuals or, more likely, with small groups, you'll no doubt see that many children begin by simply listing phrases to describe the character. Ariana, for example, began with the list in Figure III-1.

Don't be surprised that children are making lists—this should be what you expect. But when conferring, help these youngsters realize that their lists can be more specific and more elaborated. Pay attention to places where the child provides a bit more detail, and celebrate these. For example, with coaching, Ariana progressed from developing her character with a mere list of words toward doing this with phrases. [Fig. III-2]

- licks her nose with her tongue

- sometimes wears hair up half down pigtails

- puts her hair behind her ears

- she doesn't move her head when she talks

- says "well" a lot, ex—did you know that, well, the new . . .

As you confer, you will probably notice that many of the characters seem like stereotypes. This is natural. Luz, even, begins as a half-Mexican artist with dangly earrings and loose, swinging clothes. It would be tempting to teach students to think critically about the work they've done developing characters by putting their characters on trial: "Is your character a stereotype? Is your character simplistic?" I don't recommend this. For now, it is very important for youngsters to bond with their characters, and therefore we are wise to avoid treating the character or the character development work harshly. If a character seems generic, stereotypical or underdeveloped, instead of saying so, simply help the writer outgrow this surface-level character development.

For example, when a character's internal characteristics are generic, I find I can help the child open up those generic terms if I ask the right questions. If the character is "good at soccer," then I can point out that people can be good at soccer in different ways. "What is your character's *specific* way of being good at soccer?" I can even press further and ask, "What is going on inside the character that makes her so good at

---

MID-WORKSHOP TEACHING POINT · *Building the Character's Self-View* "Writers, I just must stop you! I've been thinking that as we work on creating the insides of our characters, we don't want to forget one really important thing. We need to think about how our characters feel about themselves. We know, as real people, that how we feel about ourselves is really important. It only makes sense that our characters would think something about themselves too. Does your character like himself, herself? Does the character think he or she is funny? If your character is strange, does she know she's strange? Is the character humble? Or does the character think she or he is the best thing since sliced bread?" *[Fig. III-1]*

Sally
- oval eyes
- a little curly
- tan skin
- jean capris
- red shoes

continued on next page

Sally
- obl eyes
- alittle curly
- tan skin
- jean capres
- red shoes
- blue or green shirts with a number
- long skinny lips
- small for her hight
- short legs
- long tounge

Movements
- runs really fast
- bits her nails
- sucks on her hair
- she walks fast
- talks with no exsperissons

Fig. III-1 At first Ariana simply listed phrases as she developed her character.

- licks her nose with her tounge
- Sometimes weres hair up half down Pigtails
- puts her hair behind her ears
- she doesn't move her head when she talks
- says "well" alot ex-did you know that well the new ...

Fig. III-2 With coaching, Ariana's descriptors became more detailed.

soccer?" Once the child has answered by creating some revealing details about this one dimension of the character's life, I might ask, "How does that connect to other things the character does?" It also helps to ask, "What's the downside of this?" The character who is always pushing during the soccer game may not know when to relax. In a conference, I'll ask these questions of a child, but I will also pull back and talk about the importance of asking (as well as answering) questions such as these. That is, I will pause in a conference and say, "Will you notice, for a moment, the questions I've asked you about your character because these are questions you, as a writer, need to be able to ask yourself and each other." It helps to chart these questions. My goal, of course, is for the young writer to learn that another time, he or she can ask these same questions while writing. Children can also ask these questions of each other's characters.

If a character seems wooden, I often find the youngster has been trying to make up the character out of thin air. When this is the case, I find it helps if the child learns to lend his or her own life experience to the character. A child can do this even if the character is in many ways very different from himself. For example, a child might be writing a story about an old man who has outlived all his family members. The child doesn't know much about being old, but he can think, "When I feel lonely, what do I do?" Perhaps, when no one is home and the place echoes, the child sometimes looks through sports trophies, remembering the games. Why couldn't the old man do something similar? Perhaps the youngster finds that when the house is especially empty, he finds that he waits for phone calls, and sometimes even picks up the receiver to check that there's a dial tone so that calls can come through. Why couldn't the old man do this as well? Details grounded in real life have power.

Sometimes when I confer with a child, I find that the child feels as if he or she has hit a dead end with a character. I sometimes let the child know that problems with a character's development can be early warning signals that the story idea itself doesn't fit the writer, or that the story idea has problems that need to be addressed. As a result, then, I may encourage the writer to rethink the entire story idea.

Finally, I always keep in mind that secondary characters need to be developed too! Everything that the writer has done with the main character needs to be done with the secondary characters.

---

continued from previous page

- blue or green shirts with a number
- long skinny lips
- small for her height
- short legs
- long tongue

Movements
- runs really fast
- bites her nails
- sucks on her hair
- she walks fast
- talks with no expressions

"Ariana has wisely set up two columns in her notebook. One is labeled 'attitude toward self' and the other is 'attitude of others toward her.' Some of the rest of you may want to follow Ariana's example. Before we go on, look back and see if you have included what your character thinks of himself or herself." [Fig. III-3]

Attitude toward self
- she thinks she's dumb, grumpy, rude
- and of machas she hates her lips
- she knows all of what she thinks isn't true but she still thinks that

Attitude of others toward her
- Mrs. Jorach her teacher thinks she's great in writing
- Mr. Megrache her math teacher thinks she's good in word problems

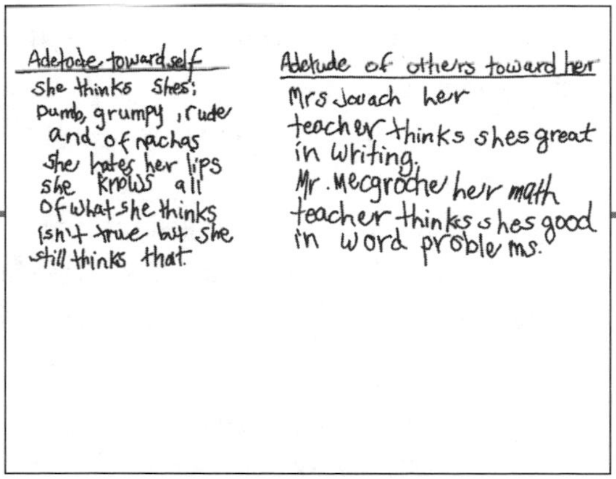

Fig. III-3 Ariana's notebook entry

SHARE

Complicating Characters

Spotlight one student who decided his character was one-sided and asked, "What's the flip side of this trait?"

"Writers, you've done some wise work today. I especially want to celebrate the wise decision Henry made when he realized that his character, Max, was too good to be true. So Henry went back to alter his early work with the character, Max. Henry had already said Max had a rich imagination. He'd already said that the character's lively imagination meant he had big, imaginative dreams, and plans and schemes, too. Henry worried, though, that Max sounded *too* perfect. He could have just added some other, less-ideal qualities, but instead he did something really smart. He thought, 'If my character has a lively imagination, this is probably bad as well as good for him.' Then Henry wrote that his character imagines everything that could go wrong, and consequently has lots of big worries and always seems nervous."

"I hope all of you learn from what Henry has done. He realized his character was too good to be true, but he didn't just jump into a list of bad as well as good things about him. Instead, Henry took one thing—that his character imagines a lot—and thought carefully about the ways this would help *and hurt* his character."

Extrapolate the larger principle. Writers develop complex characters by thinking of the bad as well as good aspects of a trait.

"Writers call characters like the one that Henry has created *complex*. With your partner today, would you look at your characters and think whether they have bad as well as good sides, and whether you've really worked through the ups and downs of your characters' personalities?"

As we listened in on partnerships, Ariana read her entries aloud and Jesse signaled with her thumb to indicate whether Ariana was showing the good side, the bad side, or a neutral side of a trait. This is what Ariana *[Fig. III-4]* read aloud.

> Seamus
> Internal Inside
> is afraid of everything
> doesn't like his father
> he likes to go on high roller coasters

You'll notice that this unit is densely packed, and that each new component of a minilesson lays out another point. There is never a time to simply share! You may decide that the sequence of these minilessons moves way too quickly, in which case you'll want to write interim minilessons. One way to do this is to take pointers that are now embedded into the Shares or the Mid-Workshop Teaching Points and use them as the teaching points in minilessons.

Although the Share session gives children one opportunity to talk about their characters, you needn't shoehorn all this thinking and talking into the writing workshop. If you want to stoke the fires of excitement that came when launching this unit, whenever you have an extra five minutes before the end of the day or before gym, assume children will be dying to talk and think about their characters and "let" them do so.

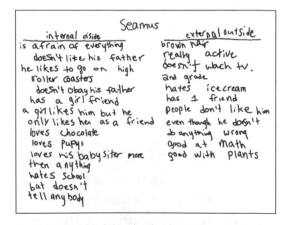

Fig. III-4 Ariana read this aloud to her partner, noticing whether she'd included negative as well as positive traits.

doesn't obey his father
has a girlfriend
a girl likes him but he only likes her as a friend
loves chocolate
loves puppies
loves his babysitter more than anything
hates school but doesn't tell anybody

External Outside

brown hair
really active
doesn't watch TV
2nd grade
hates ice cream
has 1 friend
people don't like him even though he doesn't do anything wrong
good at math
good with plants

Deveonna, meanwhile, showed Ari that she'd developed her characters by first revising her original story idea. Whereas earlier, she'd imagined that Elexa would be struggling to be chosen as a cheerleader, now Elexa struggles instead to shake off the fawning attention of Max. Beautiful, popular Elexa (the would-be cheerleader) isn't sure if geeky Max is after her or after her best friend, Lexie. This is what Deveonna wrote: *[Fig. III-5]*

> Today I was walking around the schoolyard, and I saw that Max kid, but he wasn't chasing after me, in fact he was after Lexie, and she let him catch her. Show off! She wants to be the one, so she can get the part. I wonder if I should call him over and talk and end my longest friendship over him.

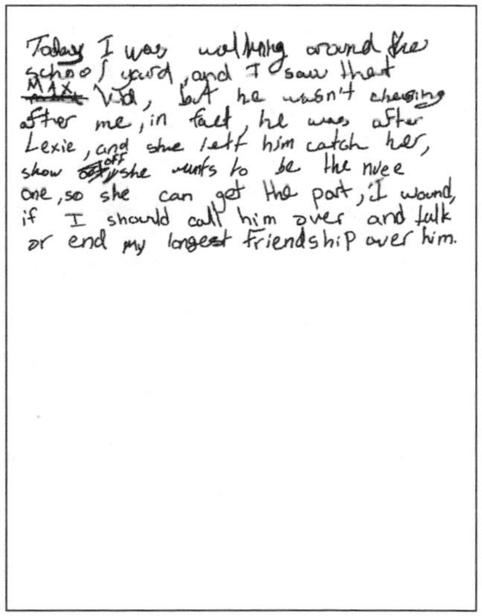
Today I was walking around the school yard, and I saw that Max kid, but he wasn't chasing after me, in fact, he was after Lexie, and she left him catch her, show off! she wants to be the one, so she can get the part, I wonder if I should call him over and talk or end my longest friendship over him.

Fig. III-5 Deveonna's revised story idea

HOMEWORK *Fleshing Out Secondary Characters* We've spent the last few days getting to know our main characters. We've made T-charts, compiled lists, and practiced writing scenes in order to bring our main characters to life. Yet we all know that there are other characters in our stories. Some of you remember from our reading work that we call these secondary characters. They are important characters and deserve our attention because they really help to make our stories believable. It's not enough for us to have a great main character if all the other characters in our story seem like we rushed through them.

Tonight for homework, take a look at the other characters in your story idea. Try some of the same work with a secondary character that you did with your main character. You can make an internal/external T-chart or you can explore different things about them that we have on our lists. Whichever you try, the most important thing to keep in mind is that writers know all of the characters in their story well, not just the main character.

TAILORING YOUR TEACHING This minilesson launches some important work with character development. You'll certainly want to spend another day or two helping children continue to flesh out their characters.

If your students need a more concrete way to get to the abstract idea that a character has an internal life . . . you could teach them that just as some writers brainstorm writing topics by sketching a heart and jotting on it the topics that the writer has in his or her heart—Mom, horses, rainy days—so, too, could children get to know a character by pretending that character does the same thing. Children can ask themselves, "What might the protagonist of my story put inside his or her heart?" Similarly, the child could imagine the people, places, or objects the character might write about in his or her writer's notebook.

If you notice that some students have lots of notes on their characters, yet the characters still feel like caricatures . . . it might help these children to see the world through their characters' eyes. You could teach your children that fiction writers sometimes find it productive to put a character in a situation where the character is all alone (waking up in the morning, walking home from school) and then to write what the character does, in tiny detail, interspersed with what the character notices and thinks and wonders and remembers as he or she goes about the small solitary activity. These solitary moments can be revealing, and meanwhile children practice writing scenes. For example, in Figure III-6, Ariana has done this:

> **In the bathroom**
>
> "Wake up, wake up," my mom calls. "Are you up yet?"
>
> "I'm getting up." I walk in the bathroom, take my toothbrush and put it in my mouth. "This tastes like tomatoes, euh!" I brushed my teeth, got dressed and walked to school.

If you have students who are game for a challenge . . . encourage them to study how authors they admire have portrayed their characters, and to let those examples serve as mentor texts. In *Night Noises,* for example, Mem Fox describes old Lillie Laceby by saying:

> Her hair was as wispy as cobwebs in ceilings. Her bones were as creaky as floorboards at midnight.

Or you could use an example from your own notebook:

> Luz looked at her dresser. She knew she should maybe put on a nice blouse or something. After all, it was picture day. Instead, she pulled out her denim overalls that had the paint splatters on the knees. Her mom hated those overalls. She thought they looked like rags. Luz loved them. They were soft against her skin, and comfortable too.

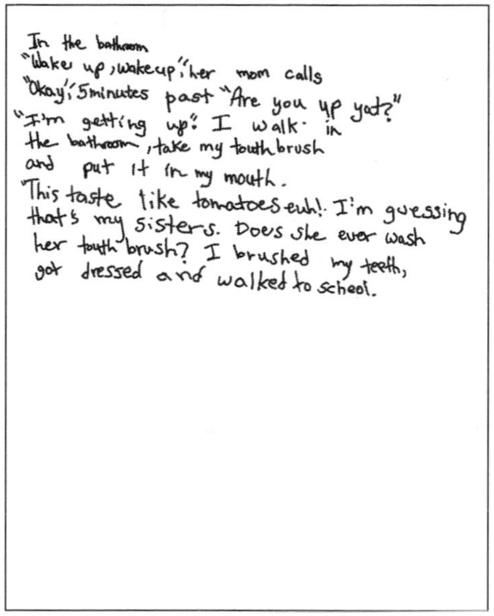
In the bathroom
"Wake up, wakeup," her mom calls
"Okay," 5 minutes past "Are you up yet?"
"I'm getting up." I walk in
the bathroom, take my touthbrush
and put it in my mouth.
"This taste like tomatoes euh!. I'm guessing
that's my sisters. Does she ever wash
her touth brush? I brushed my teeth,
got dressed and walked to school.

Fig. III-6 Ariana has written a scene, bringing her character Sally to life.

ASSESSMENT

You'll definitely want to read over your children's writing at this juncture so you can plan ways to help them. Try temporarily sorting your children's work. If you create lists of children who could benefit from one kind of help or another, then you can cover a lot more ground within the writing workshop. Examine not just their work with character, but also, more fundamentally, their story ideas. Now is the time to help children revise these, so don't wait! You are apt to see that children fit into several categories.

You'll no doubt find that some children don't seem invested in their own ideas. You'll want to work with these children one on one. Perhaps ask the child to talk to you about the story idea and try listening to it really responsively, as if it is an amazing idea and deeply suited to the child. Sometimes your commitment to an idea can help the writer become committed to it as well. But if you seem to be the only one who gets excited about the idea, then name this as a problem and help the child get started on a different idea—even if this means the child is out of step with the class.

Other children may have story ideas that contain some of the most crucial elements of story, but not all of them. Gather these children together and overview the elements that all stories usually contain (or at least those your class has studied). Ask these children to look again, thinking, "Which of these is not well developed in my entry?" Then give them a chance to flesh out their story ideas so they contain all the crucial elements.

You'll almost certainly have a cluster of children who have disregarded your efforts to channel them toward writing a *focused* short story. Their story ideas might work as ideas for a novel, but are too expansive to be contained in a short story. You'll want to bring these children together into a small group. Explain the problem, point out that the short stories they're reading at home contain no more than three scenes (or small moments). Then use what you know of each child to help that child settle on a more focused story idea.

For example, if a child has a list like Marissa's in Figure III-7 or Sofiya's in Figure III-8, help that writer zoom in on just a tiny portion of her idea.

You'll probably find another cluster of children who have each developed a fragment of a story idea, but don't yet have a complete plan. For example, this child's story idea lacks tension:

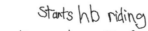

> Gwen met Summer when she moved to
> Brooklyn with her Grandparents and
> started going to school. Summer and
> Gwen always stick together.

Perhaps they've developed a character who dreams of a goal and gets it. What's still needed in that story plan is the tension, the challenge. Perhaps this is a character with particular traits and goals, and what's missing is the plot line.

Fig. III-7 Marissa's story idea

Fig. III-8 Sofiya's story idea

GETTING READY

- Chart of all the different character ideas students have developed
- Passage from a text students know well that illustrates a character's yearning
- Class story in mind that children can use for practice text
- Advice for Developing a Character chart
- Qualities of Good Personal Narrative Writing chart (from Unit 2)
- Idea for an ordinary scene with your character that you can quickly compose on chart paper
- See CD-ROM for resources

GIVING CHARACTERS STRUGGLES AND MOTIVATIONS

In today's session you will guide students into what many fiction writers consider the heart of fiction: character struggle and motivation. You will teach your students that readers will root for a character when they know what the character wants and they see the character struggle toward these goals. As Gerald Brace writes in The Stuff of Fiction, *"The first essential is the creation of believable persons who wait for something or want something or hope for something—they themselves hardly know why or what. Suspense is created by the waiting and wanting."*

We know this from our reading lives. Charlotte wants to help Wilbur, and this longing leads Charlotte to weave her web. Readers, too, want to save Wilbur. We want this so much that we flinch when Charlotte is almost discovered, and we root for a rat to bring back the much-needed newspaper clippings.

Students, like E. B. White, can rope readers in by creating characters who have desires that are intrinsic to their personalities. A shy person might dream of one day overcoming her fear of performing on stage. Encourage students to think not only about what their characters desire, but why these motivations matter so, so much. This will help children create richer, more complex characters.

In life, of course, the path is never smooth. This is true in stories, too. No one wants to read a story where the character wants something, and then promptly gets that thing. We read to find bits of ourselves in characters; and the characters we love best are often the ones whose desires and struggles mirror our own. We are more apt, then, to get lost in stories that take us on a slow journey toward overcoming a challenge or toward realizing a long-held dream rather than in the drive-through quick-and-easy stories. We want to live inside a character's shoes, facing his dragons, reaching for her gold medal. And we want to do so slowly so that we can savor the final outcome after the long buildup.

Even though students are still sorting out how they want their stories to go, this session sets them up to create the right combination of motivation and obstacles. This way, their characters can star in riveting plots.

MINILESSON

Giving Characters Struggles and Motivations

CONNECTION

Celebrate the character development work children have already done in a way that honors it.

"Writers, I feel as if a whole crowd of people came into the classroom with you this morning. You brought with you Griffen, who dreams of impressing Julie and of having a pet of his own; and Mario, who is hoping to get a chance to play jazz at his church's coffeehouse; Mrs. Randoff who has nasty teeth like an old rusty pole and who tells the black kids to get off her block; and Alex, with her horse bracelets and horse T-shirts and horse-sized hole in her life. I jotted down the sorts of details you have been inventing for your characters. Look at the list of what you have done!"

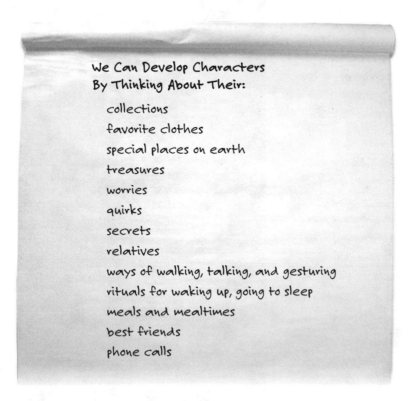

We Can Develop Characters
By Thinking About Their:

collections

favorite clothes

special places on earth

treasures

worries

quirks

secrets

relatives

ways of walking, talking, and gesturing

rituals for waking up, going to sleep

meals and mealtimes

best friends

phone calls

COACHING

Instead of beginning this minilesson by telling specific ways that I hope children have learned to flesh out their characters, I try to simply applaud their enthusiasm and show a list that records what writers have done so far. My fondest hope for the class right now is that they are absorbed in their characters, carrying these "people" with them all the time. I therefore act as if this is already happening.

Of course, I could have taught separate minilessons in which I suggest writers could think about these and other aspects of their characters, but especially by this time in the year, I try to use minilessons to teach skills and concepts that are too complicated to just mention in passing.

Name your teaching point. In this case, tell children that fiction writers must think about their characters' desires and their struggles to fulfill those desires.

"Today I want to teach you that although there are oodles of things we *can* think about as we develop our characters, there are just one or two things that we *must* think about. Specifically, I want to teach you this: Every fiction writer needs to know what his or her characters want, what they yearn for, and what gets in the way—what keeps these characters from getting what they want."

"I also want to teach you that when we know what our characters yearn for, we don't just come right out and say what this is. We *show* what our characters want by putting examples of this into little small moments, into what fiction writers call *scenes*."

TEACHING
Show students an example of a published text in which the character wants something and encounters difficulties. Show that the author conveys this through a dramatic scene.

"I learned to do this by studying how published authors—writers like Alma Flor Ada and the authors of the short stories you've been reading—write little scenes (which could be called vignettes or Small Moment stories) that show what a character yearns for and what gets in the way for that character."

"In the book *My Name Is Maria Isabel*, remember how the teacher decided early in the story that because she had two students named Maria, she would change Maria Isabel Lopez's name to Mary. Maria Isabel, of course, doesn't feel at home in the name *Mary*. She doesn't recognize when her teacher is addressing her as Mary, and so she gets into trouble. When we read the story, we come to know that Maria Isabel *yearns* to be accepted for who she is (not Mary Lopez) and to feel that she has a role to play in the class—but the author doesn't come right out and say that Maria Isabel yearns for this. Instead Alma Flor Ada shows this by putting examples of that yearning into scenes. In the chapter titled "The First Snowfall," watch how Alma Flor Ada tells a Small Moment story (or a scene) that reveals Maria Isabel's longings and also the trouble she encounters at school."

> Once she was at school, Maria Isabel kept thinking about the snow all during math . . . Suddenly she remembered that she hadn't finished her multiplication exercises, and hurried to complete her work. Maria Isabel was so busy trying to finish the page that she didn't hear the teacher call out, in an irritated tone of voice, "Mary Lopez!" When at last she realized that the teacher was waiting for an answer from her, Maria Isabel had no idea what the question had been.

This session is very full, and of course it could have been broken into separate sessions: we need to know our characters' wants; we need to know our characters' struggles (or what gets in the way of achieving their wants); and we need to show, not tell, these details. I decided to consolidate all three of these tips into one teaching point because otherwise, I felt the children's work would be odd. I didn't think it'd be valuable for children to spend an entire writing workshop listing only characters' wants, for example. Also, I'm aware that sometimes separating items that belong together can actually make them more, *not less, complicated. Notice that in an instance like this, I don't hesitate to devote a few sentences to making my teaching point as clear as possible.*

Notice that I am referring to texts the whole class already knows. It would be very rare to read aloud a new text within a minilesson. There is nothing that makes My Name Is Maria Isabel *uniquely suited to this minilesson—any story would work. Use one that your class knows well.*

Although Colleen and I have decided that during the Teaching component of minilessons, we'll often demonstrate by showing children what we do as fiction writers and that we'll often use the Luz story, we're aware it would be monotonous if every day's teaching were built upon that story. So you'll see us vary the text we use, as I do in today's minilesson. Notice that usually there are two texts in any one minilesson. One of these is a text which threads through the Teaching component of many minilessons, and the other is a text which threads through the Active Engagement of many minilessons. In this minilesson, the teaching story is a published children's book, and the story of Luz that was once Colleen's teaching text now becomes the whole class' story, used during Active Engagement.

"Well, it looks like Mary doesn't want to take part in our Winter Pageant," the teacher said. "That's all right. You can help Tony and Jonathon greet the parents at the door and show them where they can put the food and hang up their coats."

The Winter Pageant . . . Maria Isabel couldn't think about anything else on the ride home from school . . . ."I would have loved to be a shepherd. I could have used Mama's straw basket, and it would have been so wonderful . . . "

Maria Isabel turned toward the window of the school bus so that no one would see her wiping a tear.

Debrief. Mention that writers create little scenes and then piece them together like bricks. Point out that the scenes show characters in action in ways that reveal their desires and struggles.

Notice that I abbreviated the text by skipping past some of the detail. Published literature (and especially novels) will be more detailed and elaborate than anything the children can write. By letting some of the detail fall away, I share a text that more closely resembles what I'm hoping children will write. You can do the same, or you can decide otherwise. There are good reasons for either alternative.

"Some people say that fiction is like a brick wall, and the bricks that go together to make the story are scenes, or vignettes. This scene shows what school is like for Maria Isabel. When she works so zealously on her math (after being distracted by her first snowstorm), we see her resolve to do things right. And then we see how she gets into trouble simply because she doesn't recognize—doesn't hear, really—when her teacher addresses her as Mary. We see, also, how desperately Maria Isabel wants to be part of things, and how she hides her sadness."

Of course, you can decide to simplify this minilesson by letting some points fall aside. You may well want to end the minilesson by simply repeating that there are many things writers can show about characters but there are just one or two things that writers must *show: a character's wants and struggles.*

"When we are developing characters, then, we need to think not only about what our characters want and what gets in the way for them. We also need to think about how we can create little scenes that show all this."

Neil Simon has said, "Only recently did I discover that my plays didn't really take off until the main character wanted something and wanted it badly."

ACTIVE ENGAGEMENT
Rename the longings and difficulties experienced by the character in the class' story, and then have children talk with their partners to bring these motivations and struggles to life in a scene.

"Let's try this with Luz. I'll get us started by thinking a little bit about what she wants." I assumed the posture I usually take when demonstrating that I am thinking.

You have a choice. You can launch a class story that will function as a practice text throughout this unit, or you can invite children to coauthor the text that was, originally, your story. You'll notice Colleen and I chose the second option.

"Let's see, Luz is afraid of the dark. We've already decided she's going to have a slumber party but she doesn't want everyone to know she's scared of the dark. That's the story, but what does she really *want*? I think she wants her friends to think she is cool. She feels different because her father is Mexican, and she wants them to accept her."

"So will you guys imagine a scene that could show some of this? Let's put Luz somewhere—packing for a slumber party, climbing into her sleeping bag at the party—and she is doing *something* (see if you and your partner can come up with an idea) that shows that she is afraid of the dark but doesn't want to use her night-light when her friends come because she wants to be accepted by them. Turn and talk. See if you have any suggestions for how we could write this into a scene." The room burst into conversation.

Convene the class and ask a child or two to share a suggestion. Help the child to turn an explanation into a scene. Debrief to point out the process needed to make a scene.

After a bit, I interrupted. "Writers, can I stop you? What ideas did you have for a little scene we could write that might show all this?"

Sirah's hand shot up. "You could show the slumber party and she says, 'Good night' and turns off the light and then lies there in the dark, listening to the noises and worrying."

Ramon added, "Or you could have her lying in her own bed, a couple days before the slumber party, with the lights off, practicing sleeping in the dark. She could get scared and get up and leave the closet light on."

"Those are both exciting ideas," I said. "Ramon, help me actually write what you envision. Class, you'll notice that Ramon and I can't actually write a scene until we can picture exactly what happens in a step-by-step way, with all the tiny, tiny actions. So Ramon, let's picture the whole thing like a movie in our minds. Luz is lying in bed, trying not to be afraid of the dark. What *exactly* is she doing? More specifically, what is Luz doing or saying to herself that shows the reader that she is scared of the dark and shows the reader that she is practicing sleeping with the lights off?"

"She is just looking up. She looks where the lamp usually shines. She doesn't want to lie in the dark but she tells herself, 'I gotta practice.'"

"I can picture it: 'Luz stared through the darkness to where the light usually shone. "I've got to practice," she said to herself. She . . . ' What? What does she do next?"

"She closes her eyes so she won't see that it is dark. Then she gets out of bed and she opens the closet door and she pulls the light string on and she leaves the door open just a crack."

Notice that although this is the Active Engagement section of the minilesson (when it's the kids' turn to do the work), I review the facts and begin the work I've proposed. In this way I give the children a running start, passing the baton to them only once momentum has been well established. This makes it much more likely that children can be active and productive even within a three-minute Active Engagement section.

It is key to realize that once we decide on a character's traits or wants, we need to imbue these with life by writing them within a scene, as occurs here.

Novice fiction writers are apt to explain what's going on rather than to show it. Notice that I help Ramon take his explanation of what's going on and imagine the actions that a character might take that would convey this. I do this not because I want to teach Ramon (I could do that later in a conference) but because I know that by helping him, I can help most of the class.

You'll recall that this is the portion of the Active Engagement when the teacher calls on one member of the class to share what he or she just said or did. Usually we select carefully so that we call on children who help us make the point we hope to highlight. But sometimes we call on a child whose contribution is not exactly what we're after. Notice how, in this instance, I try to explicitly name the problem I have with Ramon's draft, and then coach him to revise it. This revision of one child's "writing in the air" is a helpful way to demonstrate complex, sophisticated writing work. Notice the way in which I coach him and scaffold his work. This is exactly the work you'll also do in conferences today.

"So let me try that," I said. "Class, pay attention to the power of Ramon's tiny, tiny details. I'll even add some more," I said, and quickly wrote this scene on chart paper:

> I stared through the darkness to where my lamp usually shone brightly. "I've got to practice," I said to myself. I turned onto my stomach and squeezed my eyes shut. But even through my closed eyes, I could tell that the comforting glow from my bedside lamp was gone.
>
> Climbing out of bed, I opened the door to my closet, pulled the light string on, and then closed the door partway, careful to leave a crack of light shining into the bedroom.

Debrief. Reiterate that writers put their characters into situations—small scenes—that reveal their desires and their struggles.

"Ramon and I have put Luz in a situation where we can show what she wants and what she struggles with, and we have tried to write a little scene, a small moment, that shows all of this. Notice the words we chose that really brought the scene to life: 'squeezed ... shut,' 'comforting glow,' 'crack of light.' Do you see how these words highlight Luz' struggle to overcome her fear of the dark? All of you will write lots of scenes like this for your own character today, tomorrow, and whenever you want to write fiction."

LINK
Put today's teaching point into context by reminding writers of all they now know how to do. Stress that deciding what their character wants is not an option but is essential, and add this to the chart.

"So writers, whenever you write fiction, remember there are oodles of things we *can* think about when you want to develop characters: a character's special places on earth, best friends, quirks, collections, and ways of waking up. There are oodles of things we *can* think about, but just one or two that you *must* think about: As fiction writers we must know what it is that our characters yearn for, and what gets in their way."

"We usually build the story line out of our character's motivations and struggles—so once you know what your character yearns for and struggles to have, then it's wise to create little scenes that show this. Remember how we just put Luz somewhere—in bed—and came

Notice that I accept Ramon's ideas for what could happen in this scene, but I turn his oral storytelling into text that sounds literate, or written. I act as if I'm simply restating what Ramon said. "I can see it," I say, prefacing my version of his words. The differences between Ramon's version and mine are subtle, but in this way, I'm trying to help him lift the quality of his oral storytelling to the realm of literature.

Notice that the actual writing I do in front of the class is very limited. Writing on chart paper is a slow process and minilesson time is precious!

By this time in the year, you don't need to make a fuss over the fact that, of course, students will not write Luz stories but will instead transfer what they've learned to their own story ideas.

Notice that I pick up exact phrases I used earlier in the minilesson. There are "oodles of things you can *think about . . . and just one or two things you* must *think about." Notice, also, the parallel structure. I want this advice to be memorable.*

up with something she could be doing—practicing sleeping without a light on to get ready for the slumber party—to show what she longs for? You'll want to do this same work with your story idea, not once but many times today, and you'll want to remember to do this whenever you write fiction. The scenes you end up writing today may not end up in your stories. Writing them, like making the two-column chart, is a way to bring characters to life, and that's our greatest job right now." I added the latest point to the chart of advice.

Donald Graves has said, "Fiction is really about character. It is about showing characters wanting things, having aspirations they hope will be fulfilled, or wanting a different life from the one they are living at the moment. Of course, it isn't long before all this 'wanting' produces tough choices, and negative and positive reactions from others. Usually the main character learns something about life itself" (Inside Writing, p. 36).

Advice for Developing a Character

- Start with whatever you've decided matters to you about your character. Is he/she like you? Like someone you know? A person who starts out tough?

- Put together a character where all the parts fit together into a coherent person.

- Reread often, asking, "Do these different things make sense within one person? Do they fit together in a believable way? Are these traits here for a reason?"

- Open up any broad, general descriptors—words like sensitive—and ask, "What exactly does this word, this trait, mean for this particular character?"

- If a character seems too good to be true, make the character more complex and more human by asking, "What is the downside of this trait? How does this characteristic help and hurt the character?"

- Know your character's motivations (longings) and struggles.

Threading a single chart through a series of minilessons is a great way to keep yesterday's teaching points front and center in children's minds. It is typical for a minilesson to become the latest bullet on a chart. Be sure that your charts are sensible examples of "boxes and bullets." That is, you won't want to add a tip about editing onto a chart titled Advice for Developing a Character, nor will you want to simply create hodge-podge charts.

WRITING AND CONFERRING

Showing Characters by Writing Scenes

You may find that many of your writers could benefit from a conference like the one I had with Francesca. I pulled my chair alongside her and saw she'd written the entry shown in Figure IV-1.

> Griffen likes to act like he is 13. He likes to act really cool. Sometimes he embarrasses himself in front of Julie Colings. Griffen really loves Julie. He is always trying to impress her but this boy Mikey the Bully always takes her away.

"Francesca," I said. "You've got a great idea for your story, and you've sketched out some notes on Griffen. Your next step will be to try writing some scenes which show Griffen and Julie in action—they probably won't be scenes you actually include in your final story, but writing them will help you know these characters better. Remember in the minilesson how we remembered what Luz wants, which is for kids to think she's cool and to not realize she's afraid to sleep without a night-light. So all of us imagined a scene that might show Luz doing something around those fears and wants. Ramon started off just summarizing by saying, 'Luz is lying in her bed, practicing sleeping in the dark. She could get scared,' but then he ended up making a movie in his mind that *showed* this. He had to picture it in a step-by-step way, and he started by thinking, 'What exactly is she doing?' That scene turned out this way."

> I stared through the darkness to where my lamp usually shone brightly. "I've got to practice," I said to myself. I turned onto my stomach and squeezed my eyes shut . . .

"Francesca, you'll get to know Griffen so much better if you make him come to life in a scene in your notebook. I guess you already know he wants to impress Julie. Can you think of one particular time when Griffen acted cool, trying to impress Julie?" I waited till she nodded. "Now you need to ask yourself the same question: 'What *exactly* is Griffen doing? How does it start?'"

"He and Timmy are riding their bikes and he . . . "

"So write that!" I said, dictating, "One time Timmy and Griffen . . . "

MID-WORKSHOP TEACHING POINT

Sharing a Scene That Shows a Character's Traits   "Writers, I want to show you the important work Ariana is doing. Yesterday she wrote entries about her character. In one of them, she'd written this:"

> Sally is different in front of her friends than her mom. She tries to talk really cool. Sally hates tomatoes, but her mom keeps making stuff she has to eat with tomatoes in it. That makes her mad.

"So today, Ariana decided to try her hand at writing a scene that showed this, just like we did with Luz's fear of the night. You'll remember that to get started, we began by thinking, 'Where could Luz be? What could she be doing?' and so Ariana asked herself these same questions. She knew she wanted to show that her character, Sally, sometimes gets mad at her

continued on next page

> Griffen likes to act like he is 13. He likes to act really cool. Sometimes he embarrases himself in front of Julie Colings. Griffen really loves Julie. He is always trying to impress her but this Boy Mikey the Bully always takes her away.

Fig. IV-1 Francesca's first draft of a scene

Francesca wrote this entry: *[Fig. IV-2]*

> One time Timmy and Griffen were riding their bikes and he went by Julie Colings. Griffen quickly stopped. "Hi Griffen," she said in a loving way. "Hi Julie," Griffen said almost falling to the floor. "Well bye," Julie said. Griffen could not say another word. Then he fell on the floor . . . .
>
> The next day Griffen saw some 13-year-olds skateboarding on a big ramp. Griffen wanted to impress Julie so he asked to try. Timmy told him that it was a bad idea but he did it. He landed flat on his face and the 13-year-olds teased him. Griffen was so embarrassed.
>
> Then Julie went over to him and pulled him up. "Are you ok?" she said. "Of course," Griffen said meekly. "Well bye," Julie said.

continued from previous page

mother for making her eat things with tomatoes, and also Sally acts differently when she's talking to her friends. Pretty soon she'd written this scene." *[Fig. IV-3]*

> I thump, thump, thump down the stairs into the kitchen.
>
> "Hurry, we are having tomato soup tonight"
>
> "Mom, I hate tomato soup!" I yelled
>
> "You have to."
>
> "I don't got ah" I said in a strong voice.
>
> "Go upstairs right now, young lady," she said.
>
> I thumped back up the stairs and yelled, "I hate you."
>
> That's when my mom got really mad. I picked up the phone and dialed Sarah's number.
>
> "Hello" she said.
>
> "What-up?" I said.
>
> "Nothing up, I got punished."

continued on next page

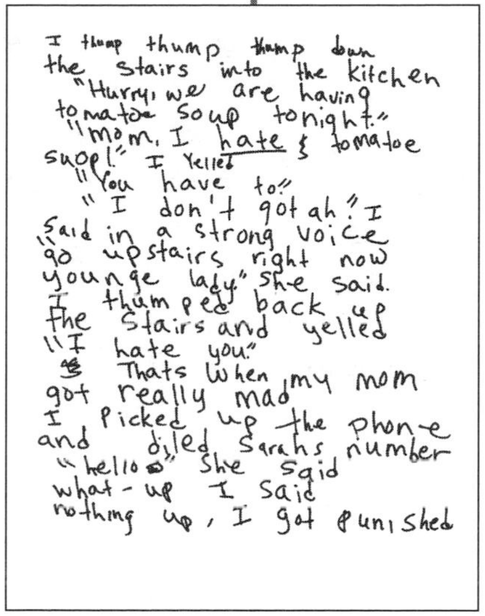
I thump thump thump down
the stairs into the kitchen
"Hurry, we are having
tomatoe soup tonight."
"Mom, I hate tomatoe
soup!" I Yelled
"You have to."
"I don't got ah" I
said in a strong voice
"go upstairs right now
younge lady" she said.
I thumped back up
the stairs and yelled
"I hate you"
Thats when my mom
got really mad
I picked up the phone
and diled Sarahs number
"hello" she said
what-up I said
nothing up, I got punished

Fig. IV-3 Ariana's scene showing her character

Meanwhile, I'd moved onto Felix who'd written reams of notes about Max. "What a lot of work!" I exclaimed, and asked Felix to give me a guided tour of his entries. They seemed to have been written in a chain-of-thought style, with one detail about a character prompting the idea for a related detail. Max was at the park saying to people, "You dropped your brain," or "Your sock is untied." "He is not a bully but no bully goes near him. He wants to be a boxer. He goes to boxing lessons." The details about Max clearly conveyed complexity. Felix wrote, "Max is very scared because there's this new kid. He's as strong as a bulldozer. He might cream Max." In addition, Max is scared of clowns and horses. Felix summarized the latter fear, saying, "Because one day Max's uncle owned a farm and they were going to ride on horses and there was a mean old one. Max still has a horseshoe scar but he puts cream on to hide it." *[Fig. IV-4]*

After taking a guided tour through Felix's ten pages of entries, I asked, "What are you planning to do next as a writer?" Felix pointed out that he'd gathered entries especially about his main character, Max, and still needed to decide on his other characters and then develop them. I asked how he planned to decide on the

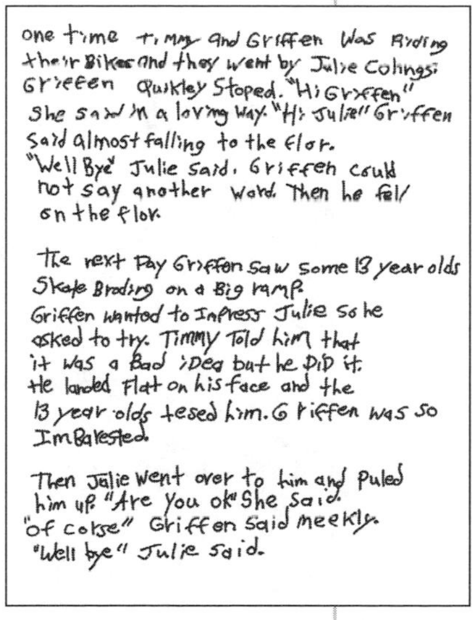
one time timmy and Griffen Was riding
their Bikes and they went by Julie Colings.
Griffen Quikley Stoped. "Hi Griffen"
She said in a loving way. "Hi Julie" Griffen
said almost falling to the flor.
"Well Bye" Julie said. Griffen could
not say another word. Then he fell
on the flor.

The next day Griffen saw some 13 year olds
Skate Brodiry on a Big ramp.
Griffen wanted to Inpress Julie so he
asked to try. Timmy Told him that
it was a Bad idea but he Did it.
He landed Flat on his face and the
13 year olds tesed him. Griffen was so
ImBaresed.

Then Julie went over to him and Puled
him up. "Are you ok" She said.
"of corse" Griffen Said meekly.
"Well bye" Julie said.

Fig. IV-2 Francesca's 2nd draft of a scene

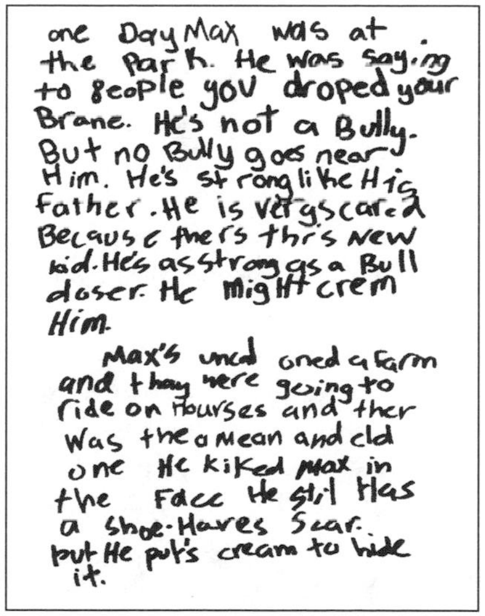
one Day Max was at
the Park. He was saying
to people you droped your
Brane. He's not a Bully.
But no Bully goes near
Him. He's strong like His
father. He is very scared
Because there's this new
kid. He's as strong as a Bull
doser. He might crem
Him.

Max's uncel oned a farm
and they were going to
ride on horses and ther
Was the a mean and old
one He kiked Max in
the Face He stil Has
a Shoe-Hores Scar.
but He put's cream to hide
it.

Fig. IV-4 Felix's entry in which he develops the character of Max.

secondary characters and he said he figured he'd need to write about Max's parents, so he might start there.

"Felix," I said. "I want to congratulate you on the fact that you've developed a really complex, interesting character. You could have just made Max into a tough boxer but you built in tension in your story idea, suggesting a new kid moves to town who could be even tougher than Max, and suggesting also that for all his cool, tough exterior, Max is still afraid of clowns and of horses. You've made him into a really human, complex, real sort of a person, and I can see why you're thinking of doing the same work for a host of other characters. You're really talented at developing characters, and I may want you to help others who struggle with this."

continued from previous page
"I love that Ariana brought her character to life, writing a Small Moment story that *showed* the kind of person she is! So when you sit with your notebook in front of you today, before you start an entry, make a choice. Will you add to your chart, listing internal and external characteristics? Will you write *about* your story idea, thinking on the paper so that your entry sounds like, 'In my story, I might show . . .'? Or will you try the new work you learned about today, and write a scene?"

Then I said, "But Felix, instead of moving on to do similar work with a host of other characters, I think you'd profit by first trying to crystallize your story. If you worked now on a secondary character, it could be someone in the park, someone he boxes with, a person at the farm . . . . I'd first zoom in a bit on the central tension of your story. I'd do that by taking some of the tensions you've created in your characters, and try to think through, 'What might end up being a turning-point moment for Max?' You could think about a time when he changes, maybe, or when he goes from being totally tough to being something else." Then I reminded Felix to zoom in on one particular moment, to envision it and to write the scene step-by-step. Before long, Felix had written these entries. *[Figs. IV-5 and IV-6]*

Should I get on that horse? No, no, no. Do it. Stop going. I won't. I will. My little brother will make fun of me. He will tell everybody in school.

I am scared of horses. What happens when it moves? Nothing. How do I stop it?

Oh no, it goes faster. Stop, stop, stop, kablam. I am not getting on a horse ever! It smells, it's ugly, everything is bad. I'd rather babysit three-year-olds. I will hate horses for the rest of my life. Why did I get on that horse?

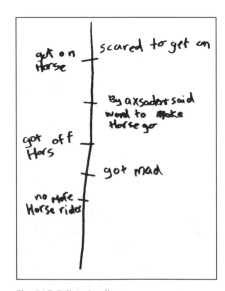

Fig. IV-5 Felix's timeline

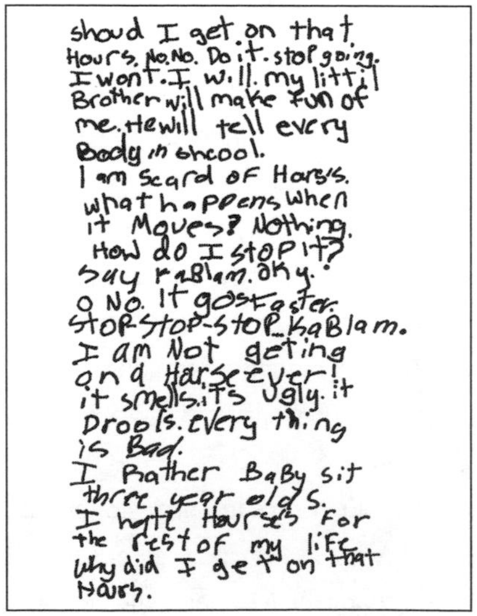

Fig. IV-6 Felix puts his character, Max, into action—riding a horse.

SHARE

Remembering What You Know About Writing Small Moment Stories

Share the work of one writer who used what he learned about writing in previous units. Explain that all writers can do likewise and invite them to begin.

"Ramon just did some important work that all of us could learn from. His story is about Marco, who knows his grandfather will leave soon for Jamaica and who wants to feel more connected to his grandfather before the old man leaves. Ramon didn't come right out and say any of this, instead he put his character—Marco—in the kitchen, cooking his grandfather some scrambled eggs as a way to do something for him. Ramon stretches out the action in the cooking scene, like all of you learned to do with your personal narratives. Marco cracks the eggs on the edge of the bowl and is afraid they'll slurp down the side of the bowl, and he's worried that the shells will go into the bowl and the breakfast will be ruined. But this is the really smart thing: When I asked Ramon how he'd thought to do this smart work, he said, 'I just wrote it like a small moment! I followed our old charts.' He keeps the charts from our narrative units on his desk as he writes."

"Based on Ramon's suggestion, I've found our chart and hung it up. Would you get with your partner now and talk about that Small Moment story chart and your efforts to write what we are calling a s*cene*? Because really, a scene in a fiction story *is* a small moment."

"If you see qualities of good personal narrative writing that you've forgotten to try to do, I don't suggest revising your writing. Instead, I suggest you take an entry you almost like and write it all over again, an entirely new version, this time using all that we learned earlier in the year to help you write it as an effective small moment."

By this time in the year, your children will be very familiar with the term Small Moment. They will therefore have an easier time understanding what a scene is if you describe it as a small moment in a story. This is also a good way to reinforce connections between units of study and between elements of writing.

Qualities of Good Personal Narrative Writing

- Write a little seed story; don't write all about a giant watermelon topic.
- Zoom in so you tell the most important parts of the story.
- Include true, exact details from the movie you have in your mind.
- Begin with a strong lead—maybe use setting, action, dialogue, or a combination to create mood.
- Make a strong ending—maybe use action, dialogue, images, and whole-story reminders to make a lasting impression.
- Stay inside your own point of view. This will help you to write with true and exact details.

It's a good idea to remind children of strategies and charts they've used in previous units of study. Students will have better results if they understand that one unit of study often builds on another and that good writing techniques apply to many kinds of writing.

HOMEWORK | *Writing an Ordinary Scene Revealing Character*   One of my writing teachers once told me the best way to get to know your character is to write a quick scene with your character in a very ordinary situation, like taking out the garbage or going food shopping or getting dressed in the morning. Then, while writing that ordinary scene, you try to keep in mind everything you know about your character as a person: their internal qualities, their external qualities, and their troubles. Remember, I already tried this with Luz, putting her in a place she goes everyday:

> Luz looked at her dresser. She knew she should maybe put on a nice blouse or something. After all, it was picture day. Instead, she pulled out her denim overalls that had the paint splatters on the knees. Her mom hated those overalls. She thought they looked like rags. Luz loved them. They were soft against her skin, and comfortable too.

I added something about how Luz loves art, tucking in what we decided about this character:

> She could fit her extra pencils and erasers for her sketches in the back pocket.

And since I knew that Luz cares about what people think, I couldn't just have her wear her overalls. I wanted her to do something to make her mom happy, so I wrote this:

> She looked at the top drawer of her dresser and thought about what shirt she could wear. She decided to go with the purple one her grandmother gave her for her birthday. It was dressy enough for picture day, but comfortable enough to wear with overalls.

I hope you noticed that I made just a tiny scene but I incorporated a lot of what we know about Luz. We may never use this scene in our story, but it helps us get to know her even better when we begin to write a little longer about her. This is something you can do when you feel like you have a pretty good idea about your character and what she or he is like.

Tonight, continue to get to know your character. Place your character in an everyday scene to see how well you know your character internally and externally. Think about something your character probably does every day, getting dressed for school or going to the store or playing with her dog. Then place your character in that situation and see how much you come to know about your character.

It's important to have kids practice placing their characters in ordinary scenes. If we teach them only to write dramatic scenes, they'll rely on the action of the story rather than digging deeply into character. When you have students reveal their characters through ordinary, everyday moments, you're showing them that in stories, the gritty stuff is often shown with small details or actions, or with internal thought or dialogue. Mastering this is tough, but it's key to effective fiction writing. The more your students practice, the better they'll get.

This homework, like so many of them, could instead be used as the heart of a minilesson.

If your students need help creating tension in their writing . . . you might want to craft a minilesson around teaching them to show, not tell, the character's struggles. To create tension in a story, the character needs to want something. Just as important, *the reader needs to discover for himself what the character wants*! If the author comes right out and names the character's motivations, we are less apt to be caught up in them. Once we grasp the character's motivations, they become our own. In a good story, we read quickly, wanting to discover for ourselves whether the story turns out okay. We read, hoping Goldilocks gets away from the bears, that the prince will spot the girl sitting in the cinders, that Jack will make it down the beanstalk before the giant catches him.

If your students are having a difficult time with the abstract concept of motivation . . . you could develop a minilesson that teaches writers that the characters in their stories—like those in the novels they are reading in reading workshop—have troubles. You might say something like, "We all know from our reading work that characters have troubles, just like real people do. Those troubles make the story more interesting and the character more realistic. The thing is, when we think about the troubles our characters might have, we don't want those troubles to come out of nowhere. The troubles need to make sense for our characters in the same way that our characters' external qualities make sense with their internal qualities. Writers sometimes look at the internal and external qualities of a character to see if these qualities suggest hidden troubles that fit with who the character is as a person." You could say, "Watch me think about the troubles that Luz encounters," and then you could flip through the pages you'd written about her and say, "I know a lot about this character, but I don't see any troubles right away. She likes animals. She lives with her mom. She is artistic. She has brown hair. At first glance, I don't really see anything . . . But wait . . . I wrote here that she's sensitive and she cares a lot about what people think. Maybe there's some trouble there. Maybe, because her clothes are casual, someone makes fun of her and it really hurts her feelings." Then you might jot these notes on a fresh piece of chart paper:

- Somebody makes fun of her clothes
- This hurts her feelings

You could show children how you press on, asking, "What else do I know about Luz that is really important? Hmm . . . I know she's artistic. Maybe her trouble comes from making art and people not liking it. Or maybe she paints a picture for an art contest and something happens. I'm not really sure yet, but I think one of her troubles could be about art because art is something that's so much a part of her character." Here you might add another bullet to the list:

- Somebody makes fun of her clothes
- This hurts her feelings
- Something bad happens with Luz's art

Be sure to debrief. Do so by saying something such as, "These are realistic troubles because they come from Luz's character. They're believable. Notice how I didn't say she was disappointed she didn't make the soccer team, because soccer is not something she really cares about. Instead, I used what I knew about her and the kinds of troubles that would make sense for her to have. I just jotted a few notes so I can go back later and see which troubles make the most sense for my story when I get ready to draft."

COLLABORATING WITH COLLEAGUES

In your study group, you'll definitely want to spend time reading. Read, read, read. Read the sort of stories you want to write. Devour stories. Read them once, twice, again. Turn them inside out and notice all the decisions the author made. For example, if you and your colleagues study Peter Reynold's picture book *Ish* (which I heartily recommend), you might notice things like these:

- Within the first few sentences, readers know who is doing what. The story begins with action; it begins with an action that reveals the main character's wants. Right away, we learn that Ramon wants to draw something beautiful—a vase of flowers. Before long, we also know why Ramon struggles—his brother laughs at him.

- We aren't told what the characters want, and what they struggle over—we're *shown* this. Leon sees his kid brother's drawing, bursts out laughing, and asks, "What is that?" Ramon crumples up the drawing and throws it across the room.

- This story is composed of scenes or small moments and also of summaries. Between the vignettes there are passages such as this one:

  > [Ramon] kept trying to make his drawings look "right" but they never did. After many months and many crumpled sheets of paper, Ramon put his pencil down. "I'm done."

- The central character experiences a journey of feelings in this story. Ramon's body language alone shows that he goes from resolve to dejection before finding his way back to happiness.

- The story is held together by a central theme. The title and page one connect to the heart of the story, as does the ending.

- Some parts of the story are described in more detail—the characters' actions are detailed in smaller steps. Notice, for example, that there is more text on the pages that are at the center of the book—"the heart of the story" or "the top of the story mountain."

You and your colleagues could also study the characters in Cynthia Rylant's story, "Papa's Parrot." This is a terrific story for character study because the characters, far from being two-dimensional, are unapologetically flawed and complex. In her opening line, Rylant writes, "Though his father was fat and merely owned a candy and nut shop, Harry Tillian liked his papa." Immediately we imagine not only the rotund papa, but a boy who sees nothing wrong with disparaging his father—what he looks like, what he does—whom he also claims to (nonetheless) like. There's humor here, and sadness, too, which is on some level the point of her piece: that we're not just one way or another—good or bad—and that life, like people, can be read in various ways.

You could teach students that Rylant probably prepared for writing this story by thinking about the external and the internal features of her character. She may have made a chart of either Harry or his father. A chart on Mr. Tillian might look like this:

Developing My Character

Outside (external features)	Inside (internal features)
Fat (blubbery stomach)	Sensitive
Candy/nut store owner	Sad
	Misses son

You could suggest to students that Rylant probably examined both the external and the internal traits of Mr. Tillian to see if they fit together. "Does the fat go with the candy and nut store owner?" she probably wondered. Then you could show children that Rylant probably thought also about whether "sensitive," "sad," and "misses son" match up.

Harry Tillian is by far a more complex character than his father, so for children who are ready for a challenge, or older, you might help them talk about how Rylant developed this character. The final scene, in which Harry both abuses his father's bird and cries for his papa, offers a great opportunity to explore the ways in which characters, like people, are often interesting mixes of seemingly contradictory traits. Harry is both soft and hard, and children might find a real connection with him imagining times when they, too, have acted one way, while feeling quite another.

When you and your colleagues think together about characters and their motivations, you'll probably notice that in most well-written stories, a character's initial desire is a smaller piece of a greater desire, one which is initially masked from both the character and the reader. As stories unfold, we watch a character's cares as they are revealed gradually. The character initially thinks he or she wants one thing, but in fact what the character wants turns out to be different. In *Charlotte's Web*, Wilbur longs for a friend, but when he learns his life is at stake, his sole desire becomes staying alive. It is only toward the end of the book, when he discovers that Charlotte has sacrificed her own life for his, that he recognizes how much he values the gift of love and friendship. In *The Lion, the Witch, and the Wardrobe*, Lucy first wants to prove to her sister and brothers that the world she's found beyond the wardrobe really exists. Once she's accomplished this, and reentered the world, she wants to save her friend, Mr. Tumnus, and when she discovers that all of Narnia is at risk, she strives to save the entire world from the witch's clutches. By the end, Lucy accomplishes her goal and through it she finds the respect of her siblings and the power of her convictions, which is perhaps what she was after in the first place.

PLOTTING WITH A STORY MOUNTAIN

IN THIS SESSION, YOU WILL TEACH
CHILDREN THAT WRITERS SKETCH
OUT POSSIBLE PLOT LINES FOR
STORIES, OFTEN ON STORY
MOUNTAINS WHICH REPRESENT
TRADITIONAL STORY STRUCTURE.

GETTING READY

- Story mountain on chart for *Peter's Chair* (used in Unit 2)
- See CD-ROM for resources

Some people imagine that writers put a pen to paper and out pours a story, or a novel, or a play, from beginning to end. In fact, that is how the writing process is often depicted in movies, giving the average person a romantic but false version of how writers work. We are fortunate to know from our own processes and through learning from countless writers over the years that the process involves as much organization as inspiration. This unit of study offers a perfect opportunity to teach children the power of rehearsal, and specifically, it gives us a chance to teach children that writers organize our ideas before we embark on a draft.

In this session, we again remind writers of a template used by countless authors to structure the plot lines of their fiction—the story mountain. As an organizing tool, the story mountain acts like a timeline or an outline. It allows the writer to step outside the details of the story to see the big picture. As children learned during the Raising the Quality of Narrative Writing unit, the shape of the mountain (as opposed to a timeline) can help writers visualize that in a story, characters journey uphill, against obstacles. By asking children to plan their plot against a story mountain, we steer them away from writing in a chain of equally important events. Instead of planning a story which involves just a string of episodes, children will plan a story in which a character reaches toward a goal, then meets and overcomes difficulty. Today's session goes farther and points out that just as in climbing a real mountain, the obstacles get harder to overcome as one progresses, with the most dramatic challenge occurring at the top. Often there is a sense that from the top, a character gains vision. Coming down from the mountain, the character probably feels more experienced.

This session also emphasizes that story mountains, like timelines, are tools for revision. Because children will be writing in scenes and not in summaries, they'll probably need to revise their story plans by zooming in on just two or perhaps three key moments.

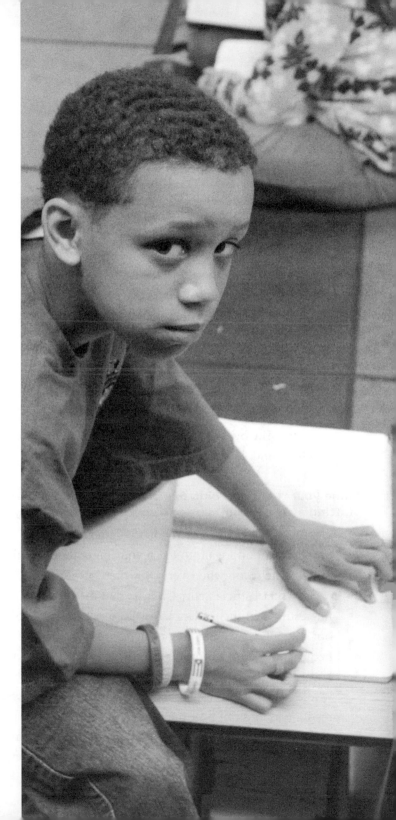

MINILESSON

Plotting with a Story Mountain

CONNECTION

Remind children that once fiction writers have brought their characters to life, we use a knowledge of the characters' wants and struggles to develop a possible plot line.

"Writers, a few days ago, I told you that fiction writers don't just go from choosing a story idea to writing a draft. Instead, fiction writers have strategies for bringing people to life, strategies like thinking about the internal and the external characteristics of the main character, the protagonist. We go through our lives thinking, 'What would my character do in this situation?' We give special attention to what a character yearns for and struggles with."

"We postpone thinking about what happens in a story, about the plot of a story, until we've done this other work. We postpone thinking about the sequence of events because eventually we take all we know about our characters—especially our understanding of what our characters yearn for and struggle with—and we use this information to create a plan for our stories."

"You'll remember that when we wrote our personal narratives earlier this year, we got ready to write by remembering what happened and plotting the sequence of events on little timelines and, later, on story mountains."

Name your teaching point. Specifically, remind children that fiction writers plan by plotting a story mountain—and specifically, by aiming to intensify the problem.

"Today I want to teach you that after we develop our characters, we draft possible story mountains. And I want to teach you something new about plotting your story, something that will help you whenever you write fiction from now on!"

"Writer Patricia Reilly Giff says that the fiction writer's job is to make every part so interesting that the reader can't wait to turn the page. She says some writers call that 'plotting,' but she calls it 'making the problem worse and worse!' Story mountains can help you do that because they remind you that you have to keep giving the characters something that makes it harder and harder to climb toward their goal. It's like each point along the mountain is just a whole new mess of trouble for your character. That's what makes readers want to keep reading, to find out how the character will solve these problems!"

"The story mountain also shows you that something is going to happen, and things are really getting tough, and then, bam, something happens right there, on the top of that

COACHING

Before now, children may have drafted scenes that put their characters into motion and revealed them as people, but those scenes will probably not comprise the start of their story. Before a fiction writer can write her lead, the writer needs to know the character, to imagine him or her in action, and to have drafted, chosen between and revised multiple plot lines for the story. Today, then, children will consider a variety of ways their stories could unroll.

We considered postponing this minilesson and this emphasis on plotting a story in order to encourage writers to spend more time putting their characters into scenes as you saw us recommending in the homework to the last session. There are lots of judgement calls to be made when designing curriculum—and you'll be in the best position to judge. So be sure you keep close tabs on your children and jettison these lessons in favor of ones you design.

Notice that I teach story mountains within the context of a bigger focus—thinking about how the story will go in general (across the pages). Only after emphasizing that the character will get himself or herself into a growing mess of trouble do I mention that this is signified by the rising slope of the story mountain. I'm trying to be sure the graphic organizer functions as a symbolic representation for the story itself.

mountain, that changes things or that solves your character's problem. After that, going along is different, easier, like your character is going down the mountain and the tough part is behind and there isn't a feeling of anticipation anymore."

TEACHING
Explain why a writer would use a story mountain to help plan a plot. Teach children that writers are not always sure of what might happen in their story when they first set out to draft a plan.

"Writers, earlier, when we were studying personal narratives, we realized that just as minilessons have a way they usually go, a pattern, so, too, do stories have a way they usually go. And we learned that usually the main character has wants, and something gets in the way of the character getting all that he or she wants. So the character encounters trouble, or a problem. And today, we learned that usually after encountering the problem, things get worse and worse, or harder and harder, or more and more complicated for a while."

"You'll remember that when we were studying personal narratives, we looked at Ezra Jack Keats' *Peter's Chair*, noticing that the story could be outlined in a story mountain that looked like this," I said, turning back to a chart the children recognized:

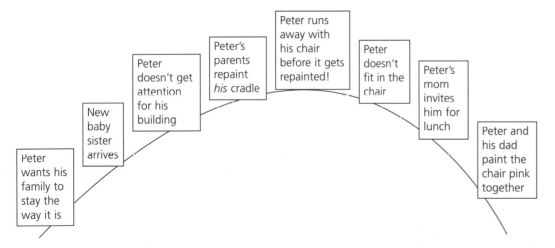

"When Ezra Jack Keats wrote this book, he probably knew he'd start it with Peter's block tower crashing down and his mother responding not by saying, 'Oh, your tower! Let me help you rebuild it' but instead by saying, 'Shush. You'll wake the baby!' And Ezra Jack Keats almost certainly knew the trouble would escalate; it would get worse and worse. But he probably didn't know, when he started to write the story, exactly what would happen. I bet he imagined one way the story might go, and another, and another."

Notice that in a single minilesson, I teach the rise and also the fall of the story arc, the story mountain. These are interrelated and need to be thought of as a broad sweeping stroke, not as discrete items. Of course, I'll need to reteach much of this!

I'm especially aware that I'm oversimplifying the resolution part of a story, setting children up to believe that in every story characters achieve all that they want which is far, far from true.

There are advantages and disadvantages to revisiting Keats' Peter's Chair. The advantage is that children not only know the book, they also know how the book can be represented as a story mountain. Therefore you can mention the book and graphic organizer in passing, and spotlight the new concept you're weaving into this session which is the idea that as one progresses through a story, trouble escalates. The disadvantage of this book is that it is not only a familiar book, it's also a story written for and about a child who is younger than your students. There are countless wonderful alternatives, if you so choose. One is Reynold's Ish, described earlier, and another is Peggy Rathman's Ruby the Copy Cat, a Scholastic book about a child who yearns to be accepted and therefore copies her idol's every move. We refer to the latter text in an upcoming session on revising one's lead. I also recommend John Steptoe's Stevie.

"Authors always know that the trouble will grow, and that characters will make choices—some of which probably won't work out. And authors know that *somehow*, in the midst of all the trouble, *somehow* there will be *something* that makes a difference. I bet Ezra Jack Keats didn't start his book realizing all the little details—he probably didn't know before he started writing that Peter would try to sit in his little chair and would find he didn't fit."

"When we plot our Luz story, I know that our character will struggle to achieve what she yearns for, our character will make choices. Some of those choices may not work out. We don't know which ones, exactly. But we do know that something will happen that makes a difference. Our character will find a way to resolve the struggle or she will change her sense of what she wants."

"And we know that just as a story mountain gets steeper and steeper, the challenges Luz faces, or the intensity of the feelings she has about them, will get stronger and stronger until finally one way or another, things will be decided. In other words, Luz will then be at the top of the story mountain."

ACTIVE ENGAGEMENT
Demonstrate planning a possible plot line based on the story idea the class has been following.

"So let's try planning our Luz story, the one that Ramon helped us start, keeping this story mountain in mind. In the draft we've already begun, we have Luz lying in bed, practicing sleeping without a light on so she can sleep in the dark at a slumber party. Then she gets up to turn on the closet light. Before fiction writers move forward to plot the whole story, it helps to rethink the start of it. Do you want to keep what we have so far as the very beginning? (This does show Luz's fears.) Or we could alter the beginning, perhaps in a way that more dramatically shows what she wants, and only then shows her fears."

"Talk with your partner and think what the first few dots on the story mountain would be. The starting scene (which will probably be the first two dots on the story mountain) must bring Luz to life, show what she yearns for, and show the trouble (which we already know will be her fear of sleeping in the dark and of being embarrassed in front of her friends). And remember, that mountain needs to get steeper, so think about how we'll then make Luz's problem get worse and worse! Turn and plan the start of our story mountain."

You'll notice that across the year, we revisit the same texts often. "Eleven" was a touchstone text for the unit, Raising the Quality of Personal Narrative Writing, *and it will resurface in* Literary Essays *and also* Memoir. *And in this instance, we bring children back to consider the story mountain Ezra Jack Keats probably made when he was planning* Peter's Chair. *It is also significant to notice that both of these texts and others that thread their way through these units are relatively simple and brief ones. When we want children to do some important new conceptual work, it's easier for them to do this when the material illustrating those new concepts is not overwhelming, complex, and gigantic.*

In this minilesson, you'll notice that the Teaching component is brief because most of the teaching is embedded in the Active Engagement. I mostly told and reviewed, and I did not show—an exception from the norm.

The story mountain is useful because it provides a concrete image for thinking about a complicated idea. When teaching students about the story mountain, I draw an actual mountain shape on a chart and model the plot points that move the character toward a moment when he or she solves a problem, confronts someone, changes, or learns something.

Many writers say that they aim to gradually raise the stakes in a story, intensifying the tension. In this instance I hope that I'm helping children imagine ways they can tweak a story plan to intensify the tension.

Annie Lamott, in Bird by Bird, *reminds us of the relationship between character development and the story mountain. "Find out what each character cares most about in the world," she writes, "because then you will have discovered what's at stake" (p. 55).*

Everyone started to talk. I moved among the partners. Marissa said, "Let's think of a different beginning, one that shows she wants friends. We could have Luz decide to hold a slumber party. Then she gets worried who'll come."

I nodded. "But try to think about that in terms of actions. What exactly might you show Luz *doing* when she decides to have a slumber party? How does the movie in your mind actually go at this starting scene?"

Marissa answered, "She realizes her birthday is just two weeks away. Then she starts writing invitations."

I nodded. "But you can't *tell* that she realizes her birthday is coming. What could she do? Imagine this as a movie. What would the character be doing that shows her realizing this?"

Marissa jumped up with excitement. "She looks at a calendar?"

Convene the class. Report on overheard ideas for how the story could begin.

"Writers, I heard some great ideas. Some of you suggested we alter the start so as to show first that Luz is hoping lots of friends come to her birthday party. Marissa thought the story could begin with Luz looking at a calendar, realizing her birthday was approaching, and beginning to address invitations. Would you be willing to have our story start like Marissa suggests?" I asked, and when children agreed, jotted an abbreviated version of Marissa and Ramon's points on the story mountain and retold those scenes from the story.

Set children up to imagine what might come next, then convene the children and add their ideas to the story mountain.

"What could come next? Remember you'd need to *show* (not summarize) her struggle and that the problems need to get worse and worse. Turn to your partner and plan."

Notice that in this Active Engagement, children are not only working on the teaching point of the day. They're also synthesizing all they know to collaboratively author a story. This is an unusual Active Engagement for this reason.

John Gardner, one of our leading novelists and the author of The Art of Fiction, *describes reading fiction by saying, "We act out, vicariously, the trials of the characters and learn from the failures and successes of particular modes of action." For fiction to do its job creating a drama in the reader's mind, it must create a vivid and continuous dream. The flow of action can't be continually interrupted by a stage manager's voice, inserting little explanatory comments. Gardner writes, "One of the chief mistakes a writer can make is to allow or force the reader's mind to be distracted, even momentarily, from the fictional dream." The writer encourages the reader to dream by presenting as many concrete details as possible. I'm trying, in this intervention, to elicit those concrete details and to remind writers that the story is carried by scenes, not summary.*

You'll see that I don't retell this conversation with Marissa in any detail to the class. I do share Marissa's idea for a lead, but I do not spotlight the way in which I coached her toward showing, not telling. In this instance, I decided it was more important to channel children's attention toward the actual plan for the Luz story. But I easily could have publicized the pointers I gave to Marissa, because they could have helped many others as well.

"The first job of a story's beginning is to start at the right time. It should not start when things are quiet, when nothing's happening, when things are much the same as they always have been. After all, the whole reason we tell the story is because something about life is new and different, something's happening that stands out—and your responsibility, as the writer, is to begin the work at that point of change" (Ebenbach, p. 60).

You'll notice that more of my pointers to you are about fiction and craft, and less about methods of teaching. This unit is a sophisticated one.

Again I listened in, and after a bit I again paraphrased what I'd heard a child suggest. Soon the story mountain contained these "dots":

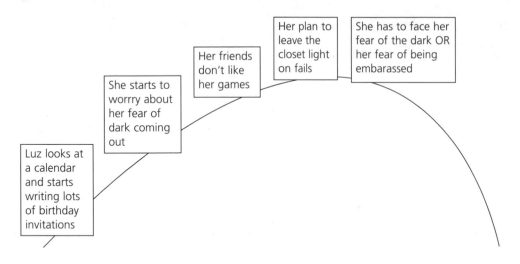

Boxes along the story mountain arc, left to right:
- Luz looks at a calendar and starts writing lots of birthday invitations
- She starts to worrry about her fear of dark coming out
- Her friends don't like her games
- Her plan to leave the closet light on fails
- She has to face her fear of the dark OR her fear of being embarassed

Philip Gerard, in his chapter, "An Architecture of Light: Structuring the Novel and Story Collection" suggests that stories have a "signature" that can be stated in a single sentence. The signature for Moby Dick is "Madman goes hunting for a white whale." This line defines what Gerard refers to as the "structural arc" of the story. He writes, "Think of the signature as the cable that hauls the roller-coaster cars up the long hill of suspense, round the hair pin turn of reversal, down the stomach-clenching fall". (p.152)

Most importantly, Gerard says that although writers begin with our structural arc and our characters clearly in mind, "almost everything will change." (p.153)

LINK
Remind writers that when fiction writers plot story mountains, we do so knowing the problems will get worse and worse.

"So writers, I hope you've been reminded today that the time comes when fiction writers plot possible story mountains. We are usually not sure exactly what will happen next, but we plan the start of the story against the shape of a story mountain, remembering that we can't just write any old thing next. In our Luz story, after she makes the invitations, we can't have her grandmother arrive and the family go to dinner, forgetting all about her being afraid of the dark and the slumber party! Instead, when we ask ourselves, 'What will happen next?' we already know that Luz's struggles to master her fear of the dark and to have friends will get worse and worse."

"So let's go—draft your story mountain, and do so, making the problem worse and worse, like writers always do!"

WRITING AND CONFERRING

Building Story Mountains

I drew my chair first alongside Caleb, who had taped a crude story mountain onto the far corner of his desk, and was now staring at a half-written page. "You've put your story mountain just exactly where Rachel, in "Eleven," put that red sweater," I said. "It's on the tippy top corner of your desk and if it could hang over the edge like a waterfall, I bet you'd push it there! Are you trying to get it out of sight, out of mind?"

Caleb laughed and assured me that he wasn't mad at the story *mountain*, just at the story. I glanced at the graph, noticing that instead of marking specific small-moment scenes into it, he'd labeled general trajectories he'd planned for the story. [Fig. V-1]

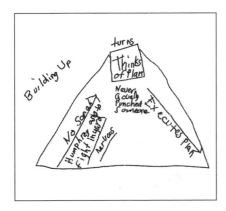

Fig. V-1 Caleb's Story Mountain

But it seemed he was preoccupied with other worries. "So what's troubling you?" I asked.

"I want to show Spencer walking to school, worrying about Humphrey, the bully. But I just keep telling what's in his brain: 'I'm worried. I'm so worried. I'm really worried.' There isn't any way to *show* his worries except if he looks up and down the block like James Bond or something," he said.

MID-WORKSHOP TEACHING POINT **Finding Story Mountains in Published Stories** "I need to stop us for just a moment and tell you something really wonderful that's going on right now. I just saw Ari get up quietly from his seat and grab his folders. Then I noticed he was going back and rereading some of the realistic fiction short stories we've been reading as a class. I wasn't sure what he was doing at first, but then I talked to Ari and realized he was doing something so smart. Ari—can you tell people what you were up to?"

Ari held up his notebook to show a rough story mountain. "I was getting a little confused as I tried to put my story into a story mountain. So I thought, well, if most stories have a story mountain, I'll go and see what other writers did. I went back to look at 'The Marble Champ' and I noticed that the story starts with Lupe getting her thumb all ready for the marble competition, in lots of different ways. So I decided to look for what would be the mountain peak in 'The Marble Champ' and to make a story mountain on that story. I think Lupe's last battle where she wins the championship is the very peak of that story mountain. Because after that she got everybody's cheers, and the trophy, and her family gave her that party, and then everything seems to calm down."

I thanked Ari, and then said to the class, "Writers, if you can pull yourselves away from work on your own story, it'd be helpful for you to try what Ari did. Consider looking for a story you can use as a model for your own story. Plot the story mountain in the text you select as a mentor text. And remember, you need to continue thinking and writing about your characters even as you plot out possible story lines."

"Caleb," I responded. "You are doing what every fiction writer—really, what every writer—does. You've identified the writing problem that your story line poses. Some stories are hard because there are lots of characters, some are hard because time jumps backward and forward. Yours is hard (or at least the start of it is hard) because you want to show what your character is thinking and feeling, and yet he's walking all alone. So the problem you are struggling with is this: How does an author reveal a character's thoughts and still show, not tell? It is really smart for you to identify the problem!"

Then I said, "What I do when I encounter a problem is that instead of thinking about what the final solution will be, I switch my brain over and think, 'What strategies could I use to at least get me started on this?' So that means, for example, I'd probably sit here and just list optional ways to solve the problem. I'd brainstorm possible ways to go about solving it. How could you *maybe* solve it?"

Caleb generated a couple of ideas, culminating in the idea to add Sarah, Spencer's friend, into this section of the story. Soon he'd begun a new draft of the lead: *[Figs. V-2 and V-3]*

> Spencer and his friend, Sarah Mayberry were walking to school together.
>
> "I have my publishing party today," said Spencer.
>
> "What story did you write?" said Sarah.
>
> "About when I caught the foul ball hit by Jason Giambi."
>
> "GIAMBI!"
>
> "The one and only."
>
> "Uh-Oh," exclaimed Sarah, "It's Humphrey Dugball and his rats!"
>
> Humphrey was the meanest bully in the history of the earth. He crushed (or gave wedgies to) everyone in his path. Humphrey was the leader of a gang called the rats.
>
> Sarah watched as one of his rats and him pulled a kindergartner's pig tails. Then they looked at Spencer and a devilish grin formed on their faces. Spencer felt like a sheep in a wolf pack.
>
> "Well if it isn't one of Snow White's dwarves," Humphrey said. "Dopey." Humphrey burst out laughing like he had heard the funniest thing in the world. "Who's that," he exclaimed pointing at Sarah. "Is it your Girl . . . augh" by the time he got to the word 'friend' he was flat on the floor.

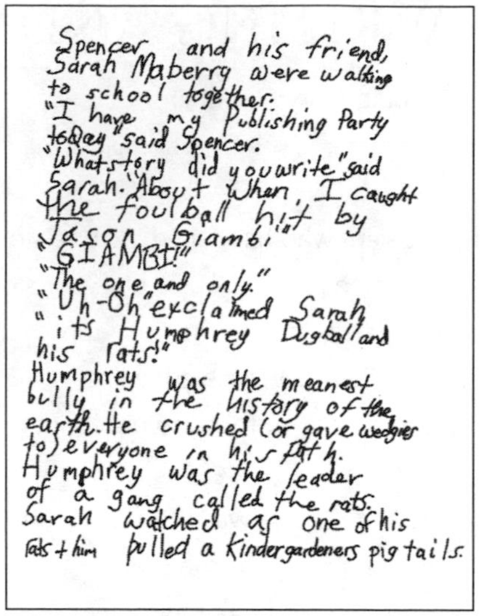
Spencer and his friend, Sarah Maberry were walking to school together.
"I have my Publishing Party today" said Spencer.
"Whatstory did you write" said Sarah. "About when I caught the foul ball hit by Jason Giambi."
"GIAMBI!"
"The one and only."
"Uh-Oh" exclaimed Sarah "its Humphrey Dugball and his rats!"
Humphrey was the meanest bully in the history of the earth. He crushed (or gave wedgies to) everyone in his path. Humphrey was the leader of a gang called the rats. Sarah watched as one of his rats + him pulled a kindergardeners pig tails.

Fig. V-2 Caleb has added a second character into his lead.

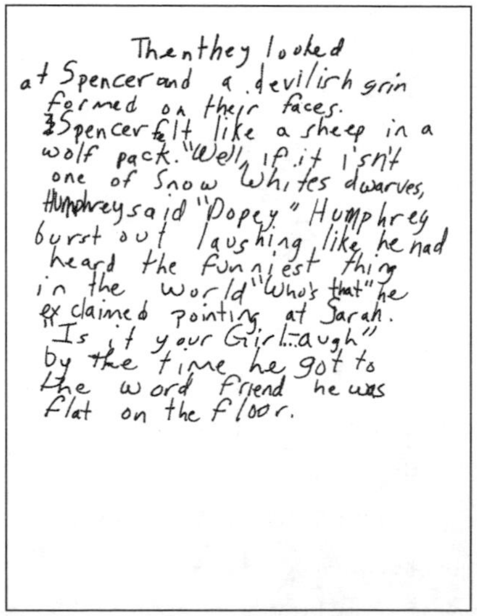
Then they looked at Spencer and a devilish grin formed on their faces. Spencer felt like a sheep in a wolf pack. "Well, if it isn't one of Snow Whites dwarves, Humphrey said "Dopey." Humphrey burst out laughing, like he had heard the funniest thing in the world "Who's that" he exclaimed pointing at Sarah. "Is it your Girl...augh" by the time he got to the word friend he was flat on the floor.

Fig. V-3 Caleb's opening scene, page 2

Once Caleb had written this lead, we again conferred. I pointed out that with the arrival of Humphrey, he'd definitely created some tension, but he hadn't really had a chance to develop Spencer's character or to show what Spencer wanted before Humphrey arrived on the scene. With that in mind, Caleb decided to revise his story mountain. "Fiction writers do that a lot," I told him. "We shift back and forth between planning possible story mountains, writing a scene or two, rereading and rethinking what we've written, and revising our story mountains."

Next I gathered a group of children together for a strategy lesson. "I want to talk to all of you together," I said, "Because each of you has a great plan for a *novel*." I added, "But I want to remind you that you are writing a very short story, and before you get much farther, you need to do some rethinking. When you plot out your story mountain, the first two dots on it will probably belong to one Small Moment story, to one vignette. And then you'll probably leap ahead to a second and maybe a third moment, but by then the story will need to be complete." Then I suggested we all look together at Felix's tentative plans, using that as a case in point. Felix had already made a timeline which began with Max winning his first boxing trophy. Then Felix shows that Max practiced to win more, followed by Max having a fight with his nemesis, Mike, followed by Max's first loss, the arrival of a girlfriend . . . [Figs. V-4, V-5, and V-6]

"You need to go back to that question," I said. "What does Max most want? Fear? Struggle toward?" The group of children helped Felix revise his plans and sketch a story mountain, and then they each brought out their own work. Soon the children had stories which were at least somewhat focused!

Fig. V-4 Felix's timeline

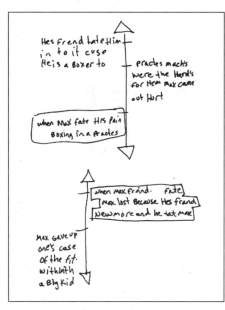

Fig. V-5 Felix's timeline, page 2

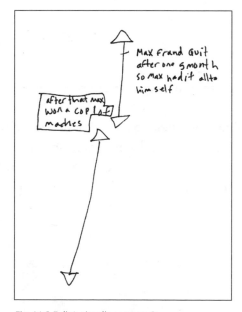

Fig. V-6 Felix's timeline, page 3

SHARE

Using Story Mountains as Tools for Revision

Share the fact that children already have strategies and tools for revision.

"Writers, I want to remind you of some work we did earlier in the year with timelines. Do you recall that we drafted timelines for our personal narrative stories and then we looked back on those timelines and asked, 'Which dot on this timeline is inconsequential to the story?" We crossed those dots out. We also asked, 'Is there one dot that's crucial?' and we often ended up rewriting that as three dots."

"We learned very early in the year that timelines are not just tools for planning, they are also tools for revision. And front-end revision is a lot more time-efficient than back-end revision."

"When we made story mountains in order to rethink our personal narratives, we again used those graphs as tools for revision. Remember how we looked between our story-beginnings, and the tops of our story mountains, and asked, 'How does the beginning relate to the real meaning of my story?' When Sophie decided her story wasn't just about going to Chuck E. Cheese's but that it was instead a story of how she and Claudia exchanged vows to be best friends, then Sophie needed to revise her lead, this time showing that en route to the restaurant, she rehearsed her proposal, feeling butterflies in her stomach."

Set partners up to share and assess story mountains with each other—and then to revise them.

"So timelines, outlines, boxes and bullets and story mountains are all tools for planning, yes, but also for revision. Would you and your partner recall what you know about stories, and look at each of your story mountains through the lenses of what you know about effective stories—then use these conversations to prompt revisions?"

Setting Yourself Up to Write Well Writers, the work you did today in our writing workshop and the work you will do tomorrow will probably be the most important work you will do in this entire unit of study. If you can start your story well, you will set yourself up for a spectacular writing experience. So tonight, your assignment is to prepare yourself. How will you do this? You'll need to decide. Write yourself an assignment, based on your own knowledge of yourself.

Are you, like Robert Munsch, the sort of writer who benefits from telling your story to one person and then another and then another? If so, recruit your family members, your dog, your sister's teddy bear to be listeners, and consciously set yourself up with specific goals before launching into a second or third rendition. Say to yourself, "This time, I'm going to try to make my mom feel how devastated he felt," or "This time, I'm going to use my words to paint a rich picture of the place."

But you may not be the sort of writer who benefits from storytelling. Perhaps, instead, you'll want to reread texts in ways that set you up to write a lead which is saturated with mood. Read then, and also write. Write one lead, and another, and another. Fiction writers often make thirty or forty attempts at beginning a story before we settle on a lead we like, and you won't have time in school tomorrow for that amount of revision.

No matter what you decide to do in the pages of your notebook—and do fill at least a page—you'll want to carry your story with you throughout the evening. Nancy Hale, in her book on fiction, describes the slow incremental growth of a story this way:

> The story continued to rise, as stories do, in my mind as I woke up in
> the morning, each day with some new addition, as though it were a
> log of driftwood that I kept pushing down into the sea only to have
> it rise again with more seaweed, more barnacles encrusted on to it.

If you go for a walk, bring your story along. If you sit on the sofa for a bit, save some space for your story to join you. Your story will be far deeper and richer because of the life work as well as the desk work you do.

● TAILORING YOUR TEACHING

If you notice some of your students appear frustrated . . . you might find that they thought they had a great story idea until they tried to show it as a story mountain. In particular, they might be wrestling with finding a good conflict to put at the top of the mountain. If this is the case, you might want to teach your students that if a writer knows his or her character very well, he or she can imagine that character in a few common conflicts. You and your students might want to brainstorm the types of conflicts they find in the fiction they read all the time. Common conflicts can be related to:

- A misunderstanding with someone in authority (teacher, parents, etc.)
- A conflict with a family member or friend
- A loss of something or someone
- A struggle to make sense of a new situation or place
- A fight with one's own conscience
- A hardship in the natural world
- A yearning for acceptance
- A deadline

Traditional ways to describe conflicts may also help students to imagine a conflict for their characters:

- Person vs. person
- Person vs. society
- Person vs. nature
- Person vs. himself or herself

If you think your students are ready for more sophisticated work thinking about story structure . . . you could let them know that not all stories have the same story mountain structure, nor are the sides of the mountain necessarily equal. You might teach your students that some story mountains have just a short climb to the crisis, and spend the rest of the story trying to come to a resolution. Other stories have a very long climb up to the crisis, with only a short time, or no time at all, for a resolution. Some stories have a series of crises and resolutions, each worse than the last—often because the "resolutions" leading up to the main crisis weren't complete resolutions of the problem. These story mountains may look like a series of peaks. Students can spend some time in their notebooks playing with story mountains of various shapes to see how the story might change based on how and where they structure the conflict. To widen their repertoire of potential story mountain shapes, they need only look at the stories all around them.

If your students are having a hard time understanding the idea of rising and falling action . . . you might want to revisit a short story they know very well, just like Ari did in the Mid-Workshop Teaching Point. Using the text of the story as your material, work with students to create a story mountain of that familiar story.

ASSESSMENT

You'll probably want to gather your children's work and try to ascertain the nature of the stories they've set themselves up to write. When you do this, try to look not at the story mountains children will have made, but rather through them to the story the writer has in mind, and the criteria for writing effective stories that the writer has assimilated. The actual graphic organizer is relatively unimportant. It's simply a vehicle, a strategy, toward a larger goal. Your real goal will be to study children's graphs, notes and entries in order to understand their writing plans.

If you find that some children seem confused by the actual format of a story mountain, then by all means show that child he or she can plan just as well with a timeline or a storyboard. *[Figs. V-7 and V-8]* Nina, for example made this storyboard about taking her sick fish to the vet. Then she wrote her story "Something Fishy." *[Figs. V-9 and V-10]*

The core structure of a short story, in a nutshell, is that a character wants or needs something (or needs to learn something) and then encounters obstacles in reaching this goal. This continues for most of the story until something happens, or someone helps, such that the character achieves that desire. The story mountain is useful visually because everyone can relate to the difficulty of climbing straight up a mountain! But other students might relate better to different graphic representations—perhaps a timeline with stars for key moments or a blank comic strip. You'll want to encourage children to use any and all means available to organize their progression of scenes.

As you reflect on students' work at this point, look for how they are using their writers' notebooks alongside their drafts to plan and organize their writing. Notice the writers who seem to "think on the page," writing out their plans for how the story might go, and then experimenting, moving items into adifferent order. By all means, celebrate this!

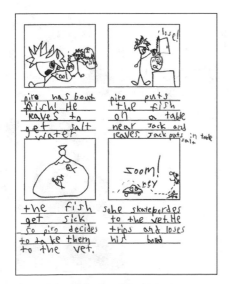

Fig. V-7 Storyboard and lead

Fig. V-8 Storyboard and lead

Fig. V-9 Nina's story

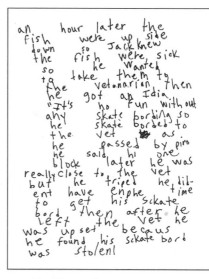

Fig. V-10 Nina's story

You will definitely, then, want to spend as much time as possible sitting alongside individuals, helping them to postpone closure on their story plans. As you teach children to brood over one idea, then another, and another, keep in mind that you are not only helping them develop a stronger story plan, you are also mentoring your students in the crucial art of revision.

You'll probably see that many of your children proceed in an all-or-nothing fashion: Either a story plan is perfect and a fait accompli or else it is terrible, and needs to be forsaken for another brand-new and totally undeveloped idea. However, it is crucial for children to learn to take a draft idea and ratchet up the level of that idea—in your assessments, try to applaud this kind of work. After all, you want to teach writers that in life, as in stories, people encounter difficulties and we persevere, eventually coming to some sort of resolution.

If you find in your assessments that children need ways to improve weak story ideas, one strategy is to teach children that a good story idea usually has the characteristics of a good mystery. When the main character encounters a problem (the mystery), the solution can't be instantly apparent and obvious to the reader; if that's the case, the story has no tension. But in the end, once the mystery has been solved, the solution can't have been utterly outlandish either. The reader should be able to look back and see that the clues were there all along.

Using these criteria, you could help children assess their own story plans, then choose one, and start drafting a lead. *[Figs. V-11 and V-12]*

Fig. V-11 Rena's story ideas

Fig. V-12 Rena's revised story idea

SHOW DON'T TELL:
PLANNING AND WRITING SCENES

Today your children will shift from planning to drafting. *You'll help them use their story mountains as guides in creating story booklets, transferring one dot from the timeline onto one page of the booklet, and then you'll help them storytell (not summarize) their plot lines. Above all, you'll help them see that show don't tell pertains to an entire draft, not just to one selected passage.*

It is easy to tell writers, "Show don't tell." But as a writer, there is never a day when I don't struggle to follow this seemingly simplistic adage. Donald Murray has referred to show don't tell as the most important quality of all dramatic writing.

In this session, you'll once again say to students, "Writers bring characters to life by setting them in motion." You'll tell children that instead of saying, "Leo was mean," a writer shows Leo kicking his cat. Instead of saying, "Sasha was upset," the writer shows Sasha tearing out of the room, calling, "See if I care!"

Your minilesson alone can't be your only vehicle for teaching children that we come to know people through actions. Watch your children, and spot one child making a generous gesture. Point out to the class that this child's actions reveal who he is as a person. "I watched Felix lend Paige his best pen, and I learned something about Felix through his actions," I recently said to the class. "I learned how generous Felix can be." Actions reveal character.

Of course, you'll also want to pause in the midst of reading aloud to talk about the character's behaviors. "He could have reacted very differently," you might say. "The fact that he did these things shows us a lot about what he's like on the inside." Then point out that in similar ways, children are using actions to bring their characters to life on their pages.

IN THIS SESSION, YOU WILL HELP CHILDREN REALIZE THAT WRITING SCENES IS, IN A SENSE, THE SAME AS WRITING SMALL MOMENT STORIES. WRITERS OFTEN BEGIN BY PUTTING THE CHARACTER INTO ACTION OR BY LAYING OUT THE CHARACTER'S EXACT WORDS, AND THEN UNFOLDING THE MOMENT STEP-BY-STEP.

GETTING READY

- A snippet of conversation between children about their writing illustrating that it's time to write
- *The Three Billy Goats Gruff* or whichever published text you've been using so far
- See CD-ROM for resources

MINILESSON

Show Don't Tell: Planning and Writing Scenes

CONNECTION

Use an overheard comment about writing to illustrate that there comes a time when writers need to move from planning to drafting.

"Writers, while you were lining up to come in this morning, I heard Emily tell Rachel that she can't figure out exactly what her character will do all along the way in her story. Emily *knows* her character wants to dance a solo in her dance recital and that every time she performs in class, she messes up—but Emily can't decide exactly *how* her character messes up."

Remind children that when the time comes to write, writers can use paper in a way that flows from the organization they've set out. In this case, tell children that writers can use a separate page for each point on their story mountain, and demonstrate by transferring dots on the class story mountain onto the early pages of a booklet.

"So I told Emily something that I want to teach you, that yes, there comes a time when writers need to stop planning, and write. Sometimes it's easier to plan once we are already writing. Often the best details are those that come out of our pens, surprising us."

"So today, I want to remind you that when we want to write a story, it helps to think carefully about the paper we'll use. In this case, I suggest we write our stories in drafting booklets that have one or two pages for the opening scenes of the story, and then several pages for the heart of the story, and a page or two for the ending scene. You may put a labeled dot from your story mountain on each page as a way to plan the contents of that page. Then we know where to start and where we're going, roughly. Writers always try to make our materials support the plans we have for writing."

"We already know that narratives are made up of scenes, or Small Moment stories. Many fiction writers get ourselves ready to write a draft of a story by gathering a booklet of paper, and thinking through plans for what we'll probably write on each page of a booklet. I usually give myself a different page, a different piece of paper, for each point on a story mountain. Two of those points usually comprise one focused, Small Moment story, so I stretch the story

COACHING

Obviously you won't tell your children about this particular overheard conversation; this was the conversation Colleen overheard, and you'll refer instead to a conversation you hear your own children saying to each other. The important thing is that you keep your ear to the ground, and that you hear evidence that your children's work on their stories is becoming the "talk of the town." Engagement matters tremendously, and it deserves your attention.

In perhaps a quarter of our minilessons, the main goal is to shepherd children toward the next steps in the writing process. In these minilessons, it is tempting to forgo a usual teaching point. Instead of saying, "Today I want to teach you that writers often . . . ," it is tempting to say, "Today, I'd like you to . . . ." When the work is complex and multifaceted, it's especially tempting to use the minilesson as a forum for giving directions and assigning work. Notice that despite the ambitious agenda she has for the day, Colleen clings tenaciously to the idea that minilessons provide opportunities to teach strategies that writers use often—meanwhile, however, she manages to lay out her particular hopes for today's work.

You'll probably use the word scene synonymously with small moment. By scene, we mean a bit of continuous drama—as in one part of a play. In your own mind, think of a scene as a Small Moment story, and keep in mind that it includes a flow of related mini-events.

across two pages of my booklet. It helps to label at the top of the paper the dot from the story mountain which will go on that page."

Looking at the first page of a chart paper booklet (on which she'd already written a dot and a sentence), Colleen said, "Marissa helped us realize we could start the story with Luz looking at a calendar, realizing her birthday is two weeks away, and sending out invitations. We realized she'd definitely be dreaming of all the friends who'd come, but she'd be nervous too."

Then Colleen said, "I copied the lead Marissa helped us write onto one page of our drafting booklet." Then she turned to page two and, drawing on the story mountain, Colleen said, "I think time will need to jump ahead until it's the day of the sleepover and Luz is getting everything ready and starting to worry about her fear of being revealed, so I put a second dot on the top of this page and wrote, 'Luz got ready for her party.' Later, after I use my story mountain to set up this whole drafting booklet, I'll come back to this page and write this dot as a Small Moment story. But for now, let me move on to thinking about what might happen later in the story."

"Writers, after you've planned out your story, you'll want to work on a lead. Before you do, I want to remind you that throughout most of your story, you'll be writing in scenes, not summaries."

You could, of course, decide against encouraging your children to write in story booklets, steering them instead toward notebook pages. We chose the booklets because they are a concrete way to encourage children to take their time, stretching out the story. But there is nothing sacred about writing in booklets.

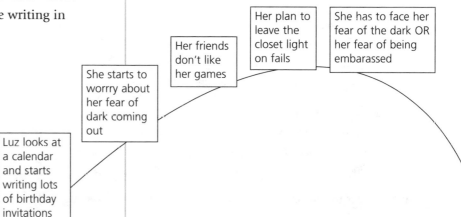

Name your teaching point. Specifically, tell children that fiction is composed of scenes, or drama, and that sometimes a line of dialogue or a small action ignites a dramatic scene.

"I want to remind you today that when we want to create a scene, we are creating drama. We sometimes use a line of dialogue—we make a character talk. Or we describe a small action—we make the character move or react physically to what is going on in the scene."

If you feel today's teaching point is not a new one, you are right. This time, Colleen has put a new spin on the now-familiar lesson of storytelling versus summarizing, but essentially this is a repackaged version of a minilesson that I've taught before. It might be interesting to contrast this version with earlier ones.

TEACHING
Illustrate the difference between summary and scene by telling a familiar tale in two contrasting ways.

"Let me remind you of the difference between writing summaries and writing scenes," Colleen said. "Listen while I tell the story of *The Three Billy Goats Gruff* in a summary way, like a stream of words rushing past."

> It's a story about three goats who are trying to cross a bridge to go eat some grass on the other side, and there's this troll who wants to eat them. So as he goes across, each goat tricks him by promising he can eat the next goat who is even bigger. The troll's greedy so he waits for the next one, but the biggest goat pushes him in the water, so they all get across safely. The end.

"Didn't you feel like that story just rushed by you? Didn't you want me to slow down and give the troll a voice, and make some sound effects, and put in some suspense to help you see and hear what is happening?"

"Now listen as I write in the air a scene from that story."

> "That's the greenest green grass I've ever seen in my life," said Third Goat. "Can we go over to that hill to eat some, pleeeeeeese?"
>
> "Yeah, we're hungry!" said Second Goat. So First Goat placed one foot gingerly onto the little wooden bridge that would carry them over the rushing river to a delightful afternoon snack. The bridge felt good and sturdy. "Nothing's stopping us! Follow me!" And First Goat stepped out onto the bridge toward the grassy hillside.
>
> "No No NO!" boomed a voice. "Who dares to cross my bridge?" Suddenly, First Goat felt the hot breath of a troll on his muzzle!

"Can you hear the difference between that stream of words, just telling, telling, telling what happened, and then the sound, when my characters talked in their character voices?"

Colleen told this story in a purposely hurried, monotone way, emphasizing the summary feeling. She does this for two reasons. First of all, it is easier to tell a story using story language and dramatic flair once the storyteller or writer has some sense for the bare bones of the story. Telling the story in summary fashion acts rather as a timeline, scaffolding the storytelling which will follow. She also summarizes the story because she wants to define what a story is by highlighting what it is not. A story is not a discussion, a summary. As Brace writes in The Stuff of Fiction, "Fiction is not an explanation or a summary or an argument. Exposition is almost no good in fiction. Visible action and audible speech are needed. The reader must see and hear . . . the purest form of fiction is drama where everything is presented directly to the senses—the stage to be seen, the actors to be watched, and heard".

As Colleen stretches out a moment from the story, she uses her voice purposely again, this time to give body to the words and help children really hear the difference.

There is a reason why we're appealing to the listener's sense of sound, of voice. We believe some children need to learn about story almost viscerally, from soaking it up. Mem Fox describes how she learned story; saying, "It came from the constant good fortune of hearing great literature beautifully delivered into my ear, and from there into my heart, and from my heart into my bones." Mem goes on to write, "All this makes me wonder whether we, as teachers of writers, focus too much on the mind: have we forgotten, or did we ever know, the explosive power, the necessity of focusing also on the ear?"

ACTIVE ENGAGEMENT

Set children up to storytell a moment from their stories to each other. Then share one child's summary, inviting the class to reimagine it as a story.

"Let's try it together. Will each of you think of a moment from your story mountain—perhaps the moment that could become the start of your story? And will you turn to your partner and take turns saying your little moment first like a summary of what's happening?"

"Okay, great! Let's listen to Caleb's summary, and see if we can help him reimagine this as a story."

> This guy named Spencer really wants to do great in
> school 'cause he wants to go to the same college as his
> big brother, but his friends think he's a geek for reading.

"Whew! That story flew by, didn't it? I want to hear what Spencer sounds like and what the other guys say to him and what books he's reading, don't you? Before you try to turn this summary into a scene, remember that during our personal narrative work, you learned that it's easiest to do this if you begin with a line of dialogue or with a small action."

Remind children that when you turned the summarized fairy tale into a real story, you started it with dialogue. In this way, help your children have success storytelling their classmate's summary.

"Remember that I began my *Three Billy Goats Gruff* scene with a line of dialogue? I said, 'That's the greenest grass I've ever seen in my life!' When a character talks first thing, it can make the scene come alive *instantly* in the reader's ears and mind."

"A second way that writers begin their scenes sometimes is with a small bit of action. Usually the story doesn't start with the main action, giving everything away in the first sentence, but with a tiny action that causes the reader to picture that movement in his or her mind's eye. So, for instance, I could have begun my Billy Goats scene by having First Goat put out his little hoof to test how steady the bridge was. So it would sound like this."

> First Goat gingerly placed one hoof onto the wooden bridge and leaned
> his weight into it. It seemed sturdy enough. "Let's cross to the other
> side and eat some of that greeny, green grass," said the First Goat.

It might be hard for children to mentally shuffle through their entries, settling on one in which they summarized a tiny moment rather than storytelling it. For this reason, we know from the start that we'll soon draw on one child's example and ask all children to help the one child reimagine a moment he's summarized, writing it as a scene.

You'll notice that this Active Engagement section involves another round of demonstration. Colleen made the decision to do this because we think children need lots of scaffolding to go from summarizing to storytelling. There are no set laws for how minilessons must progress. The most important thing is that these lessons are helpful—and our job, as teachers, is to do whatever is needed to make them so.

Ask each child to try telling the story idea as a story, not a summary.

"Okay, now let's all try to write in the air, and help Caleb turn his summary into a little scene. You can choose to make the first sentence a line of dialogue or a small action to pull your readers in right away." Colleen listened in on the children. "You've got it! I can picture so many of the scenes I heard, as if they were on movie screens in front of me! Let's hear the way Caleb rewrote his own scene."

> Spencer peeked out from behind the science portable and looked both ways. Good. No one in sight. He sat back against the wall of the portable and pulled his football jersey out of his backpack. He opened the jersey and there, hidden safe and sound, was a piece of heaven: <u>Harry Potter</u>.

Debrief by reminding writers to show their characters by putting them into action.

"Can't you see Spencer peeking out to see if any of those tough guys are around? That's the way to bring the reader right into the heart of the scene. Show us what your character is doing or saying."

LINK
Send children off to work, reminding them of the many points you've made today. And tuck in a reminder to carry these lessons with them always.

"So writers, your job today is first to transfer your story mountain onto a story booklet, and then to use that booklet as a support for storytelling your story. Try telling it so that each page or two of your booklet contains a Small Moment story. When you are ready, start working on your lead. Make sure when you start writing a scene today that the scene sounds like a story. Create a kind of word-movie with dialogue and action. Let's get to work, writers!"

In a school where I've recently been working as a staff developer, teachers have piloted the units of study described in these books, and they are accustomed to writing their own minilessons. We've been working on the Active Engagement components of their minilessons so that the teachers scaffold some aspects of these little practice-sessions, supporting and channeling children's work so they are able to have success with the one new tool or strategy the teachers will have just taught in the minilesson. In a similar fashion, you and your colleagues may want to do an inquiry into just this component of a minilesson. If you examine Active Engagements, notice the blend of support and of space we try to give children.

You can see from this Link that today's session is loaded with little lessons. Colleen could have made a different decision, choosing to end the minilesson by simply highlighting today's new point. But we wanted to help children synthesize all the particular points they've been given into an organized, multifaceted understanding for the process of writing.

Children will understand right away what you mean when you tell them you can picture their scenes being on movie screens. Their world of entertainment is largely one of moving images: television, video games, movies, etc. You can take this image further by talking about the sounds of your children's writing, the tones of voice you imagine their characters having, the ways in which they move, their facial expressions. "All this," you might say, "came from the words you chose and the way you decided to put them together!"

WRITING AND CONFERRING

Moving from Summary to Story

You'll want to make sure that every student is now drafting scenes rather than using writing as a way to think about and plan the scenes they'll soon write. Bits of story should be taking shape; they should pop off the page at you as you confer today. If students have trouble moving from entries that are *about* the story to entries that *sound like* story, you may find that it helps for you to model. Listen to the child's story, tell the child your observation about his or her work, and then say, "So I imagine it might sound like this," and rewrite the child's summary into the start of a story. Pause after just a bit to say, "Of course, I'm just making this up and *you* know how the story really goes. So now you try it. Tell it like a story." Help the child get started writing in the air.

If the child says a summary statement, quietly prompt for more specifics. You'll find that when students rehearse bits of a story out loud, with you coaching right beside them, saying things like, "What did she do? What did he say back?" students get started saying aloud beautiful stories. Jot down what the child says as a way to synthesize it and then say it back to the child. The writer will hear the difference between the first and the later version:

> I got home. I was exhausted. I went to bed.

becomes:

> I flicked on the light so that I could see my way to my bed. It looked like it was miles away from where I was standing. I closed my eyes. I wanted more than anything to be carried to my bed. Instead, I had to walk. I dropped my backpack on the floor with a thud. Then I used my feet to pry off first one shoe, then the other. The idea of bending over to untie them was just too exhausting. I trudged to the edge of my bed, step by step. "You can make it, just a few more steps," I told myself. Then I was there. I began to fall onto my bed, unable to even pull the covers back. My eyes closed as I fell. The last thought I had before I fell asleep was, "I should have taken off my jacket."

> **MID-WORKSHOP TEACHING POINT** — *Revise, Revise, Revise*   "Writers, can I have your attention for just a moment?" Colleen said. "The work you all are doing seemed so important that I can't resist doing similar work. I could just move on to the next page, but I know that beginnings matter. So I'm going to reread page two one more time." Colleen read:

> > On the day of my slumber party I put everything I would need into a corner of our family room. I propped my sleeping bag up against the corner, and my pillow on top of it. Above the pillow, I laid out my cute new pajamas. Then I added my secret night-light to the pile. I was afraid of the dark and nobody knew it.

> "Hmm . . . I *could* just go on to page 3, but I like to revise as I write. This scene is about Luz getting ready for the party. I want to make it really clear that she wants people to like her, and that she's a little insecure and embarrassed about being afraid of the dark. I think I can make my character's wants and struggles a bit clearer," Colleen said. Dictating as she wrote, Colleen scrawled out this revised page:

> > I checked all my stuff at least three times. I made sure my secret night-light was pushed all the way to the bottom of my pillow case where no one would see it. Then I walked over to the table and rearranged the napkins.

> > Everything on the table was yellow. Yellow wasn't my favorite color, but a lot of the girls coming to the party wore yellow all the time, so I thought they'd like it.

> *continued on next page*

Your conferring today will be crucial. As important as the adage "show don't tell" is to all writing, it's even more important to fiction. Fiction writer Shirley Jackson ends her *Notes for a Fiction Writer* by summarizing all that she's said in the article. She concludes, "Just remember that primarily, in the story and out of it, you are living in a world of people. Suppose you want to write a story about what you might vaguely think of as 'magic.' You will be hopelessly lost, until you turn your idea, 'magic,' into a person, someone who wants to do or make or change or act in some way. Once you have your character you will of course need another to work in opposition, a person in some sense, 'anti-magic;' when both are working at the separate intentions, dragging in other characters when needed, you are well into your story."

Help children reread their own work, noticing times when they tell the reader something that they could instead have shown. For example, Sofiya's story about a girl named Elizabeth who is afraid of snakes includes a fair number of places where she summarizes or talks about the character and the events. You and Sofiya could find those places, and work together to rewrite them. *[Fig. VI-1]*

Once there lived a little girl. Her name was Elizabeth and she lived with her mom and dad. Elizabeth was in first grade. One day her class went on a trip. The class had to sit in a circle. When the class had been there for about half an hour or so, the lady that was working with Elizabeth and her class brought out a snake. Elizabeth, who was terrified of snakes, stared wide-eyed at the snake. She heard the lady tell the class that they may touch the snake. Elizabeth got even more terrified. When the lady with the snake reached her, Elizabeth felt her hand touch the snake. Oh, how frightened she was! Poor Elizabeth thought the snake would bite her hand off, or poison her! Little Elizabeth was delighted when she didn't feel the snake harming her. The rest of Elizabeth's trip was a lot of fun. When Elizabeth got home, she told her parents all about the trip. She also exaggerated the snake part a bit, but her parents knew that.

continued from previous page

Colleen shifted back to her role as teacher. "Did you notice that I could have gone on to page 3, but instead I reread page 2, and remembered what I knew about stories and revised it. I tried to show what Luz wants and what obstacles keep her from getting what she wants."

"I hope you notice, writers, that to start drafting, I first set up a draft booklet based on our story mountain. Then I copied our lead, and wrote another page and revised that page. Fiction writers revise as we progress!"

"So writers, before you move from one page of your story booklet to another, remember to do as I just did and revise. I revised to bring out our character's wants and struggles even more, but you could revise toward any goal that seems to you to be an important one."

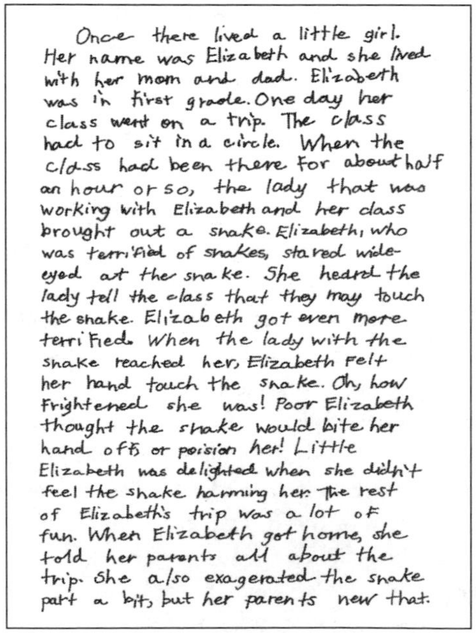
Once there lived a little girl. Her name was Elizabeth and she lived with her mom and dad. Elizabeth was in first grade. One day her class went on a trip. The class had to sit in a circle. When the class had been there for about half an hour or so, the lady that was working with Elizabeth and her class brought out a snake. Elizabeth, who was terrified of snakes, stared wide-eyed at the snake. She heard the lady tell the class that they may touch the snake. Elizabeth got even more terrified. When the lady with the snake reached her, Elizabeth felt her hand touch the snake. Oh, how frightened she was! Poor Elizabeth thought the snake would bite her hand off or poision her! Little Elizabeth was delighted when she didn't feel the snake harming her. The rest of Elizabeth's trip was a lot of fun. When Elizabeth got home, she told her parents all about the trip. She also exagerated the snake part a bit, but her parents new that.

Fig. VI-1 Sofiya's draft contained bits of summary.

In her next draft, Sofiya left off the most obvious instances of telling/summarizing, as you can see in Figure VI-2. What an important step ahead!

Elizabeth felt her hand touch the long, mean-looking snake. Its gleaming, coal-black eyes sparkled in the light as it stared at Elizabeth not even blinking. The snake kept sticking its blood-red, forked tongue out of its mouth. Elizabeth felt coil or something like scales under her fingers. Elizabeth knew that it was the snake's rough skin. She wasn't surprised that it was rough because she thought that snakes are rough and so is their skin. Elizabeth noticed the pattern on the snake's back. How she liked it! It was also the only thing she liked about the snake! Golden gleaming and sparkling diamonds on the same kind of coal black surface.

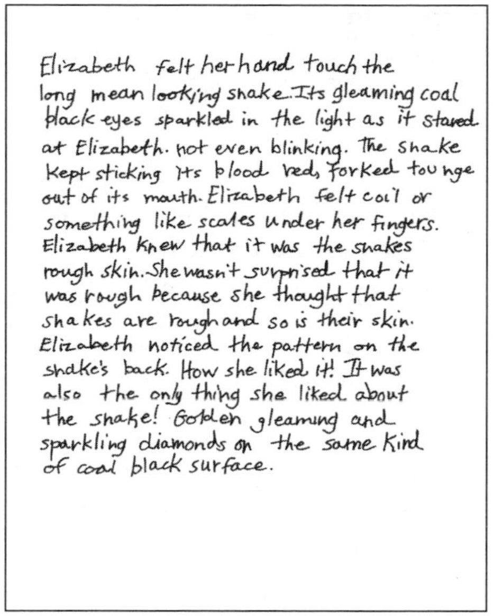

Elizabeth felt her hand touch the long mean looking snake. Its gleaming coal black eyes sparkled in the light as it stared at Elizabeth. not even blinking. The snake kept sticking its blood red, forked tounge out of its mouth. Elizabeth felt coil or something like scales under her fingers. Elizabeth knew that it was the snakes rough skin. She wasn't surprised that it was rough because she thought that shakes are rough and so is their skin. Elizabeth noticed the pattern on the shake's back. How she liked it! It was also the only thing she liked about the snake! Golden gleaming and sparkling diamonds on the same kind of coal black surface.

Fig. VI-2 Sofiya tried to rewrite so that her summaries became scenes.

SHARE

Acting Out Writing

Ask several students to direct fellow classmates in the scenes they've written to see what revisions, if any, are needed to make them "camera ready."

"Writers, I wish we had the movie cameras rolling on some of these scenes you've got going! But why don't we pretend that we *do* have movie cameras filming our scenes. Let's try acting out a couple of your scenes to see how they look and sound, to see how that helps us revise them!"

"I'm going to choose five students to be the directors of their little scenes." Colleen named them. "Will you find actors for your scenes? You have five minutes to give them the directions so they know what your characters are saying and doing, and then you all can rehearse the scene once, really fast! Then another group of kids will watch the scene you develop and see if it feels ready for filming or if the scene needs some revision. Okay, choose and rehearse fast!"

Reconvene the class. Tell a story about children resolving to do superbly well, even while knowing today's best draft will be revised.

"Ariana and Gabe and Francesca are working on a dance for the talent show. They're practicing every day after school for this whole week. Do you suppose that on Monday they grab any CD and start doing any old dance moves, saying to themselves, 'We don't need to make this good till Friday?'"

"No! Ariana and Gabe and Francesca worked really hard so that when they met on Monday, they had already chosen the song they thought would work and the moves they hoped would be perfect. As the group practiced, I hear they came up with even better dance moves—but that doesn't mean that on Monday they aimed for anything less than their best!"

"The same needs to be true for all of you as you move forward in your draft. I know you will aim to make this draft of your lead gorgeous and spectacular and significant. We've learned that writers first plan how their stories might go, sketching out possible lines of development on one story mountain after another. We try on leads, and use those leads to test out what our stories might be like if we write in one voice or another, if we start in one place, at one time, or another."

If you've never had your students practice acting out parts of stories or using their bodies and voices like this before, you may find this Share a bit chaotic. But when students are accustomed to role playing and to performing Readers Theater, like these students are, this provides a powerful way to give body and voice to the words on a page. When writers see real human beings trying to carry out the action of the scene, they realize quickly that they have important revision to do so the scene works better. (And the good news is, this comes at the end of the workshop, and you can end it early if you feel you need to!)

Capturing students' attention matters. Colleen knows that this group of students cares about the challenge of getting a dance number ready, choosing a CD, and rehearsing with friends. It strengthens her lesson about writing when she links writing to the creative endeavors that children care about most.

First Colleen makes the point that when composing a dance, children resolve to do their best from the start, despite knowing their best will turn out to be only a rough draft. Then she makes a parallel point about writing, suggesting that to do their best from the start, students must resolve to work toward all the goals they've learned so far.

Living in a Character's Shoes   Writers, tonight when you have supper, you'll be having supper not just as a child, not just as a son or daughter, but also as a fiction writer. You'll remember from earlier this year Cynthia Rylant was once asked to describe her writing process, and she said, "It is about going fishing as a writer, having relatives over for supper as a writer, walking the aisles of Woolworth's as a writer." So when you pull up a chair at the supper table, you need to think to yourself, "I wonder who my character sits with at supper?" When you plop your backpack down in its regular place in your bedroom or your kitchen, you need to pause for just a second and think about the teeny tiny rituals in your character's life. Where does your character keep his or her stuff?

Fiction writing isn't just desk work, it is life work. We carry our story ideas and especially our characters with us always, letting them grow with time and attention.

So right now, as you read this assignment, pause for a moment. Think to yourself, "Where does your character sit in order to read?" Look up at the space around you. Think to yourself, "What does your character see when he or she looks around?" And as you go about your life this evening, try to let something new about your character pop into your mind. Then remember: You could easily forget these thoughts. Tonight, when you live like a fiction writer and grow new realizations about your character, please jot those into your writer's notebooks so you are sure to hold on to them.

⊙ **TAILORING YOUR TEACHING**

If some of your writers need concrete reminders of the elements usually found in scenes . . . you might offer them a clear checklist of things to include. Even though your students spent a lot of time during earlier narrative units working on small moments, which are essentially scenes, some students will find the idea of scene writing in fiction a little risky. You might consider creating a chart or a handout that offers a bulleted list of things writers include in scenes.

If your students are struggling with the concept of scene versus summary . . . you might teach them that writers study texts others have written, noticing not only what the author says but also the structures in which the author writes. For example, a writer of short stories might reread a familiar short story, keeping an eye out for places where the author writes in summary and where he writes in scene. The writer might box each section and code it with notes to themselves like *sum* for *summary* and *sc* for *scene*, and then look between those sections in order to notice the differences between the two kinds of writing.

Things Writers Include in Scenes
- A beginning, middle, and end
- A setting
- Characters who want things
- Characters who feel and think
- Obstacles that get in the way of what characters want
- Action
- Dialogue (most of the time)

ASSESSMENT

You will definitely want to linger late in your classroom, with a cup of coffee (or whatever lifts your spirits) on hand. Expect that you'll be there still when the afternoon shadows become long. Give yourself the opportunity to really look closely at your children's work. Their leads, after all, represent the drafts they are angled to write. Just as leads are a sort of contract with the reader, they are also a contract between the teacher and the child. By blessing the child's lead and letting the child go forward, you are putting a seal of approval on the life work the child has taken on. So take the time to read the leads your children have written, and arrange for time tomorrow to talk with children about the problems and the promise you see in their work. You'll probably need to meet with a child or two before school, and another cluster during lunch. Investing this time will set children up for success and make the entire unit work better.

You will probably find that at least half a dozen children have begun their stories far from the main event. My friend Ralph Fletcher cautions writers, "Start when you can hear the waterfall around the next bend." Some children will need you to convene a strategy lesson and teach them this.

In order to help these children, show them that part of the story they have planned is backstory. I recently worked with Carrie whose story began with a detailed description of a girl, also named Carrie, whose best friend, Kim, was a foster child. Then Kim was adopted by an out-of-state family, and moved away, leaving Carrie feeling lonely. Then—good news! (I say this tongue in cheek) Kim's adopted family rejected her, she returned to being a foster child, and Carrie was reunited with her friend and is no longer lonely. In Carrie's original draft, the story began before the adoption, and was poised to drag on and on. I interceded to point out that the story could begin much, much later; perhaps with the lonely heroine going to the mailbox in search of a letter from her distant friend. Carrie and I studied the

start of both *Because of Winn-Dixie* and *Journey*, noticing that in both those books, before the story actually begins, a great deal has taken already place.

I also find that when I look at the leads of children's drafts, some of them raise issues about values. When you read over their leads and study their story plans, you find that sometimes the values that children weave into their stories are ones you want to question. After one afternoon assessing writing, I made an appointment to confer with three girls who were each writing a version of the same story. The story line was this: three girls go to the mall. A classmate, Kayla, is there, drinking a smoothie, carrying on about the fact that her drink contained natural ingredients. The three girls are disgusted with Kayla, and decide to retaliate. The grand climax of the story comes with the three girls inventing a way to retaliate—they fill Kayla's locker with poop and cockroaches, and when she weeps at the sight, they spray whipped cream in her face. Reading the story, the teacher and I were speechless and convinced that part of the problem was our decision to let the girls plan a story collaboratively and to include so many characters in it. The gang-mentality was shielding them from seeing the viciousness of their heroines' actions. The teacher and I decided we couldn't live with these girls investing a full month writing and role-playing such a story. So I pulled the girls together, and said, "I read your lead and I see this is a story about a gang of really vicious girls who first gang up on an undeserving victim (at the mall) and then, the gang's behavior gets much much worse and they act in really violent and hateful ways. So what do you think will happen—perhaps in the midst of that awful attack—to change your characters? How will they learn a lesson? Will one girl look Kayla in the eyes and suddenly come to her senses, or what?" In this fashion, I subtly but firmly steered the children toward work I felt would be more helpful for them.

FEELING AND DRAFTING THE HEART OF YOUR STORY

IN THIS SESSION, CHILDREN WILL LEARN THAT FICTION WRITERS CREATE OUR BEST DRAFTS WHEN WE EXPERIENCE THE WORLD THROUGH OUR CHARACTER'S SKIN, LETTING THE STORY UNFOLD AS IT HAPPENS TO US.

GETTING READY

- Example of a well-known text, such as *Fireflies!* in which students have probably experienced "becoming" the character
- Current lead for the class story
- Current story mountain for the class story
- Idea for a scene for the class story you can use to demonstrate writing by pretending to be the character
- See CD-ROM for resources

In this session, you'll set children up for something quite magical. When writing, we plan and chart, deliberate and select. But then the day comes when we do none of this. Instead, we "let it rip." We "go with the flow." We write fast and long, our eyes glued not to charts admonishing us to do one thing or another and not to mentor texts that demonstrate what's possible; but instead, to the drama that unfolds before us as we follow our characters into the thickening plot.

Frankly, it's not easy to figure out how to pass along the equation for the magic that happens when a writer finds that words and characters lead us toward meanings we didn't even know we knew! To some extent, I always approach this particular minilesson knowing my teaching will be hopelessly inadequate. But we carry on, as best we can, knowing that children can learn from their words as they appear on the page, if not from the minilesson.

In this session you will try to equip children to experience the power of what some people refer to as a "discovery draft." One way writers do this is to empathize with our characters, imagining ourselves within another's feelings, situations, and thoughts. By stepping into the character's skin, right into the story, the writer watches and listens and feels what is happening as the story unfolds—writing the story down as it happens.

Set children up to expect that as they write, their character's problems will get worse and worse, the stakes will rise. Teach them to hold their hats, expecting quite a ride! In this session, then, we'll teach children that writers draft by empathizing with our characters and letting that empathy determine the course of the story.

MINILESSON

Feeling and Drafting the Heart of Your Story

CONNECTION

Celebrate that your children have created story mountains and characters and best yet, they've begun bringing these to life on the page.

"It's a rather amazing process, isn't it? You plan, list, choose, sketch—like the old woman making that gingerbread boy. She probably thought, 'What will I use to show his eyes?' 'Will his shirt be a button-down shirt?' 'Will he wear suspenders?' But then the day comes when the gingerbread boy springs to life, calling out, 'Run, run, as fast as you can. You can't catch me, I'm the gingerbread man. I am, I am!'"

"You have each created a gingerbread child who has sprung to life. Hannah's character, Jane is standing in Central Park near the carousel, with her two friends circling her, taunting, 'Jane is scared, Jane is scared.'"

"The blood rises to Jane's face, she feels circled, caught, so she snaps back, 'At least I'm smarter than you guys!' and she huffs away. The amazing thing is that Jane's creator didn't know that Jane would snap back like that. One thing led to another, that's all; Jane was caught and she dug deep into herself and found a kernel of self-respect and shot back with, 'At least I'm smarter than you guys!'"

"This is the magical power of writing fiction. Our characters, like that gingerbread man, spring to life and suddenly we, as writers, are following them, trying as best we can to catch up."

Name your teaching point. Specifically, tell children that once writers are actually drafting, they worry less about writing and focus instead on reliving the drama.

"So today, what I want to teach you is this. Before writers actually get going on a draft, we think a lot about ways to make a draft into a really good story. But once we're actually in the midst of the story, most of us try, above all, to lose ourselves in the story. We become the characters, and writing is a bit like a drama, happening to us."

COACHING

Faulkner has said, "There are some kinds of writing that you have to do very fast, like riding a bicycle on a tightrope." Another time, he used a different analogy to convey the same message, "A writer writing is like a man building a chicken coop in a high wind. He grabs any board he can and nails it down fast." You are setting children up to draft, fast and long—and more than that, you are setting children up to produce a draft that they regard as temporary and improvable.

Once dancers and writers have produced the start of a work of art, the time comes to worry less about ratcheting up the level of their composition and to focus more on letting the dancing or writing flow.

TEACHING

Remind children that when reading, we lose ourselves in a story, becoming the character. Explain how this is true for writing as well. Give an example.

"You all know how, when we read, we feel almost like we become Gilly or Opal or Melanin Sun or the narrator in *Fireflies!* We read the words and suddenly we are that boy at the dinner table, looking out the window onto our backyard at dusk, seeing the dots of light flicker by the dark shape that is our tree house—seeing through his eyes and living in his self. We hardly need the words of the story to tell us that the boy pushes away his plate and asks, 'Can I be done?' and then rushes to get a jar for catching fireflies."

It could be a fruitful inquiry to look at all the minilessons focused on drafting in all the Unit of Study books. I believe fast-writing works to help students draft. You may not, in which case you may want to suggest that some people draft slowly and cautiously. Regardless, there is a cyclical curriculum underlying these units, and you can learn from studying it— and also from questioning it! Any one line of work is but one choice among many.

Tell children that readers can more easily walk in the shoes of a character if the writer has done this first.

"Readers can do that—we can read words on the page and suddenly be in the shoes of the character because writers first do the same. Gerald Brace, in a book called *The Stuff of Fiction*, says it this way:"

> It is not enough for a writer to tell us about a person or a place; he must give us the illusion of being the person ourselves . . . the basic failure in much writing is the failure of the writer's imagination: he is not with it . . . not trying hard enough to live from moment to moment in the very skin of his characters.

"We, as writers, need to try to do this work—live in our characters' skins as we draft their stories!"

I'm reminded of tobogganing as a child. We line up the toboggan just so at the top of the hill. We anticipate its journey. We call for folks to clear the path. We give ourselves a running start. But then at some point, momentum takes over and we simply hold on tight, traveling fast. To me, drafting is a bit like tobogganing—the time for control and choice ends, and the pace quickens.

Demonstrate to show how you go from envisioning to enacting to drafting.

"And so today, I'm going to reread the latest lead to our Luz story. At one point we'd said we wanted to start it earlier, as she writes invitations, but now we've settled on this lead, I revised it a bit since you last saw it. Today, I'm not going to be re-thinking the lead so much as writing more. To do that, I'm going to pretend to *be* Luz." Colleen reread the latest draft, written on chart paper:

> On the day of my slumber party I put everything I would need into a corner of our family room. I propped my sleeping bag up against the corner, and my pillow on top of it. Above the pillow, I laid out my cute new pajamas. Then I added my secret night-light to the pile. I was afraid of the dark and nobody knew it.

So far, Colleen has given a little lecture on the virtues of envisioning and role playing as part of the writing process. She could simply shift now to the next phase of the minilesson. Instead, she demonstrates what she's just described in the hopes that this will provide more ways to support children. You can decide whether to explicitly tell, to demonstrate, or to do as Colleen has done and combine both teaching methods.

I checked all my stuff at least three times. I made sure my secret night-light was pushed all the way to the bottom of my pillow case where no one would see it. Then I walked over to the table and rearranged the napkins. Everything on the table was yellow. Yellow wasn't my favorite color, but a lot of the girls coming to the party wore yellow all the time, so I thought they'd like it. And like me.

First Marta came in. Then Joy and Tish walked in together, helping each other carry all their sleeping stuff. I helped carry things to the corner of the room where my mom and I decided we would keep the stuff until it was time to go to sleep.

"So what are we going to do first?" Joy asked.

I looked around at all my friends. I was so excited that my party was finally happening that I almost forgot the games I had planned.

"I'm going to keep in mind that the next dot on the story mountain says, 'Her friends arrive and don't like her games and I'm going to remember that Luz wants desperately to feel popular,'" Colleen said, referring to the story mountain.

"But mostly I'm just going to try to *be* Luz." Colleen picked up her pen and began scrawling on her pad of paper, saying aloud the words as she wrote them. Pulling back from writing, she said to the children. "I just that second made up the idea that the games were brand-new and I pretended they were junk. I have no idea what, exactly, will happen next, so I'll reread what I just wrote and just let something come to me."

Soon she'd added (and voiced) this scene:

> "What do you wanna do?" I asked, waving with feigned carelessness to the stack of games on the table. They're all old," I said, hoping I'd taken the price tags and cellophane off each of them.
> "TWISTER?" Tish said, her voice incredulous. "My mom played that when she was a kid. That's such a stupid game."
> I felt the blood rise to my cheeks. "I know," I said. "I don't know why we even have it."

"Let your story move as naturally and as easily as possible," Shirley Jackson urges young writers. "Suppose you are writing a story about a boy and a girl meeting on a corner; your reader wants to go to that very corner and listen in; if, instead, you start your boy and girl toward the corner and then go off into a long description of the streetcar tracks and a little discussion of the background of those two characters—you will lose your reader and your story will fall apart."

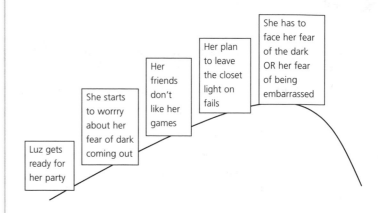

Notice that Colleen tucks little insights into her demonstration. This is important to do. Some children will hear these fleeting tips, some will probably learn only from the demonstration as a whole. The subordinate tips make the minilesson more multileveled.

ACTIVE ENGAGEMENT
Recap specific tips you hope children gleaned from the demonstration.

"Writers, do you see that when we write—when any fiction writer writes—we keep in mind the big plan for how a story will probably go, but we let the details emerge from the specific, exact actions we take. Usually, our scenes involve two characters, and one does or says something and then the next one reacts."

Set children up to extend the class story by putting themselves into the unfolding scene. Then call on one set of partners and add their work to the class story.

"To continue writing our Luz story, you need to *be* Luz, gesturing with disgust at the stack of games, pretending you agree that they're junk. You need to keep in mind that Luz desperately wants the party to go well. She's got it all planned—the games she's dismissing were her best hope for keeping everyone happy."

"Right now, pretend *you are* Luz. Picture her. The games are out on the table. The one friend has just looked in disgust at Twister. What does Luz do (remember—actions matter, not just talk). Turn and tell your partner the next bit of the story." To get them started, Colleen reiterated the last scene:

> "TWISTER?" Tish said, her voice incredulous. "My mom played that when she was a kid. That's such a stupid game."
> I felt the blood rise to my cheeks. "I know," I said. "I don't know why we even have it."

The children talked with their partners, and soon Colleen had called on one partnership and added this to the story:

> I jumped up to put the entire stack of games into the closet. The other kids, however, surrounded me, and Joy and Marta were shaking dice to see who'd go first in a game of Mousetrap.

LINK
Remind children that drafting is a form of acting on the page, and send them off.

"Writers, I want to remind you that writing is a lot like drama. Once we've written our lead, we need to reread it and become the main character. We need to stand in the character's shoes, to see through her eyes, to blush with her, and to hope with her. This way our readers will also be able to experience the story we put onto the page."

"You'll probably do as I did today, and reread your lead, then turn to page 2 of your story booklet and to the second dot on your story mountain, and act out—write out—that story."

Over and over this year, we've told children that a writer "makes a movie in the mind" and records what the writer sees. In this minilesson, Colleen brings children into this concept more deeply by inviting them to explore the close link between drama and writing.

The emphasis in this minilesson is on showing, not telling. You may determine that other qualities of good writing will help your children more. Scan students' work as they draft. The emphasis in the minilesson grew from the fact that despite all our best efforts, some students were still summarizing when they should have been writing scenes or small moments. That said, there are times when summary is the best tool a writer has at her disposal. Teach students that when we are drafting there are times when we want to show the reader everything—those are our scenes. There are also times when we might choose to summarize. Fiction writers usually summarize when they want to pass by a lot of time, when something routine happens (such as brushing teeth or putting on shoes), or when they want to quickly transition from one scene to the next by using transition phrases like the next day *or* that afternoon. *Readers don't need to see a character pack his backpack at the end of the day, unless something compelling and unusual, like a fight, has occurred and is related to that action. In that case, we'll want to see it as a scene!*

Notice that after children turn and talk, we do not hear from one child after another after another.

WRITING AND CONFERRING

As you confer today, you'll want to help writers make significant revisions in their story mountains and their leads. When working with children around both of these things today, help them envision what's happening. Often writers will need to go from summarizing to storytelling. If a child has written something like, "Elisabeth woke up and listened to her parents fight," you'll want to point out that this is still a summary. "Pretend you are Elisabeth," I said to Sofiya. "You are lying in your bed sleeping. Now you begin to wake up, just a bit. You hear something. What is it?" Coaching, I said, "Maybe you hear voices. Then what do you do? Sit up in bed, and listen some more? This time you make out a voice you know—whose? Can you make out any words the voice is saying?" In this way, I helped Sofiya rewrite her draft so that she storytold in a step-by-step fashion—and relived her character's experience of that morning.

As you confer with your children, remember that you are a talent scout, searching for what each child does well so that you can solicit that child to teach his or her peers. Then set children up to lead little seminars. For example, when I read Chris' work, I was blown away by his ability to convey the reciprocity and intimacy in a friendship between two best friends. And so I called a group of children together, who, like Chris, were writing relationship stories, and I asked them to study Chris' writing closely, just as we'd studied texts by other authors, and to pay special attention to Chris' talent for making a relationship seem very real. He'd written, for example:

> Jerod wasn't in Boy Scouts because it met at a church; he was Jewish and his mom didn't want him experiencing another religion. Luke understood and never brought it up.

MID-WORKSHOP TEACHING POINT · *Matching Writing with Story Mountains*

"Writers, I want to remind you that when we worked on our Luz story, we had our story mountain out beside us, and before we picked up our pens and stepped into Luz's shoes, we first checked our story mountain so we'd keep in mind the main event that we knew would happen next. Before we wrote the story of Luz bringing out the stack of games, we checked our plans. As we wrote, we kept in mind the overall game plan—one page about playing games, another page in which Luz's worries over being liked get worse and worse. Make sure you're keeping your own story mountain beside you as you write and that page 2 of your booklet is the second dot on your own story mountain." Then I added,

continued on next page

When a text provides such precise detail, readers believe the story is real. Above all, children noticed Chris' culminating metaphor:

> He and Jerod were like a chain. If it breaks, it's just two pieces of metal always looking for the other piece.

When I find a child who has done something marvelous, it is incredibly powerful if I let that child's good work become a subject for study. Once I saw Chris' beautiful metaphor capturing his character's friendship, I asked Chris if he could help revise the Luz story so that it, too, contained a beautiful metaphor. We found a possible place. The text read:

> Then, just like that, the lights were out. It was dark. Luz tried to find some light, somewhere in the living room.

With Chris' help, we rewrote this. We thought, "What else looks for something the way Luz is looking for a light? Hmm . . . she's starting to feel a bit frantic . . . ."and we wrote:

> Luz searched the dark living room like a sailor lost at sea searches for land on the horizon.

Then Chris taught a cluster of other children to do similar work on their drafts.

continued from previous page

"Remember that as you move from page one to page 2 of your story, your character's troubles escalate. They get worse and worse."

"Caleb has already started to move into the next scene in his story about Spencer, the boy who decides to face up to the big bully and meet him on the playground. Listen to the beginning of this first scene, how he sets up the problem: There is going to be a confrontation with that bully." *[Fig. VII-1]*

> I tried absent-mindedly to walk away so that the oversized tiger wouldn't prey on me. I'm as skinny as a wire and a main target for bullies.
>
> My puny frame was no match for Humphrey's bulging one. I wanted to shrink and shrink until he couldn't see me anymore.

continued on next page

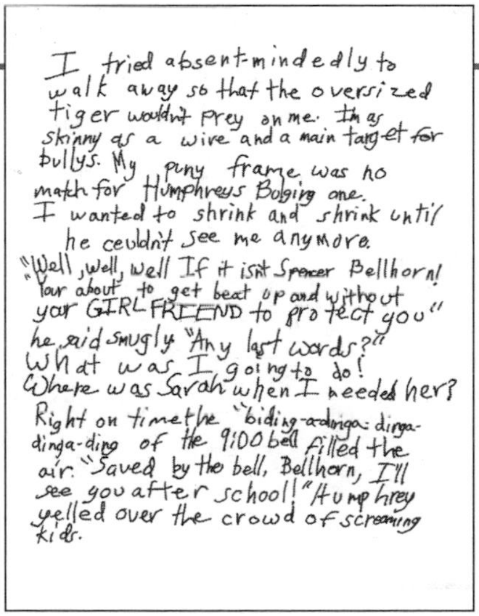
I tried absent-mindedly to walk away so that the oversized tiger wouldn't prey on me. I'm as skinny as a wire and a main target for bullys. My puny frame was no match for Humphreys Bulging one. I wanted to shrink and shrink until he couldn't see me anymore. "Well, well, well If it isn't Spencer Bellhorn! Your about to get beat up and without your GIRL FRIEND to protect you" he said smugly "Any last words?" What was I going to do! Where was Sarah when I needed her? Right on time the "biding-a-dinga-dinga-dinga-ding of the 9:00 bell filled the air. "Saved by the bell, Bellhorn, I'll see you after school!" Humphrey yelled over the crowd of screaming kids.

Fig. VII-1 A snippet from Caleb's draft

Of course, children, too, need to be talent scouts. You can help them find talent among their classmates and among the authors whose books they admire. Becca came to me with this section of *Journey*, by Patricia MacLachlan, announcing, "Know what's amazing? It's the best description in the world and it only has two adjectives in it!"

> The first letter that wasn't a letter came in the noon mail. It lay in the middle of the kitchen table like a dropped apple, addressed to Cat and me, Mama's name in the left-hand corner.
>
> I'd watched Cat walk up the front path from the mailbox slowly, as if caught by the camera in slow motion or in a series of what Grandfather calls stills: Cat smiling; Cat looking eager; Cat, her face suddenly unfolding out of a smile. She brushed past me at the front door and opened her hand, the letter falling to the table.

I looked with her at the passage, agreed with her analysis, and pointed out to her that when I was studying with Don Murray, he gave me a list of editing tips. "Check to be sure you are writing with strong precise nouns and verbs, not relying on adjectives and adverbs to prop them up—the *young* dog is a puppy, and if the man walked *quietly*, he tiptoed."

continued from previous page

Can't you just see them? Caleb has really set this scene up, and it feels dramatic. What will happen? Will the bully hit him or not? Listen to the next scene that Caleb made." *[Fig. VII-2]*

> I couldn't pay attention in math class because I was thinking of a plan, a plan to defend myself against Humphrey. I could run away! No he would get me the next day. I could set a trap! No time.
>
> Then a thought crossed my mind. Humphrey had never actually hit someone, he had just threatened to! So why should I be afraid? A light bulb lit up in my head. I had a plan.

"Can you hear how Caleb is making a plan for how to stand up to the bully? Make sure that as you write your stories, you keep in mind where the story is going . . . but that like Caleb, you take your time getting there."

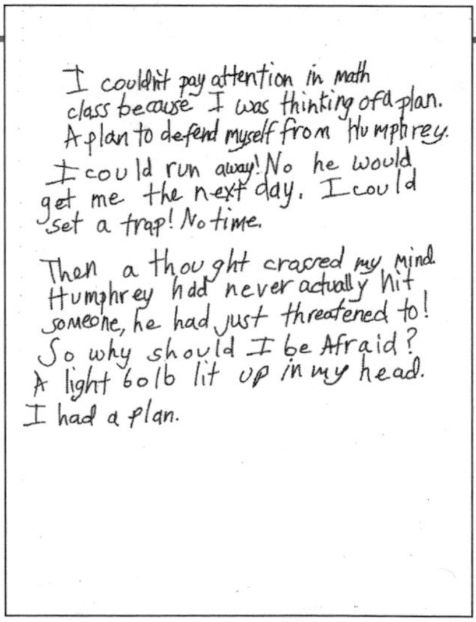
I couldn't pay attention in math class because I was thinking of a plan. A plan to defend myself from Humphrey. I could run away! No he would get me the next day. I could set a trap! No time.

Then a thought crassed my mind Humphrey had never actually hit someone, he had just threatened to! So why should I be Afraid? A light bolb lit up in my head. I had a plan.

Fig. VII-2 Caleb's draft, page 2 of his story booklet.

SHARE

Revising Leads

Tell children that you can't move fast enough to help each writer, so you'll teach them how to be writing teachers for each other. Explain that it is more efficient to revise earlier rather than waiting to revise the whole story, and tell children that they need to look at leads asking, "What story does this set up?"

"Writers, I've been racing around, conferring with lots of you. But your stories are so long and complex and interesting, that I'm not moving fast enough. And I want every single one of you to have the chance to confer with someone about your story, so that you can revise before you get a lot farther into your draft. It's much easier to write a page or two and then look at those early pages and say, 'Whoa! Let me rethink this,' rather than writing a whole ten-page draft, then rereading it and saying, 'Whoa! Let me rethink this!'"

"So right now, I want to teach every one of you how to be writing teachers for each other, and then I'm going to suggest you each meet with your partner, and try to confer in ways that help both of you rethink your lead *and your story*."

"You see, when you help each other revise your leads, you are really thinking, 'If this keeps on going and becomes a whole story, what problems might the story encounter?' I think I may have told you about the time I wanted to put a new carpet on our living room floor. But I didn't want to buy a big carpet, install it, and *then* say 'Whoa!' So I got a sweater the color of one possible carpet. I put it on the floor and I looked at it, squinting in such a way that I imagined that sweater as a whole big carpet touching the walls, and I thought, 'How would this look if it were big?' Then I put a different sweater on the middle of the floor, stepped back and squinted at it, imagining *that* sweater as a whole big carpet."

"We can reread the early pages of a story like I looked at those sweaters, thinking, 'What might this look like when it's a bigger text?' When you do this for your own writing and for each other, reread the draft and think, 'What will happen next in the story?' Talk and think about the story that this particular lead sets up."

Remind children of the common problems they're apt to see when they look at each other's and their own leads.

"Often you'll decide that your first draft starts too far from the turning point, and you'll decide the next draft needs to zoom in on an event that is closer to the main action. On the other hand, sometimes you'll decide that you've told the whole story right at the start from

I find that a unit of study on fiction quickly becomes a unit of study on revision. In part, this is true because writers are so eager for the chance to write fiction that they fill pages upon pages in short order. Then, too, there is so much involved in getting a story off to a good start that it's inevitable that children will write a less-than-ideal draft and that we'll want to ratchet up the level of that draft by helping the child make significant revisions. So ready yourself to put a lot of weight behind the importance of revision, and prepare to act utterly dumbfounded if a child announces he or she doesn't want to revise. Act as if you've never heard of such a preposterous idea! Unheard of!

As your children become more experienced as writers and as students of writing, their abilities to confer well with each other will grow in leaps and bounds. Whereas during the early portion of the year, you probably hoped that in their peer conferences, children functioned as audiences for each other (only), by now, you can expect children's conferences with each other to include assessment, planning, and suggested strategies.

beginning to end, leaving nothing for page 2 or 3. In this case, you'll need to back up and work on your story mountain again. Ask yourself, 'What episode (or Small Moment story) could occur next to show the predicament? What episode could make the predicament get worse and worse?'"

Set children up to practice conferring by asking them to consider how they'd respond to a child you describe who's written just the lead of a story. Then launch partnership work.

"Imagine, for example, that you are Rena's partner. She brings her draft to you. I'm going to read you page 1 and 2 of her story booklet and would you think to yourself, 'How will this look once she's written an entire story?' Ask yourself, 'What problems might Rena run into once this becomes a whole big story? Has she started too early in the sequence of events? Has she spilled the beans too early?'" [Fig. VII-3]

> "I got both of your invitations . . . same day . . . don't know what to do . . . can't make . . . anyone feel bad . . . ," Morgan panted after running up to Cassandra in the school yard.
>
> "Who? Wha–"
>
> "Your birthday party is on the same day as Amy's. I can't miss either, I just can't," Morgan said firmly.
>
> "Why? It's OK if you'd rather go to Amy's," says Cassandra humphily.
>
> "That's the point though, that's the point!" Morgan wailed. "Oh I just can't stand making either of you feel bad. Plus, the parties sound like so much fun, so I can't miss both, but I just can't only miss one!"
>
> Cassandra smiles and nudges me. "Hey calm down, I was only joking. Like I care if you go to Amy's . . . It's my own fault I planned it on the same day during the same hours. Plus I'll still know you're my friend."
>
> Morgan shook her head vigorously, "I can't risk offending either of you. Uh-uh, no way. I won't."

Soon the class had agreed that if they were Rena's partner, they might tell her that she'd not only conveyed the problem, she also came very close to solving it! Within just this first page, the character got herself into and out of a little scrape. So the children suggested Rena could now go back to the drawing board, quite literally, and think again about the story mountain of her story. They suggested she needed, also, to take a bit of time to allow readers

Fig. VII-3 Rena's lead

If you're accustomed to reading children's efforts to write narrative, then you'll probably have the eyes to see that Rena has made a big effort to intersperse small actions throughout the dialogue. Often children begin to do something as writers that needs to be celebrated—and extended. I think Rena needs to be more clear where the interchange is taking place, and what, exactly, her characters are doing, holding, and so forth. If Rena were clear about this, she could add actions and setting in a way which grounded the dialogue. Then she could hear your suggestions about tenses!

to identify with and care about the protagonist. "Show her in agony over the decision," they suggested. "Then make it get worse and worse." Rena agreed to return to the stage of planning and drafting her story.

With this experience as writing teachers behind them, partners convened and tried to give similarly dramatic help to each other.

HOMEWORK *Revising Story Mountains* When my sons were young, they spent much of one summer building a tree fort high in the branches of a lakeside tree. Long before they put the first logs into place, they sketched out their plans. Starting in the middle of winter, they worked on their architectural drawings. Should the fort be one story, or two? Should the second story be above and parallel to the first, or jutting out on a higher branch? What sort of stairway might link the floors?

My sons began sketching and dreaming and problem-solving in February and kept at it through the entire spring. Writers in a writing workshop don't have as much time to mull over story mountains, but it is still really important to imagine alternative ways that a story (like a tree fort) might go. John Gardner, author of *The Art of Fiction*, describes this stage of the writing process this way.

> Plotting is ordinarily no hasty process but something the writer broods and labors over, trying out one approach, then another, carrying the idea around with him, musing on it casually as he drifts off to sleep. (pp. 170–171)

Tonight, try a few different story mountains, and be sure that with each different sketch, you take the time to envision how that version of the story might unroll. Does it get to the heart of the action right away? Does the tension increase slowly until it is unbearable? Come to school tomorrow with a diagram of your story that feels like it's a viable plan.

If your students are rushing along in their stories and you want to give input to help their endings . . . you could say to them, "Writers, I think Patricia Reilly Giff would be proud of the heap of trouble you have all gotten your characters into! I'm out of breath just thinking of climbing your story mountains! But now we've all created some gigantic problem mountains, and we're stuck on top! How will we get our poor characters out of the situations they are in?"

Then you could tell children that realistic fiction writers work very hard on what they call the resolution. We work hard to make sure the resolution of the problems makes sense and doesn't seem to come out of the clear blue sky. It's not like a comic book, where Superman can just fly in to save the day. A good resolution feels like it fits with the rest of the story, and makes our character learn something or change in ways that feel tailored to the character.

If your students are working through this unit for the second or third year . . . you could spend some time teaching them the difference between first person, second person, and third person perspectives in writing. Second person, the "you" voice, often feels forced or too familiar. The third-person voice allows students to distance themselves from the characters and reinforces the idea that this is fiction, not personal narrative. The first person often sounds more natural, and using it can make it easier for students to integrate an internal narrative. You can teach children that writers often experiment with different perspectives before settling on one. To do this, writers would write the same scene in first, second, and then third person. Then, we choose which perspectives have the effect on the reader we prefer, and hold to that point of view. Writers could try this in partnerships.

ASSESSMENT

You'll definitely want to collect your children's work and study it. It's easy to look at student work for signs of trouble, and that will be important to do. But give yourself firm orders to first look for signs of growth. Since the start of the year, your children will have often picked up their pens and spun stories onto their pages. Look back on the earliest September entries and contrast them with the writing they did today. The fact that September's writing was personal narrative and this is fiction shouldn't detract from the comparability of these texts. What progress do you see?

I suspect you'll see that children are writing with vastly more fluency, voice, detail, and structure. If so, you'll want to point this out to the child. Bring out the first entries and contrast them with the child's latest work. "Look at the difference!" you need to say.

But you also need to point this out to yourself, because your children's growth should help you believe in the power of instruction. And the evidence that your children have already made important gains can renew your energy to teach. Be willing to look at children's writing and to see what they are almost but not quite doing.

There are a few problems that you should expect to see. These won't be new problems—chances are, they were also present during the personal narrative work. Many times, you'll see that even your most skilled writers try to carry their scenes through dialogue, not action. This was the case in the lead to Rena's story we studied in the previous share session, and you'll see the problem remains in this new effort she made to write a whole new story. *[Figs. VII-4 and VII-5]*

"Butthead!" Cassidy says seething.

"I didn't do anything," Carly, the sensitive one of the three is on the verge of tears.

"Did so! You kept on hurling pine cones at me when I told you to stop, and then you played keep-it-away-from-Cassidy with my favorite hat and now it's halfway downstream because

you tried to throw it across the spring to Morgan and it landed in the spring."

"I was joking," says Carly looking down. "It was funny."

Ideally, you will want to see your students weaving together action, thought, dialogue and setting to create the scenes of their stories. As you read through their work, notice which of these elements your students do and do not use.

For example, I noticed that in this section of Joey's draft, when he tried to convince his mother to give him money to buy a bicycle, he relied exclusively on dialogue:

"But Mom," Gary said. "I really want that bike."

"Sorry, but you can't afford it," Gary's mom said.

"Can't you give me the money? I'll pay you back."

"And how exactly do you think that will work?"

> If... Two friends Cassidy and Carly are fighting
> Then... I would get both to laugh about something like a funny memory and make up.
> "Butthead!" Cassidy says, seething.
> "I didn't do anything." Carly, the sensitive one of the three is on the verge of tears.
> "Did so! You kept on hurling pine cones at me when I told you to stop, and then you played keep-it-away-from-Cassidy with my favorite hat and now it's halfway downstream because you tried to throw it across the spring to Morgan and it landed in the spring."
> "I was joking," says Carly, looking down. "It was funny."
> "Remember that time when you guys were both at my house and my little brother got into my mom's make-up and marched into dinner in her evening gown and lipstick, eyeshadow, and mascara?" Morgan says." Carly looks up and giggles escape her mouth.

Fig. VII-4 Rena's lead

> "Remember, Cass?" she says. "He went full out. He smeared Morgan's body glitter on too. And the nail polish—all that nail polish—on his cheeks, up his nose.

Fig. VII-5 Rena's lead, page 2

This would have been a much stronger image if Joey had added thoughts and action and setting. Revised, it might have gone something like this:

> "But Mom," Gary said, "I really want that bike. Gary sat at the kitchen table finishing his · homework as his mother cooked dinner.
>
> "Sorry, but you can't afford it," Gary's mother said without looking up. Her voice was strong and final, but Gary wasn't ready to give up."
>
> "Can't you give me the money? I'll pay you back."
>
> Gary's mother stopped cooking. She turned and looked at her son. She stood with her arms folded as if she was firmly resisting his pleas. "And how exactly do you think that will work."

Children need us to give them examples of what we imagine. If we simply tell them to add actions, they don't necessarily grasp the way in which we envision setting the words into a scene. So plan on actually showing them how a bit of their text could be rewritten, and plan also on extrapolating the larger principles from this. Once we rewrote a few sentences of Joey's draft for him, we could point out that in the new version a reader could see that Gary's mother is not at all agreeable to Gary's plan, and that Gary is relentless in his pursuit to get a new bicycle.

You will probably also notice that if your students write with setting at all, they put one big blob of it at the beginning of their story and let it sit

there. The characters walk past the setting, but the setting doesn't further the main action of the story. Joey's original draft started like this:

> It was a sunny day. Gary walked through the park towards school. The ground was covered with leaves and the trees were bare. People were walking their dogs and drinking coffee. There was a chill in the air, but Gary was wearing his new fleece so he was warm.

Joey has created a sense of place at the beginning of the story, but as his story unfolds, you can see that the setting has little to do with his story line. If revised to make the setting serve his story, his beginning might instead go like:

> Gary rushed through the park toward school. It was a sunny day but Gary hardly noticed. He was too intent on hurrying. People were walking dogs and drinking coffee and chatting, but Gary's only interest was getting to the bike shop before school to catch one quick glimpse of his favorite BMX bike.

As you read through your students' writing, you'll learn what you need to know to plan your future teaching.

STUDYING PUBLISHED TEXTS TO WRITE LEADS

IN THIS SESSION, YOU'LL REMIND WRITERS OF VARIOUS STRATEGIES FOR WRITING EFFECTIVE LEADS. YOU WILL ALSO REMIND CHILDREN THAT WRITERS REREAD LITERATURE, LETTING IT TEACH TECHNIQUES FOR WRITING.

GETTING READY

- Leads of two short stories kids are familiar with
- Lead that invites further revision
- Two examples of dialogue, one empty and one revealing, written on chart paper
- See CD-ROM for resources

If you look across all the units of study that we've detailed in this series, you'll see that time and again, we ask children to draft and revise their leads. The goal in making a great lead isn't the lead itself. The goal is to imagine a work of art, and then to write a lead which points the course toward and is worthy of that larger enterprise. Opening scenes set up the drama of what will follow. We plan our leads with an eye toward all that we believe is essential for the larger experience to work.

This session, then, aims to help children remember that after drafting a lead, it's important to step back and ask, "How might this lead set up the larger text? Is that the way I want the larger text to go?" As writers revise this opening paragraph or two, they also revise the larger text.

We ask children to revise their leads because front-end revisions are vastly easier for children to embrace and more likely to lift the level of entire drafts than back-end revisions, which are much more time consuming. And by investing a minilesson (and therefore an added day) in early revision work, we slow children's progress, making it more likely that we'll be able to confer with more children at this crucial just-starting stage. Once children are deep into the first drafts of their stories, they become more and more committed to the road they've taken, and it is harder to deter them from that pathway. Soon, children won't want us to confer in ways that help them imagine other paths their story could have taken.

When we ask children to revise their leads, we aim to remind them that writers consider and reconsider not only the content of their stories, but also their craftsmanship. When a writer shifts from planning a story to writing a draft, the writer needs to think not only about what will happen in a scene (in this instance, in the opening scene), but also about how to write the scene well. Children are much more apt to write well if, just before they pick up their pens, something occurs that stirs their hearts, that raises their hopes, that fills them with a sense of momentousness. So we tell them, "Study the work of other authors"—and secretly, we say, "Put yourself under the spell of other authors. Let their magic rub off!"

In today's session you will show students how they can study the work of published writers to help them craft enticing leads for their stories.

MINILESSON

Studying Published Texts to Write Leads

CONNECTION

Celebrate that your children have begun their stories, and do so by conveying the essence of a couple of stories to the class.

"Writers, you'll see from today's schedule that the read-aloud we've scheduled for later will be a special one. Instead of me continuing to read our chapter book aloud, some of you will read aloud the leads to your stories. Something extraordinary is happening in this classroom, and we all need to be a part of it. Stories are literally coming to life in your story booklets. You need to know each other's stories!"

"You need to know that just as that gingerbread boy came to life, there are characters coming to life right in this room. You need to know that a girl named Elexa is surveying the playground, hoping against hope that the geeky boy who stalks her hasn't caught a glance of her. Elexa sees her best friend—but oh no! She is frantically gesturing that someone is close by, and with a sinking heart Elexa realizes she's been spotted."

"You need to know that Spencer is getting ready to confront his nemesis, Humphrey Dugball, the meanest bully in the history of Butts, Missouri. And you need to know that right here in this room, Jane's friend Amy has asked her yet again to sleep over, and Jane is frantically coming up with yet more excuses."

Name your teaching point. In this case, teach children that by revising their leads, they revise their entire stories, and remind them they could emulate the work of another writer.

"Today I want to teach you that just when a writer is most fired up to write, most ready to charge into page after page of writing, we force ourselves to pause. We pause, rewind, and then we listen to what we've written. And we revise it. We revise our lead because by doing so, we revise our entire story. Sometimes, we do this with help from a pro."

COACHING

Your job is to help children fall in love with their own stories and with the fiction writing workshop itself—and to then channel their energy and zeal for writing into revision. Notice that the impetus for revision is not discontent, but instead pride and commitment.

Notice that the message to children today is, "Your stories are riveting! I'm dying to learn how they turn out." It's important for children to aim toward writing riveting, absorbing stories that draw in readers.

Children can learn as much from their friend's work with a draft as they learn from your work with a demonstration text. So be sure that you help them learn vicariously by following the drama of each other's progress.

A unit of study on fiction writing is also a unit of study on rehearsal and revision. Fiction writing is such a complex enterprise that there is no way we can preteach kids all they need to know to get off to a good start. By emphasizing revision, we give ourselves opportunities to double or triple the amount of instruction we can give to our students. Meanwhile, children will experience the power and pay off of real revision.

TEACHING

Tell children that to write leads that draw readers into a story, it helps to study the leads published authors have written.

"You already know that the beginning of a piece of writing, any piece of writing, is called a *lead* because these sentences are the way an author *leads* readers into the text. A good lead functions like the Pied Piper. You remember the story of the Pied Piper, walking through town playing his flute? People would listen up, and soon all the villagers were following along wherever he led them."

"This morning, I told Francesca that I always work hard on my lead because I want it to draw readers along. But she asked the crucial question—how can a lead do that? What techniques do writers use?"

"Of course, you know how to answer that! When we writers want to learn how to do something, we study texts written by authors we admire. After we look really closely at exactly how other authors pull something off, we try the same techniques in our own writing."

When teaching skills, we need to anticipate that we'll often revisit earlier lessons. It's a challenge to find new ways to teach a familiar concept. In this instance, I've found a new way to describe the role a lead plays in a story.

Tell the class that you and one student studied the leads from familiar stories. Read one aloud, listing what the student noticed about it and then showing the resulting revisions in her own lead.

"Francesca and I decided to study leads. We first reread the lead to *Ruby, the Copy Cat*, which you'll remember is a picture book by Peggy Rathmann. The story starts like this:

> Monday was Ruby's first day in Miss Hart's class. "Class, this is Ruby," announced Miss Hart. "Ruby, you may use the empty desk behind Angela. Angela is the girl with the pretty red bow in her hair."
>
> Angela smiled at Ruby.
>
> Ruby smiled at Angela's bow and tiptoed to her seat.

"Looking at this story reminded Francesca of things she'd learned earlier: It often helps to start with the exact words one character is saying (or with a small action); and, in a short story, it's important to start close to the main event. If there's a waterfall in the story, start when you can hear the falls. The main tension in this story revolves around Ruby wanting Angela's approval, and she will try to earn this by wearing a red bow, just like Angela's . . . and by worse examples of copying too! Notice that the lead of the story hints at what will come later."

F. Paul Wilson has said: "I don't know how it is with other writers, but most of the time when I finish [reading] a story or novel, I may be pleased, I may even be impressed, but somewhere in the back of my mind I'm thinking, 'I can do that.'" The act of apprenticing oneself to a respected and more experienced practitioner is an age-old tradition.

There is nothing special about this particular story. We also use Peter's Chair, Stevie (by John Steptoe), or "Merry Christmas, My Friend," a short story from Chicken Soup for the Kid's Soul. Select any text that works!

Set children up to listen to and then talk with partners about what the one child did as she revised her lead.

"So Francesca thought about her story. She already knew that the heart of the story revolved around Griffen, the boy in her story, trying to convince his father he could take care of a pet. She remembered that often it helps to start a story with dialogue, so she decided to try a lead in which Griffen says something about getting a pet to his dad. Listen to what she wrote: *[Fig. VIII-1]*

> "Dad," Griffen said.
>
> "Can I get a pet?"
>
> "Well, a pet is a lot of responsibility," Dad said.
>
> "Please," Griffen said.
>
> "If I see that you are responsible enough you can get a pet," said Griffen's dad.
>
> The next day, Griffen told Timmy. He was amazed.
>
> "I bet we can show that we are responsible enough," Timmy said.

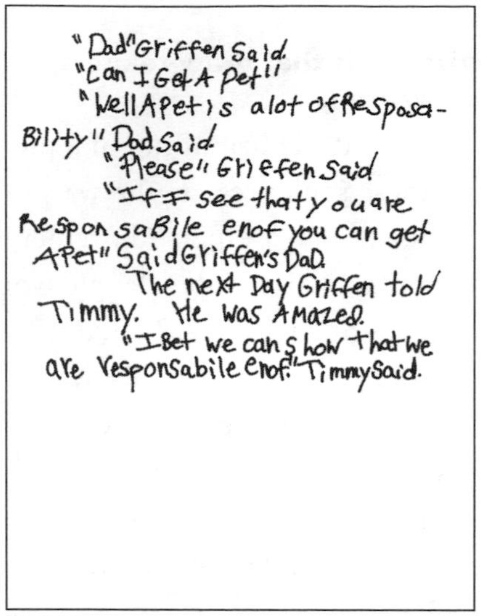
"Dad"Griffen Said
"Can I Get A Pet"
"Well A Pet is alot of Resposa-
Bility" Dad Said
"Please" Griefen Said
"If I see that you are
Responsabile enof you can get
A Pet" Said Griffen's DaD
The next Day Griffen told
Timmy. He was Amazed
"I Bet we can show that we
are responsabile enof" Timmy Said.

Fig. VIII-1 Francesca's lead

This is not a spectacular example of a lead. Francesca is a very capable writer, as you will have seen from following her progress throughout the year. Don't be surprised if your children's writing, like Francesca's, is not as impressive when they are writing fiction as when they wrote personal narratives. As this session unrolls, you'll point out ways to enrich this writing.

Active Engagement

Share a second lead, this time asking the class to list to a partner what they notice about it that Fransesca, and all of them, could try.

"Then Francesca and I looked at a second lead, this time from Julie Brinckloe's *Fireflies!*" We were pretty sure this story would teach us more techniques, so we read it really closely. Reread it with me now, and think, 'What has Brinckloe done that we can learn from?'"

> On a summer evening
> I looked up from dinner,
> through the open window to the backyard.
> It was growing dark.
>
> My treehouse was a black shape in the tree
> and I wouldn't go up there now.
>
> But something flickered there, a moment—
> I looked, and it was gone.
>
> It flickered again, over near the fence.
> *Fireflies*!

You've probably noticed throughout this series that I use the same texts in my minilessons over and over again. These are texts that I have read to the children, texts that they know and love, carefully selected for their teaching potential. Returning often to the same text shows students how very much we can learn through the study of one beautiful story. Keep a stash of these texts to use as demonstrations during small group and individual conferences, too. I've sometimes led workshops to show teachers how we can weave any one text into fifty very different conferences!

"Don't let your dinner get cold," said Momma.

I forked the meat and corn and potatoes into my mouth.

"Please may I go out? The fireflies—"

Momma smiled and Daddy nodded. "Go ahead," they said.

"Brinckloe's used lots of techniques here; the lead is one we could examine and talk about for hours. So let's reread it again. As you listen this time, let a section of the lead stand out for you, and then when I finish reading it, turn and point out that part to your partner. Name what Brinckloe has done that you could emulate."

I reread the lead, and reminded children of what they each needed to do in his or her own mind. After giving them a moment or two of silence, I queried, "Ready?" and when they nodded yes, I directed them to share with a partner. I listened in as the children talked.

Convene the class to talk as a group about what they noticed in the lead. Do this to lift the level of partner talk which will be continued soon.

After a moment, I said, "Who can get us started on a conversation about the techniques Brinckloe has used in her lead?"

Deveonna's hand shot up. "It has less talk."

"Hmm . . . that's interesting," I said, looking at the text. "That's a smart thing to notice. But class, do you see that if there's *less* talk, there is *more* of something else?" I asked. Then I named the larger principle. "Writers, when I try to learn from other authors, I push myself to name what a writer *has* done, not just what he or she *hasn't* done, because it's easier to emulate something positive. What *did* Brinckloe do instead of writing dialogue?"

"She takes her time showing where the story takes place; the evening is coming and the treehouse is a black shape and all?" Ramon said.

"She doesn't start with dialogue." Ari added. "First there's just the backyard, then a flicker by the fence."

"So this author first creates the setting," I confirmed, providing Ari with the words he seemed to be reaching for. "But also, even before we see the backyard, we see the narrator, sitting at the dinner table, looking outside. The backyard is growing dark . . . . It's not the author who describes the setting is it? It's the boy, the narrator, who notices the setting. And what do you make of the flicker? Why did the author write the setting in such a way that there is a flicker right from the start?" Then I said, "Let's again try to talk with partners and this time really name what Julie Brinckloe has done in this lead." I sent children to talk in pairs about this.

Convening the class, I again called on a few children.

Notice that when teaching strategies, I am careful to describe each step in sequence. I don't simply suggest that children "talk about what they can learn from this author." Instead, in order to set children up to make a reading-writing connection, I ask them to reread the text, let a part stand out for them, then point to that part and name the technique the author has used in this part that they can emulate.

This is unusual. I'm asking for a child to launch a whole-class conversation within the minilesson instead of simply retelling what I heard a child do. The teaching component of this minilesson was brief so I saved enough time for this.

The way I ratchet up what Deveonna has said is a way you too can try. I could have simply agreed that there is less talk and then asked, "What takes the place of that talk?" But whenever possible, I try to explicitly teach concepts that might apply to other situations, and so I first point out the generalizable principle—that children will learn more from looking for positive features, features that are present rather than absent.

Of course, the decision to select a story that is filled with such a sense of place and of mood, too, was not accidental. I'm hoping to expand my students' repertoire. I agree with Janet Burroway who writes, in Writing Fiction, *"Your fiction must have an atmosphere because without it, your characters will be unable to breathe. Part of the atmosphere of a scene or story is its setting, including the location, period, weather, time of day . . ." I agree, too, that we most effectively reveal setting through detail. Burroway cites this example of how a detailed movement can create the larger setting: "The bugs hung over the black water in clusters of a steady hum." I refer instead to the examples in* Fireflies!.

"I think there is action, but it is just the flicker of the firefly."

"I think some stories start with the setting, and with making a mood. That's what this lead does 'cause we know it's evening outside."

"You've noticed a lot of techniques!" I said, and listed a few on my fingers:

- Sometimes stories begin not with a big action but with a small action, and this can be an action in the setting, as when the firefly flickers on and off.
- Some stories begin by creating a mood and a place, and only afterward does the sequence of actions begin.
- Sometimes the time and the place are revealed slowly, bit by bit, as the character sees or moves into the setting.

Channel children to use what they notice an author has done in order to help one child again revise her lead.

"Let's all listen again to Francesca's first lead and think whether the techniques we've learned from Brinckloe could help Francesca as she gets ready to again revise this lead. Listen again, then tell your partner if you have suggestions for Francesca."

> "Dad," Griffen said.
>
> "Can I get a pet?"
>
> "Well, a pet is a lot of responsibility," Dad said.
>
> "Please," Griffen said.
>
> "If I see that you are responsible enough you can get a pet," said Griffen's dad.
>
> The next day, Griffen told Timmy. He was amazed.
>
> "I bet we can show that we are responsible enough," Timmy said.

After the children talked with their partners, I called on Shariff, who said, "Francesca, I'm not sure, but I think maybe your first lead had *too* much talk. You could add in where you are, and put some setting in with it and take some talk out."

Hannah added, "Another idea is you could start the story earlier, before this when he's just sitting and dreaming about getting a pet, and have Griffen be alone, like the kid in *Fireflies!*—then he could go to his dad next. That'd show his wants more."

You could decide to create a large chart with a favorite passage from a mentor text on the left, the words children use to describe what the author has done in the center, and examples of two or three children's efforts to write similarly in the far right column. This chart could form a cohesive link, tying together several days of inquiry and apprenticeship. I recommend this sort of chart in the Authors as Mentors *book within the* K-2 Units of Study *series, and you'll see charts like this elsewhere in this book.*

I deliberately selected a student whose lead invited further revision. I wanted to make it easy for children to imagine ways they could incorporate more setting.

Restate the options your children have for today, reminding them of the step-by-step process they might take to revise their leads.

"So writers, I want to tell you a surprise—Francesca and I came to the same conclusions when we studied her lead. Francesca tried two other leads; let me read them to you." [Figs. VIII-2 and VIII-3]

First Revision

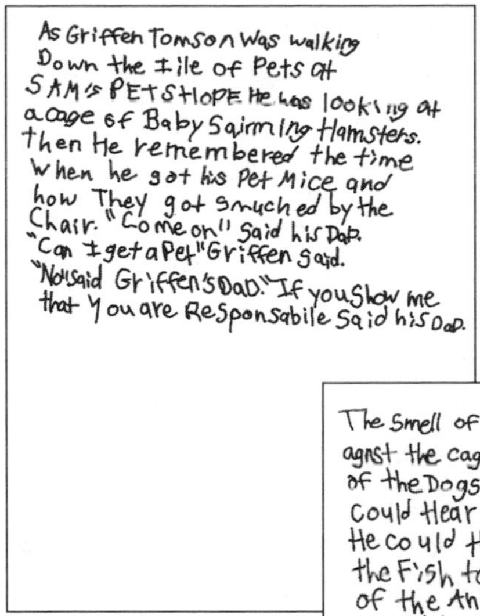

As Griffen Tomson was walking down the aisle of pets at Sam's Pet Shop, he was looking at a cage of baby squirming hamsters. Then he remembered the time he got his pet mice and how they got squashed by the chair. "Come on" said his dad. "Can I get a pet?" Griffen said. "No" said Griffen's dad. "If you show me that you are responsible," said his dad.

Later Revision

The smell in the air of the pets' fur rubbing against the cage. The smell of the dogs breath panting. Griffen could hear the hamsters squeaking as they ran. He could hear the running water in the fish tank. It felt like all of the animals were his pets. He could hear the cat's purring and he could hear the turtles walk. It smelled like dog and cat fur. He could hear the birds squawking and making loud noises. He could see the little turtles rest under their mom. He saw one little turtle all alone under its shell. He saw it go under a big rock like a cave. He wanted to take the little turtle home!

"Do you see what she learned from other authors in her own lead? Today, each one of you needs to decide what you need to do. Some of you are probably realizing that in order to write with this sort of detail, you need to rethink your story plan, figuring out how you can zoom in more on just two Small Moment stories. Some of you may decide that you need to do some revisions that are similar to those Francesca has done. Some of you will want to study published leads for yourself, learning more techniques. All of you will be drafting and revising leads, but you'll decide how to go about doing that. You're the boss of your own story!"

Of course, I could have told the children that Francesca decided to revise her lead by adding more of the setting and by working to create a mood, and then asked them to reread their leads and to consider whether Rathmann or Brinckloe's leads could help them imagine ways to improve their own leads. I would work with children's own leads if the class I was teaching was filled with resistant writers or with writers who struggled to get anything much on the page. In either case, setting the children up to decide upon and rehearse for the revisions they'd soon do could be very helpful. I didn't do this in this instance because I think it is more ideal for children to work collaboratively to revise a model, and then to disperse and initiate a review of their own leads.

Fig. VIII-2 Francesca's first revision of her lead.

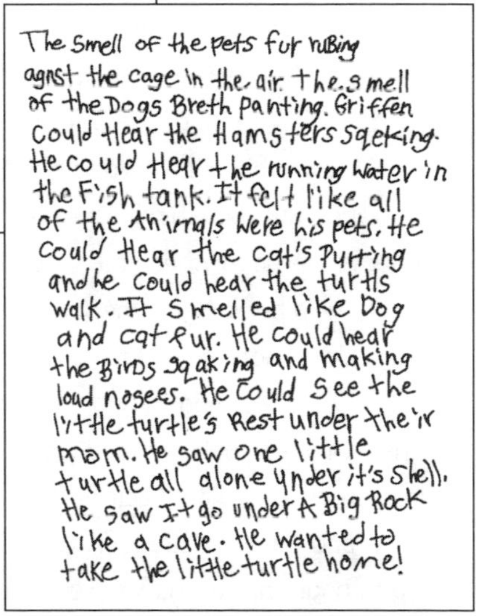

Fig. VIII-3 Francesca's second revision of her lead.

Writing and Conferring

Learning from Mentor Texts

As you move among your writers, you may want to carry a couple of short stories or picture books with you so you can refer to these often as you work with children. Keep in mind that the same text can be used to help writers with a wide array of goals. This means that your resolve to help children use mentor texts needn't control the course of a conference. Instead, you'll want to open your conferences by asking, "What are you working on as a writer?" Presumably many children will respond that they're trying to learn from Julie Brinckloe or from another author.

Don't act as if this answers your initial interest in understanding the writer's intention. Instead, press on. "And what, exactly, are you admiring about your mentor author's text?" you can ask, channeling the child to at least point to a favorite part. Appreciate that section of the text. But then quickly shift from oohing and ahhing toward helping the child think, "What has the author done in this text that worked so well?"

That's a tricky question for a child to answer. If the child makes any attempt to articulate the replicable and transferable strategies the author has used, plan on accepting and building upon whatever the child says. Act fascinated by the child's observations. "Huh! That's so interesting!" you can say. "Explain more, 'cause you are onto something!"

On the other hand, be ready to demonstrate the sort of response you hope the writer might produce in case the child says nothing. If a child says she liked the lines, "It was growing dark," "My treehouse was a black shape," and "But something flickered there, a moment . . . It flickered again, over near the fence," and if the child doesn't respond when you nudge her to articulate what Brinckloe has done that she, too, could try doing, you might help her imagine the sort of response you hope she provides. "Were you especially impressed by the way Brinckloe made us feel that *her character* was the one noticing the backyard? Was that it? You loved that we got to see the setting through the boy's eyes? Was that the aspect you especially liked?" Give the child some options. "Or were you impressed with the way Brinckloe made the setting, the place, more interesting by setting it into motion, having it be active? The backyard grows darker, doesn't it, until the tree house is just a black shape . . . and then something flickers." Then restate your question. "Were you impressed that we saw the setting through the character's eyes or that Brinckloe made the setting active, or what?" By this time, the child will probably be able to indicate which of those two options impressed her more, or she'd grasp the sort of

> **MID-WORKSHOP TEACHING POINT** **Using Dialogue Deliberately** "Writers, can I stop you? I know by talking to many of you about your pieces and by looking over your shoulders that you are using a lot of dialogue in your stories. Give me a thumbs up if you have dialogue in your story." Most of the students gave a thumbs up.
>
> "That's great. We know that fiction writers use dialogue all the time, so it makes sense that we're using it. I just want to give you one caution. When we use dialogue in our stories, there has to be a reason. We usually use dialogue because we're trying to show something about a character. It's important that we don't just use dialogue as filler. For example, look at this piece of dialogue." The students looked at lines I'd written on chart paper:
>
> *continued on next page*

response that was expected and could contribute something of her own. Either way, ask if the writer was thinking of trying to do similar work in the next draft of his or her lead. It was this sort of conference that led Francesca to revise her lead. *[Figs. VIII-2, and VIII-3]*

Although your minilesson today was erudite and set children up for ambitious work, don't fool yourself into expecting that all your conferences will be aimed towards making good leads into great ones. Today's session gives you a final chance to check in with each student, making sure that each child has embarked on a project that is at least in the ball park that you have in mind. You are sure to find some children who, like Jasmin, have resolutely refused to follow any of your advice! Look at Jasmin's story mountain and her rough drafts of some leads: *[Figs. VIII-4, VIII-5, and VIII-6]*

Jasmin's first lead:

> "What are you doing?"
>
> "Nothin . . ." Chaos said quickly, "For now."
>
> Chaos's eyes shifted side to side. "Really?" Akyra asked, a little suspicious. I nodded. Chaos, Death, and I zoomed up the stairs. Lora and Ashley closed the door of the basement. Even though I started to hear weird noises from the basement, I kept walking. As Lora, Ashley, Akyra, Chaos, and Death walked ahead of me I turned the flashlight and laughed maniacally, "MUAHAHAHAHAH!"

Jasmin's second lead:

> I saw Death and Chaos open the door of the basement. They walked down the stairs. I tilted my head for a second, then I followed them.
>
> Chaos, Death and I were stuck in the basement . . . thanks to Death. Chaos and I looked at Death. We both yelled to Death, "NICE GOIN' IDIOT!" I thought of this situation as, DEATH'S FAULT!

continued from previous page

> "Hi" I said.
>
> "Hi," he said.
>
> "How are you?" I asked.
>
> "Fine, how are you?" he replied.

"Does everyone see how this part of dialogue doesn't do anything to help us learn more about the characters? It doesn't even move the story along. Instead, we can simply summarize what they said and write dialogue that deserves to exist, like this:

> After we exchanged greetings, I said what I had been meaning to tell him for days. "Mike," I blurted out. "I can't stand the way you pick on me all the time."
>
> "I had no idea," Mike said quietly. "Why did you wait so long to tell me? I would have stopped a long time ago."

Fig. VIII-4 Jasmin's story mountain

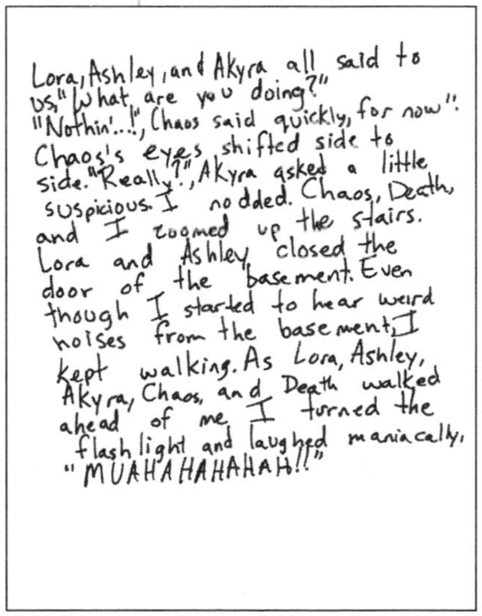

Fig. VIII-5 Although Jasmin's been directed to write realistic fiction, this is her first lead.

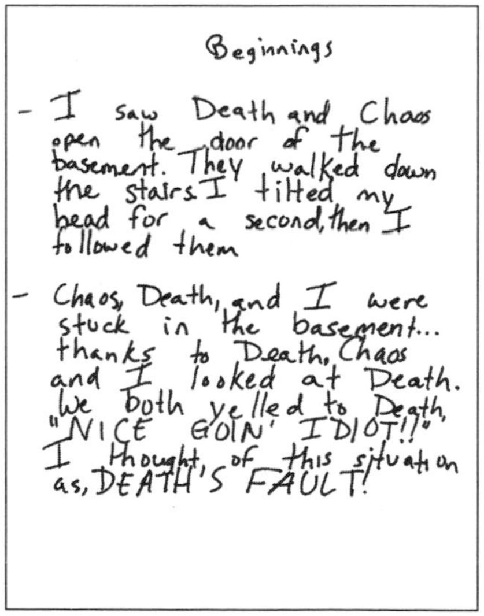

Fig. VIII-6 Jasmin's revised lead is close to the first version.

When I reminded Jasmin that we were studying *realistic* fiction, she immediately pointed out that her characters' names—Death, Chaos, and Spike were really their nicknames, and that underneath the nicknames, these are really just three normal fifth graders named Marilyn, Steven, and Lilly. "And underneath the bits about zombies and so forth, what's the simple, human story line?" I asked.

After some convoluted explanation, I finally extracted the fact that Spike-Marilyn follows the other two kids but is ambivalent about their tendency to always push boundaries and get in trouble.

"This is incredible!" I said, once I finally pushed past all the overstated drama. "Now I get it! What an incredible idea. So Marilyn wants to be friends with these kids. Do they seem to her to be powerful? What's their allure?"

Jasmin and I talked a bit more, and then I put all her drafts of the Death, Chaos, zombie story inside her folder, and pushed it to the side. I gave her a new blank sheet of paper and said, "You are definitely going to want to plan and write this story," I said. "Where will Steven and Lilly go? What sort of trouble will they get into?" Then I said, "Choose a place you know, a place you go to so that you can include realistic details, like Brinckloe did when describing the backyard."

This is the draft that Jasmin started that day: *[Fig. VIII-7]*

Lilly, Steven, and I walked through Chinatown. "So . . . many . . . shops," I thought. Steven pointed to the fish market. "Let's go there," he said. Lilly sighed, "Ok! What about you Marilyn?"

"Whatever . . ." I responded, as I shrugged. We all ran to the fish market. I could smell the seafood. It didn't really smell so bad. Lily swung the door open. Steven froze. "Look at the fishy goodness," Steven said. His eyes widened. I wasn't really amused. Lilly ran toward the fortune cookies.

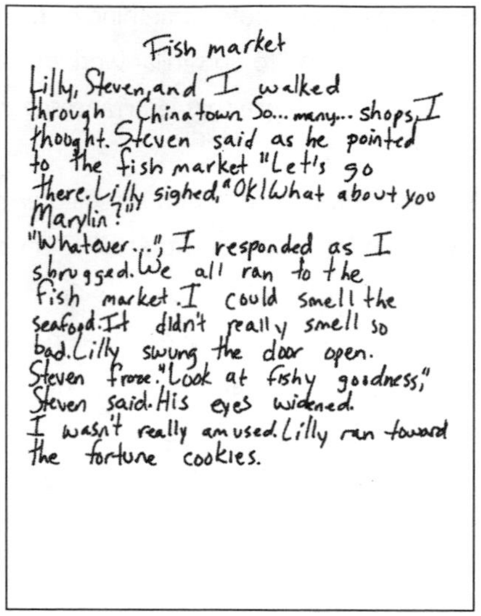
Fish market

Lilly, Steven, and I walked through Chinatown So... many... shops, I thought. Steven said as he pointed to the fish market "Let's go there. Lilly sighed, "Ok! What about you Marylin?"

"Whatever...," I responded as I shrugged. We all ran to the fish market. I could smell the seafood. It didn't really smell so bad. Lilly swung the door open. Steven froze. "Look at fishy goodness," Steven said. His eyes widened. I wasn't really amused. Lilly ran toward the fortune cookies.

Fig. VIII-7 Jasmin is now launched in a much more realistic story.

SHARE

Playing Out Leads

Remind your children that as they reconsider various leads, they are actually reconsidering various ways their entire drafts could go. Ask them to write in the air the way the next section of their story would go if they selected one lead, or another lead.

"Writers, by now many of you have written several leads, several different first scenes. I want to remind you that each of your leads will get you started telling a different story. Would you share one of your leads with your partner, then see where your lead, leads? Write in the air to help your partner imagine how that particular lead will set up your story. After that, share a second lead, and again see where it leads. Use this as a way to figure out which lead sets you up for the story you want to tell."

I listened as Valerie read first one lead to her partner, then another, pausing each time to dictate the story that would follow each lead. *[Figs. VIII-8 and VIII-9]*

Lead #1

It was a dark and gray day, kids were screaming and running inside puddles of water. All of them were screaming "Yahoo!" because school had just ended. The last day of school was sure a bad one, maybe it wasn't so bad for the other kids but it was pretty bad for Summer. She was sitting on the monkey bars wishing that school hadn't ended yet. In the back of her head she was thinking, "Oh, man, do I have to go to Catskills with Grandma & Grandpa?" Summer ran back home as fast as her feet would take her.

Lead #2

I was sitting on the school porch thinking and thinking and thinking about school. School was ending. Kids were happy. They were going home. Some of them were going away for the summer with their grandparent or their parent, others were staying home for the summer, but I was going to the Poconos with my grandparents and for me that was a disaster.

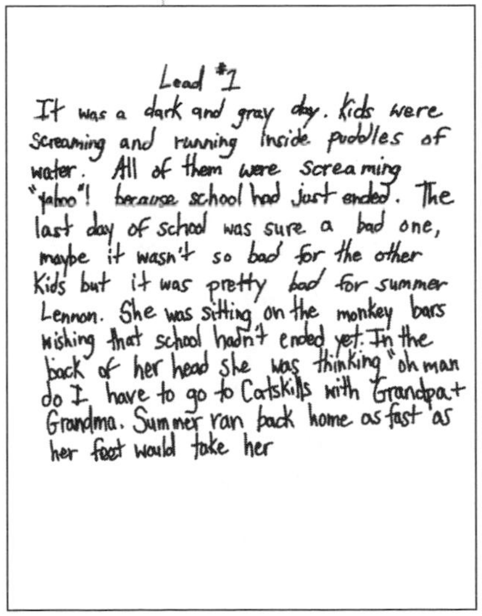

Leads set the path for the story to follow, so playing out each lead's story before choosing one is necessary work. The lead is not only a hook for the reader, it is also the rudder for the whole story.

Lead #1
It was a dark and gray day. kids were screaming and running inside puddles of water. All of them were screaming "yahoo"! because school had just ended. The last day of school was sure a bad one, maybe it wasn't so bad for the other kids but it was pretty bad for summer Lennon. She was sitting on the monkey bars wishing that school hadn't ended yet. In the back of her head she was thinking "oh man do I have to go to Catskills with Grandpa + Grandma. Summer ran back home as fast as her feet would take her

Lead #2
I was sitting on the school porch. thinking and thinking and thinking about school. School was ending. kids were happy. They were going home. Some of them were going away for the summer with their Grandparent or their parent others were staying home for the summer but I was going to the Poconos with my Grandparents and for me it was a disaster.

Fig. VIII-8 Valerie has written this lead in third person.

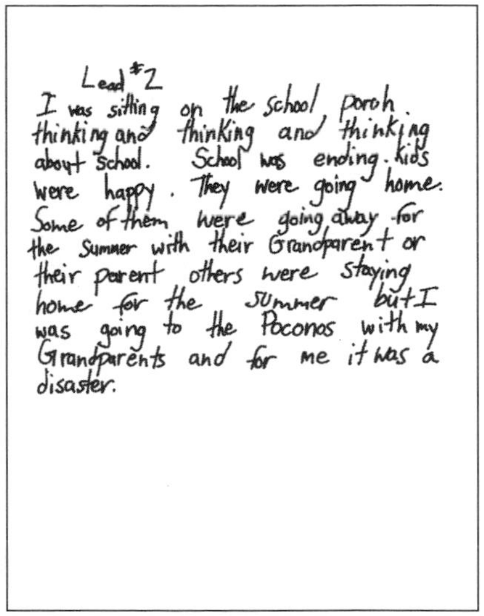

Fig. VIII-9 Valerie has written this as a first-person lead.

The girls talked over the differences, and Valerie decided she liked writing in first person, but wanted to create a mood as she'd done in the first lead. With her partner's help, she began writing a third lead which eventually looked like this: [*Fig. VIII-10*]

Lead #3

Huge lightning bolts were in the dark gray sky. Thunder was booming in my ears, rain was hitting the ground like little bits of hard rocks hitting the windows. I was standing outside and getting soaking wet. I wasn't the only one who was out in the huge storm. For some weird reason I didn't like going home, at least that's what most kids thought. Well, I thought it was a good reason. Going home to your two boring grandparents wasn't fun, especially if one of them was really fussy, grumpy and mean.

"Writers, I need to stop all of you," I said, interrupting the partner conversations. "Your leads are beautiful. Listening to them, I thought if your leads weren't handwritten, it'd be hard for me to tell which leads you wrote, and which leads had been written by professional writers! Remember, writers test out our leads as one way to help us choose and revise."

⊙ | HOMEWORK | **Reading the Work of Other Authors for Inspiration** Sometimes, when fiction writers are starting a new story, we stop and take some time to get inspired. We reread some of our favorite fiction stories and we look for some new stories we've never read before. We do that for a few reasons. We do this in order to find techniques that other authors have used that we can emulate, sure, but we do this for another even more important reason. We read other writers' work because this can change what we're feeling inside. When I reread parts of some of my favorite books—like *Because of Winn-Dixie* or *Roll of Thunder, Hear My Cry*—I get goose bumps. I get excited because those books are just so good. I want to make things that are that good, that give people goose bumps in the way Kate DiCamillo and Mildred Taylor give me goose bumps.

It might be convenient for you to take these three leads and turn them into a lesson that offers children an example of how they can try out different ways to draft and revise leads. You might also use these leads to hold a discussion with children about which leads work the best for which purposes. Children could also work together to revise these leads toward different ends, either as a class or in partnerships, and then compare and contrast their revisions.

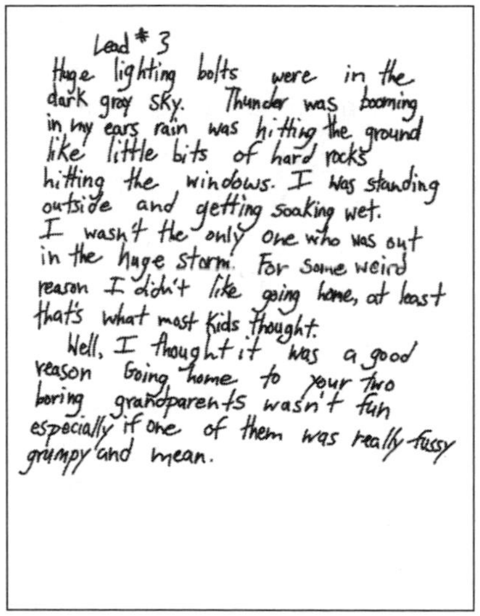

Lead #3
Huge lighting bolts were in the dark gray sky. Thunder was booming in my ears rain was hitting the ground like little bits of hard rocks hitting the windows. I was standing outside and getting soaking wet. I wasn't the only one who was out in the huge storm. For some weird reason I didn't like going home, at least that's what most kids thought. Well, I thought it was a good reason. Going home to your two boring grandparents wasn't fun especially if one of them was really fussy grumpy and mean.

Fig. VIII-10 Valerie aims to write in first person and to create a mood. She moves deeper into her story line.

Writers, give yourselves the time to be inspired by the fiction writers you know and love. Tonight pull out a book or two that you've read before and loved. Don't just limit yourself to chapter books either. Often, some of the best stories you can find are in picture books. Look through those books, and put a sticky note wherever you find a place you love. Read that part again and again. Read it aloud. Then put the book aside, and bring out the drafting booklet containing your story. Reread what you've written so far. Perhaps you'll find yourself revising!

TAILORING YOUR TEACHING

If you want to write another minilesson supporting reading-writing connections and revisions of leads . . . you could begin this way: "You know how when you go to the library or a bookstore, you read the first few lines or paragraphs of a book to see if you want to take it home? How many times do you recall passing up a book because the beginning just wasn't interesting enough? That's why it's crucial that we each write the best lead possible for our stories. Think of a lead as a hook on a fishing rod. If the bait is tasty enough, you'll catch the fish! Today I want to help you learn to write really effective leads. One way to do this is to study the leads of authors you admire. You already know that writers choose our words carefully so as to paint a picture. But writers also write for the ear, choosing words which have a rhythm. Think about the lead to Karen North's *Hot Day on Abbott Avenue*:"

> Hot day on Abbot Avenue. Too hot to even flutter a fan. Buster, snoozing, barely flicks flies at his ears. The cat keeps to herself under the house.

"The author could have just written, 'It was a very hot day on Abbott Avenue.' Instead she created a sort of rhythm out of the heat. Listen, it almost sounds like a poem. Notice the rhythm and notice also that the author, Karen North, has picked precise words that make you feel that awful heat, like 'flutter' and 'barely flicks.' Notice the repetition of words that begin with the letter 'f' (this is called alliteration): 'flutter a fan,' 'flicks flies.' This lead pulls you right into that hot, lazy day and makes you want to read on, doesn't it?" Then you'll want to reread, and to perhaps invite children to reread. You may later want to direct children also to the lead of Donald Crews' book, *Shortcut*. It's so simple:

> We looked . . .
>
> We listened . . .
>
> We decided to take
> The shortcut home.

You may want to point out that although this lead is simple, it is also suspenseful. As a reader, you're left wondering, "What are these characters looking at? What are they listening to? And what's so special about the shortcut home?" You could point out to children that Donald Crews did this intentionally; his writing style conveys that the children in the book are as apprehensive about taking the shortcut home as the reader is about what lies beyond these four short lines.

In the same minilesson, you will want to remind children that a lead should relate in some way to the heart of the story. Heat is central to the tension between the two girls in Karen North's book, *Hot Day on Abbott Avenue*, just as taking a chance—by taking a dangerous shortcut home—is central to Donald Crews' book, *Shortcut*. Leads aren't arbitrarily selected. It doesn't work just to pick an enticing opening line. The lead you write must fit in some precise way with the rest of your story, giving the reader a hint of what's to come and convincing her that she's at the start of a fascinating ride.

If students are struggling with making the leap from the story mountain to the draft . . . you can teach them how to use storyboards, just like filmmakers do. Students can take each point from their story mountains and draw a thumbnail sketch about it, then write a quick sentence or two about that scene. When they are done, the sketches will look a lot like comic-book panels. Each sketch helps students visualize what they want to happen in each scene. Often, as students sketch, they realize that some points can be consolidated or others need to be added.

MECHANICS

During the first few days of this unit, many children will have spent their time jotting lists rather than writing passages. By now, your children will have had plenty of time for writing narratives, and this means that you may want to look at their drafts with an eye toward noticing which conventions of written language have become so second nature that children are using them with automaticity even in their early drafts.

Notice, for starters, whether all your children use end punctuation and capital letters as they write, rather than seeing periods as something to scatter across the page of finished drafts. The question is not whether they use these absolutely correctly, but whether they have the instinct to punctuate as they write. If you emphasized to children earlier in the year that writers say a thought to ourselves, then write that sentence without pausing, adding a period at the end of the thought as a culminating action before pausing, then you should see that children by now show that they have the instinct to write with end punctuation.

You may notice next whether or not children use a variety of end-punctuation. If they write with periods only, then you'll definitely want to help them see the relationship between punctuation and intonation, learning that the same words can assume different meanings based on punctuation. For example, it means something very different for a child to write, "Punctuate?" or (Punctuate) rather than writing, "Punctuate!"

Notice whether children are using punctuation to show dialogue. My colleagues in the Teachers College Reading and Writing Project studied punctuation across New York City schools and found that by spring of their

first year in a writing workshop, an astonishing number of children used punctuation correctly . . . and we decided that children grasped these conventions easily because they'd *first* learned to make people in their stories talk. Once stories contain lots of dialogue, it is not hard to teach children to punctuate that dialogue.

You'll want to study children's rough draft entries in order to decide on two or three tools that you believe will especially help them write more conventionally. You may decide that children need help writing in past, present and future tenses (without shifting recklessly between these). The prospect of teaching verb tenses can feel like a daunting one, but if you set children up in little role plays, you'll find they have very little trouble with tenses. If you say, "Pretend you are at a soccer game. Use your cell phone to tell a friend what's happening in the game as you watch it," you'll see that children talk in present tense. If you say, "Pretend you called your grandma and you want to tell her about an event that happened a month ago," children will talk in past tense. Once you realize that your children really do know something about tenses, then teaching them to write in consistent tenses is less scary. We can admonish them to listen to their writing, to hear whether it sounds right, and to correct it when needed.

Then, too, you may decide that there are a dozen irregular verbs that continually cause your children difficulty. Perhaps you'll want to put word pairs such as, *say, said* and *run, ran* and *think, thought* on your word wall, teaching children that these words deserve to become part of children's sight vocabulary.

IN THIS SESSION, YOU WILL REMIND WRITERS THAT AS THEY WRITE, THEY NEED TO "STAY IN SCENE," MAKING SURE THE ACTION AND DIALOGUE ARE GROUNDED IN THE SETTING.

GETTING READY

- Anecdote or metaphor you can tell to describe the disorientation caused by lack of setting
- Scene containing almost nothing but dialogue, copied onto chart paper
- Revised scene showing more story details
- Passage from the class story, on chart paper, for whole-class practice with setting
- Passage from a favorite read-aloud story that communicates setting well
- See CD-ROM for resources

ORIENTING READERS WITH SETTING

When teachers discuss predictable issues their students have had, someone invariably says, "Kids love fiction. They'll write for pages. The only problem is it's all dialogue. I can't make heads or tails of it!"

Be sure you recognize that the dialogue which swamps the pages of many drafts represents a gigantic step ahead for these children. They are no longer summarizing the main events in their stories; instead, your authors are making mental movies and recording what happens in those movies—or at least, they are recording the sound track to those movies! This is a gigantic step ahead and your children are poised to write spectacular texts. You simply need to teach them one further step!

In a spirit of "your work is halfway there," then, convene children and tell them that you can see they are making mental movies, enacting events in their minds as they write. But point out that although they can no doubt see the character walk, gesture, turn, grimace, those parts of their envisioned stories have yet to reach the page.

Once your children begin to ground their stories in precise settings, all of a sudden it is as if the stories become real. Everything becomes grounded. One character grabs her shoes, runs to the ocean's edge, then stands ankle deep in the waves. "Come in," her sister—waist deep in the waves—beckons. Before the character can join her sister, she tosses her shoes on the dry sand. One falls near the water's edge, and before the character can reach it, a wave washes over the shoe. When writers write with setting, people carry real shoes, and those shoes need to be put somewhere before the character can wade waist deep into the ocean. When we write with setting, we need to remember to put down our shoes before we go into the water.

Today, you'll teach your students that fiction writers use settings to ground our stories. We use places, like living rooms and swing sets and forests; we use the weather, like heat waves and fog and lightly falling snow; we use times, like midnight and sunrise and lazy afternoons. Our students can often orally describe the setting of a story, but those details rarely make it onto the page. Part of the bargain that writers make with readers is that the characters will take action within a very concrete, specific world. Best yet, when children learn to write with setting, they learn not only that setting allows us to anchor characters and plots. They also learn that developing setting can help them to convey tone, and hint at a character's mood, feelings, insights.

MINILESSON

Orienting Readers with Setting

CONNECTION

Tell about a time you were awakened in the dark and felt disoriented. Liken this to the disorientation some readers feel when drafts don't include enough setting.

"Last night I was sleeping, and the phone rang. When the phone woke me up, my whole room was dark and I didn't know where I was. I couldn't see anything. I couldn't tell if I was dreaming or awake. Has that ever happened to you? You wake up and for a minute, you can't remember where you are?"

"When the phone rang again, I looked at where the sound was coming from and saw a light blinking, and it dawned on me that I was in my bedroom and that I'd just been woken by the phone. My eyes got used to the dark and I saw the dresser that held the phone."

"That unanswered phone call ended up helping me. Because when I was abruptly woken in the middle of the night like that and didn't know where I was, this made me realize that sometimes readers experience our drafts as if the events in our stories happen in the dark. The sounds—the voices—come out of nowhere, and readers are disoriented and need to ask themselves, 'Wait, where am I?' and 'What's going on?' and 'Where's that sound coming from?' Readers can hear the words a character says, but it's like the words come out of nowhere."

Name the teaching point. In this instance, let children know that writers need to show the setting in a story so that readers don't feel disoriented.

"Today I want to teach you that we need to be sure that we 'turn on the lights' in our stories, to show the place and the time, so that our readers don't have that disoriented feeling, asking, 'Wait, where is this? What's going on?'"

COACHING

This little episode actually occurred the day before I wrote this minilesson. I was in a hotel which added to the sense of disorientation, but that detail seemed like a distraction. Just as writers live wide-awake lives, expecting that tiny everyday events can be grist for the writing mill, so do teachers. And of course, our teaching takes on special immediacy and intimacy when we bring the tiniest little events of our lives into minilessons. Sometimes teachers don't realize they can do this. They say to me, "But I'm not a writer. My life doesn't contain writing lessons!" So I try to show them that even a phone call in the dark can bring new life to a minilesson.

This is really a lesson on improving the quality of our students' fiction writing, and there are, of course, zillions of possible topics for this minilesson. Students' stories will inevitably be very different from the stories that mature, experienced writers produce. I selected this particular point because students' drafts frequently contain a stream of dialogue, with very little setting for orientation. Often it's as if student writing provides only the sound track for a movie. Then, too, I'm focusing on setting because this is something important that we haven't addressed very seriously yet in these units of study. I've addressed the overreliance on dialogue, of course, but before now suggested the solution lay in adding actions. Now I spotlight a second solution. The truth is that most qualities of good writing can be taught within any genre, and the decision to highlight one or another is partly arbitrary.

TEACHING

Tell children that when writing scenes, it's easy to rely only on dialogue, resulting in characters who don't seem to be anywhere in particular. Give an example of an all-talk scene in which the characters are nowhere, leaving readers struggling to feel oriented.

"Sometimes when we're writing a scene we get so caught up in our dialogue that we forget everything else. Let me give you an example. Ryan, a high school writer, wrote this." I showed a short, generic excerpt that I'd copied onto chart paper.

> I didn't know what to do. I looked at her. "Hey, are you mad at me?" I asked.
>
> "No. Are you mad at me?" she asked.
>
> I took a deep breath. "No. I don't think so," I said.
>
> "Great, then let's race," she said.

"Some things work in this scene. Characters are talking. We can tell how they're feeling. But the characters are floating. The story produces the same feeling I had when I woke up in the middle of the night and I didn't know where I was. We can't tell where the characters are, and we're not sure what they are doing."

Tell children that the child revised the scene by adding action and setting, then show the resulting next draft.

"To make sure the lights are on for our readers, we need to always include two things: action and setting. Watch how Ryan's draft became much more clear when he added action and setting."

"Ryan didn't actually know what his characters *were* doing. When he wrote the draft, his characters were just talking. So he decided to revise his draft so his characters were walking home from school. He decided it'd be a gray, rainy day. That way, one of the characters could do stuff with an umbrella and the other character could step in puddles. Ryan expected the actions would be fillers, really, to hold up the talk, but the actions ended up revealing the real story in very important way. Listen to Ryan's next draft:

> "Are you mad at me?" I asked as we walked down the sidewalk together.
>
> "No. Are you mad at me?" Zoe responded.
>
> A car whizzed passed us, kicking up water from the rain-

I deliberately chose a very brief excerpt. I know this will more than double in size when it is revised, and I want to keep my minilessons brief. Little is gained by showing large expanses of text in minilessons.

Watch the ways in which I weave threads from earlier sections of the minilesson into the later sections, creating cohesion. I believe that all writers do this, and that the aspects of a text that reoccur are central to the text's message. This is why, when I teach readers, I put more of an emphasis on helping children see intratextual connections (those that occur within a text) rather than intertextual (or text-to-text) connections.

filled gutters as it went. I thought about what Zoe was asking, and shifted the umbrella so that it protected her as well as me. With my other hand, I tugged on my back pack straps. My bag was heavy from all the homework our teacher had given us.

"No. I'm not mad," I said.

She smiled at me from beneath her yellow rain hood. "Good. Then let's race!" She took off ahead of me, splashing through every puddle on the sidewalk. The rain streamed down on her. I pulled in my umbrella, and took off after her. I caught up with her, then loped easily in her wake.

You'll recall that earlier in this series, I talked about Chris Raschka's Caldecott Honor winner, Yo! Yes? as a book that can help us teach children that their stories cannot be carried by dialogue alone. The words of that book are simple, one-word exclamations or questions. The dialogue alone isn't easy to comprehend. The book works because the author-illustrator provides pictures that describe each character, providing the gestures and body language that need to support the dialogue. Because readers can rely on the pictures as well as the dialogue, the story actually "reads" more like this: "'Yo!' called the basketball player, as he stood with a swagger, chest out and hands on his hips. Nearby, a little nerdy boy in a suit coat shrugged, hid his head, and meekly responded, 'Yes?'" With that book, it would be easy to point out to children that because their stories rely on words alone, their words need to do the work done by Raschka's drawings as well as his text. This lesson would be as appropriate now as in that previous unit. You may decide to use this book and make this point again here, even if you also used this suggestion before.

Debrief, tucking some extra tips into your description of what the student did to revise. Point out that when trying to supply the setting and actions, the writer discovered important new interactions and meanings.

"Writers, do you see how the characters are not in the dark anymore? We can really picture them. We can see what they're doing and where they are. And you know what? When Ryan wrote this, his only plan was to have the two of them walking home together. He only made it be a rainy day because he figured he could describe the rain. Then, as he wrote the scene, adding in the actions, stuff started happening between the characters that Ryan never planned for at all—it just happened on the page! It surprised Ryan that his main character decided to move the umbrella over to shield Zoe, and he was totally surprised when her 'Let's race' response left him standing behind like a fool with that open umbrella! He recovered, though, and caught up with her, but didn't need to show her that he was the faster runner. All this drama came out in the story simply because Ryan realized that he needed to get his characters out of the dark, and to rewrite the story, showing the characters as they moved and interacted in the setting."

The lessons that I tuck into my minilessons are often more advanced than the teaching point itself. I know in this instance that the writing-to-discover work that Ryan has done is beyond the reach of most of the writers in this class. He is a high-school student, and this is skilled work. But I do still want to expose all writers to the richest and deepest ideas, because who knows what will "click" for a child! And meanwhile, I am usually confident that my main teaching points are within reach and pertinent for everyone. The little subordinate tips one weaves into a minilesson are one of the ways our minilessons become multilevel, providing differentiated instruction.

ACTIVE ENGAGEMENT

Ask children to reread the Luz story from the chart paper while asking, "Will this make sense to readers?" When they encounter a passage that might be disorienting, ask them to revise it with their partner, adding setting.

"So let's try it. Let's read this section of our Luz story—I've been writing some more of it—and as we read, let's ask ourselves, 'Will this make sense to my readers? Is this clear?' If we come to a place in the story where the words seem to come out of the dark, a place where we suspect that readers might feel disoriented, you and your partner will have a chance to write in the air, sprinkling references to the setting and to small actions that characters do in that setting, into our next version."

I retrieved the draft and read a section of it aloud—a section that I knew was well-lodged into the setting and amplified with actions. I read:

> "Cake!" my mom called from the kitchen. All of us raced to the table which my mom had decorated entirely in yellow.
>
> "Everything looks so cool," Marta said as she reached for a thick slice of the yellow cake with chocolate frosting. I couldn't help grinning. I had been right to choose yellow. It was a cool color. Since I didn't really have a favorite color it didn't really matter anyway.
>
> I had barely swallowed the last bit of my cake when the other girls started to jump out of their seats to toss their party plates in the trash.
>
> "Let's go, first one there gets dibs on spots," Trish called out as she ran.

"Could you picture what was going on?" I asked. "Did you see the place?" Children gave me a thumbs up. "So let's read on," I said, and this time read the upcoming section (a part I knew was underdeveloped):

> "Here's my place," said Beccah
>
> "I'll be near," I said. "We can talk. But let's move closer to the closet."
>
> "No, this is nice."
>
> "Weellll . . . "
>
> "Can we fit in," three others said.
>
> "I'll move over," I answered.

Notice that, instead of beginning the Active Engagement by saying, "Could you rewrite this scene so that . . . ," I instead ask readers to begin by rereading a fairly large passage of the Luz story using the lens of "Is this clear?" By backing up and starting with this, I not only get the chance to synthesize all the points I have made in this minilesson, I also demonstrate to writers how they might position themselves to do this work in the first place.

Notice that the whole-class text has, in this unit of study, served alternatively as the teaching text as well as the text used in the Active Engagement.

The children talked to their partners, and after a moment I intervened. "Writers, please don't simply *comment on* how you'd go about rewriting this to add setting and actions—write the new text in the air."

Ask one partnership to share their new version, and set up other children to act out the new version.

"Let's listen to Francesca and Jamal. While they write in the air, I'll record it. But can I have someone who will play the part of Beccah and act out what they say, and someone who'll be Luz? Are there three of you who'll be the three others who want to join?" Soon the improvisational drama was ready to begin, and the children began improvising the new story. "The first character to do something is Beccah," I said, and gestured for her to step forward on the "stage." "What exactly is she doing?" I asked Jamal and Francesca. With that, they began spinning out a story, while the actors moved about accordingly:

> Beccah got her sleeping bag and found an empty spot of rug behind the sofa. She unrolled her sleeping bag. Then Beccah said, "Here's my place."
>
> I grabbed my stuff, and sat on the floor beside Beccah. "I'll be right here," I said. "We can talk." But as I said that I knew I wouldn't be able to sleep there. I couldn't see the closet where the light was on, so I knew I had to move. I tried to talk Beccah into it and said, "Let's move closer to the closet."
>
> Lying down, Beccah said, "No, this is nice."
>
> I wasn't sure. I looked over to a nice spot right beside the closet, and was about to try again to get Beccah to move closer to the closet. Then three other girls came. "Can we fit?" they asked.
>
> "I'll move over," I said, and picked up my stuff and went over to the empty place.

Ask the class to end the scene in a way that is informed by the acting.

"What could happen to end this scene?" I asked. "What might Luz watch that group of girls doing together?"

"They could all be huggin' each other and all so she feels left out?"

"Okay, but remember, we have them arranging their sleeping bags and getting ready for bed. Could they do those actions in a way that accomplishes the same thing in the story?"

If you look back on the instructions I gave children, you'll see that I originally told children to write in the air to show how they'd revise this. If our words are going to mean something, we need to speak up when children ignore our instructions.

If you and your colleagues are looking for a way to lift the level of all these units of study, you might try to incorporate more drama into the entire series. I believe there is a very powerful connection between drama, reading, and writing. I'm convinced that these minilessons do not harvest the power of drama as much as they might.

These seemingly innocuous little prompts actually are fairly controlling. My question channeled the text in ways that made it much better. The children believe they've written this on their own, but meanwhile I've been directing.

Soon the class had written this ending to the scene:

> I watched as the group of girls figured out how to
> arrange their sleeping bags so they could all be close to
> each other. I heard Eliza say, "This way we can whisper
> together all night."
>
> I turned my back away from them, toward the closet
> where the light shone.

Debrief, highlighting the sequential steps you hope writers use with their own texts. Emphasize that revisions that begin as corrections can become entirely new creations.

"Writers," I said, "you've done some amazing revision. You reread this part of our draft and realized that readers might feel disoriented, as if the scene were taking place in the dark. So you sprinkled in a little information about the characters' exact actions in the setting, and as you did this, you—like Ryan—ended up surprising yourselves and finding that things are happening between the characters that we didn't even realize when we planned the story!

"This is what writers do. Our revisions start out as corrections and they end up as creations!"

LINK
Remind writers that today they'll shift between drafting and revising, and that to revise, they'll want to reread their draft with specific lenses.

"Writers, today you'll continue to draft and revise your stories, shifting between the two processes. And when you revise, you'll reread for all the goals that have become important to you. You'll make sure your characters feel real. You'll keep an eye on the deeper meaning of your story. You'll make sure you don't leave your readers in the dark. If there is a section of your story that seems disorienting, you can revise it like you've done today, adding more setting and actions to the scene. Please be sure that if you expect to *correct* your draft, you do so knowing that revisions that begin as corrections often take on a life of their own and become creations. Let your characters do things to and with each other that you'd never expected they'd do. Run along behind them!"

You may want to look at several minilessons and notice all the different ways in which we debrief after teaching. My hunch is that even though the debrief segments are usually brief, you'll find they are almost always sequentially organized, retelling a sequence of steps as one would in a how-to text. Although these sections where we debrief are summaries, they are also examples of how a writer can organize thoughts.

I suspect that this last line is one that deserves more attention than I give to it: Revisions start out as corrections and become creations. So true, if we let it be true!

Since the sentence—revisions that begin as corrections often take on a life of their own and become creations—will probably go over some students' heads, I may want to capture it in print and invite children to talk and think about it another time. This brings up a larger question of note-taking during minilessons. Be very careful that you don't emphasize this in a manner which slows down your minilessons!

WRITING AND CONFERRING

Weaving Together Action, Thought, and Dialogue

Beccah was busy at work adding in sentences here and there to her story. I approached her and said, "Beccah, I can see that you are busy revising your story. Can you tell me about the work you're doing?"

"Well, I realized that I don't have a lot of setting in my story, and so I'm trying to add in some setting so that my reader knows where my characters are."

"That sounds like great work, Beccah. Can you show me a place where you've done that?" I asked as I scanned Beccah's draft.

Beccah turned to the last page of her story and skimmed the page. "Right here," she said. "This is the part where Chloe and Samantha walk away from Niki and leave her standing alone. The first time I wrote it, it went like this:

> "Sorry, Niki," Chloe said.
>
> "Let's go," Samantha said, smirking at Niki. Together they turned and walked away from Niki. Niki just stood there.

"And then, I revised it by adding in setting. Now it goes like this:"

> "Sorry, Niki," Chloe said.
>
> "Let's go," Samantha said. They all stood in the hallway looking at each other. Doors were opening and closing as kids went to class.

I thought to myself, "Yes, Beccah has certainly added setting to her story. Even this little bit helps orient the reader." But I also thought about the fact that so many of my students saw revision as adding in a word or a sentence here and there. I wanted to celebrate this kind of revision but I also knew many of my students were capable of much deeper work. In this case, for example, I knew I could teach Beccah that people are affected by their environments and that adding setting to a story can be a tool for revealing what a character is feeling. This could teach Beccah about how to add in setting in a more effective way, but it could also teach her that revision is about helping oneself see more deeply into a character or situation, and that it entails more than adding a sprinkling of sentences. Beccah looked up at me and waited.

MID-WORKSHOP TEACHING POINT *Using Mentor Texts in Revision* "Writers, I want to tell you about the smart discussion Ryan and I just had. He decided to study how Julie Brinckloe lets us know where and what is going on in *Fireflies!* and so he noted all the tricks he saw her use that he could use." This is Ryan's list:

"If you aren't sure that readers will know exactly what's going on in your stories, look at your draft and ask whether you do the same things that you find in the mentor text you study. Ryan realized he hadn't done many of them. Now he knows just what his work can be. You can try the same thing he tried, now and anytime you write."

Sentences from Text	Strategy Brinckloe Uses
On a summer evening I looked up from dinner, through the open window to the backyard.	tells where narrator is/what he's doing right away
On a summer evening I looked up from dinner, through the open window to the backyard. It was growing dark. My treehouse was a black shape in the tree . . . fireflies flickered.	tells big feeling of place, weather, time, right away
• forked food into mouth • asked to go out • found a jar • polished it . . .	She tells a whole sequence of actions, of events.
First he's at kitchen table near window. Then he runs to cellar. Then he runs back upstairs. Then he returns to house . . .	Every action has a place.

"So you've let the reader know that your characters are in the hallway, and you've added in details that show what's going on around them. That works for sure," I said, and then added, "As I read this, I could see that you are ready to do even bigger revision work. What do you think?"

"Okay," There was hesitation in Beccah's voice.

I continued, "You know, Beccah, when story writers revise our writing, we are often trying to show a little more of what our characters are experiencing on the inside as well as the outside. That's what we saw Ryan do—right? He added setting but did so in a way that brought out his characters." I looked at Beccah. "When you add setting to your writing, this gives you a powerful way to reveal your characters. What happens on the outside definitely affects us on the inside, right? A rainy day might make us feel down, a stadium filled with screaming Yankee fans might make us feel excited. So, when you add setting to your writing, you need to think about how the details you add can help your reader understand what your character is experiencing on the inside."

Turning to Beccah's draft, I said, "So let's look at the part of your story where Niki is watching her best friend, Chloe, walk off with her arch-enemy, Samantha. How is Niki feeling here?"

"Well," Beccah reread the part and then said, "She's feeling all alone, and sad. She's feeling like, 'Wow, I just lost my best friend.'"

"Hmm . . . so she's standing in the hallway feeling alone. Let's think about how you might use the setting to show that Beccah feels alone."

I knew as I said this that I could always show Beccah a published text where the author does this, and there are so many—*Fireflies!*, *Owl Moon*, *Fly Away Home*. I chose, instead, to coach Beccah as she thought through her work. You'll decide how to proceed depending on how much scaffolding you believe students need.

Beccah spoke up, "Well, maybe I can show that she's feeling lonely and the halls are all empty because everyone has gone to class and she's just standing there with no one to talk to or walk to class with."

"So how might you write that? Let's turn to your draft." We both reread the part that Beccah was working on. Then, Beccah said, "Well maybe it can go like this:

> "Sorry Niki," Chloe said.
>
> "Let's go," Samantha said to Chloe. Niki watched as they walked through the blue, metal doors. She looked around, but the halls were empty. She was all alone with no one.

"Yes, Beccah, that definitely works. You are on your way! You are letting the setting reveal how Niki is feeling. Always ask yourself how your revision work is helping you dig a bit deeper into whatever you want to say—and you are definitely doing that. Nice job!"

As you confer with children, show them that it helps to shift between action and thoughts, not just record a stream of thoughts. So if I wanted to describe my worry when my son, who recently got his driver's license, returned home late, I'd write in a way which intersperses thoughts with actions. To do this, I'd create a set of tiny actions which mirrored my thoughts and feelings:

> I looked at the clock: 6:08. "Where could Miles be?" I thought. I went to the door and glanced out at the empty driveway, then at the road. Empty. "What could have kept him?" I worried. I went to the phone, picked up the receiver, and heard the dial tone. "Good. The phone's working and there have been no calls," I thought, and recalled last summer's awful phone call.

A few children in your class may well write in running commentary that sounds almost like free association, as Laurel has here *[Fig. IX-1]*:

> "Oh my god, Jessie is that you?"
>
> "Lex? Oh my god. I haven't seen you in such a long time."
>
> "I know," Jessie said. "So what's up?"
>
> "Nothing."
>
> "Like fifth grade?" Jessie asked.
>
> "It's different."
>
> "Are you still in touch with Sophie, Ali, Caitlyn, Beccah, Jamie and Alex?"
>
> "Of course. They are my best friends. So how is Hanna?" Lex asked.
>
> "Not as annoying. You know how younger sisters are from Sam. And by the way how is she?"
>
> "She is good. Just like Hanna."
>
> "How is Jenna? I almost forgot about her."
>
> "Totally great."

Free writing will end up being a wonderful skill that children can lean on, but writing always involves some coloring inside the lines (or working within the constraints) as well as some free expression. For now, these children's writing skills will come out best if they take each scene of their story, think of it as a Small Moment story, and then plot the main sequence of actions (not the thoughts) on a timeline. Some children may want to

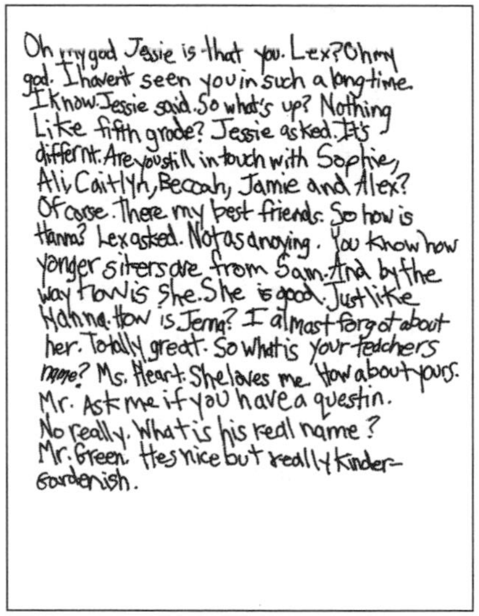
Oh my god Jessie is that you. Lex? Oh my god. I haven't seen you in such a long time. I know. Jessie said. So what's up? Nothing Like fifth grade? Jessie asked. It's differnt. Are you still in touch with Sophie, Ali, Caitlyn, Beccah, Jamie and Alex? Of corse. There my best friends. So how is Hanna? Lex asked. Not as anoying. You know how yonger siters are from Sam. And by the way How is She. She is good. Just like Hanna. How is Jenna? I almast forgot about her. Totally great. So what is your teachers name? Ms. Heart. She loves me. How about yours. Mr. Ask me if you have a questin. No really. What is his real name? Mr. Green. Hes nice but really Kinder-gardenish.

Fig. XI-1 Laurel has been free writing her story and needs to instead focus on a small moment or two.

make double timelines, with one timeline summarizing the actions, the other, the parallel thoughts or comments. Then ask children to write, alternating between dialogue, action and setting. See Laurel's second draft: *[Fig. IX-2]*

> "Let's go look at the animals first so then on the sky ride, we can retrace where we were," Jessie said. "Ok" her mom said. They were zooming along 70 mph. Hanna and her mom were singing "Ninety-nine bottles of beer on the wall. Ninety-nine bottles of beer take 1 down pass it around ninety-eight bottles of beer on the wall." When they got to sixty-six Jessie yelled "Enough! Let's play the quiet game whoever talks first loses. Ok 1, 2, 3." They stayed quiet then their mom said, "I hear that they have rides and games where you can win prizes." "And?" "We are there." They jumped out of the car and ran for the animals.

When conferring with children who struggle to pin down their free associations, I'd be apt to share my draft with them, or even to show a child how I might rewrite his or her draft. We might read a line or two and ask, "Where exactly were you? What exactly were you doing?" After the child answered, I'd say, "I asked those questions because you might want to shift between retelling your very specific actions and recording your thoughts. For example, your draft might go like this . . . " and then I'd get the child started by showing how I might start the draft, weaving between action and thought, action and dialogue. I often summarize this teaching by saying to children, "For every thought or piece of dialogue, you need to add a narrative or action." I realize this sounds like a recipe, but for students who've resisted your more generalized suggestions, this can help.

I recently pulled students who struggled with creating setting into a small-group strategy lesson. I gave each student a copy of the Luz story with a lot of white space between each paragraph. Then I modeled how to add some setting to the Beccah section, adding the sentence, "Beccah got her sleeping bag and found an empty spot behind the sofa . . . " As I modeled this, I wrote it onto my copy of the story, in the white space where it belonged.

Then I asked children to work with a partner, filling in some other setting details for the next paragraph, where the narrator speaks. I coached the partners, encouraging them to use actions and setting to help us picture what the character was doing, and where characters were.

Soon I shifted them to do similar work, adding details that allowed them to show the characters in their own pieces. I checked back with them as they continued the work after I left, prompting them. "Remember how you and Shiv worked on helping us see the room here? You wrote that 'Luz spread out her sleeping bag on the floor beside Beccah.' You said, 'Luz couldn't see the closet from where she was because the sofa was blocking her view.' Those details helped us picture this place. Are there other places in your draft where readers will be in the dark?"

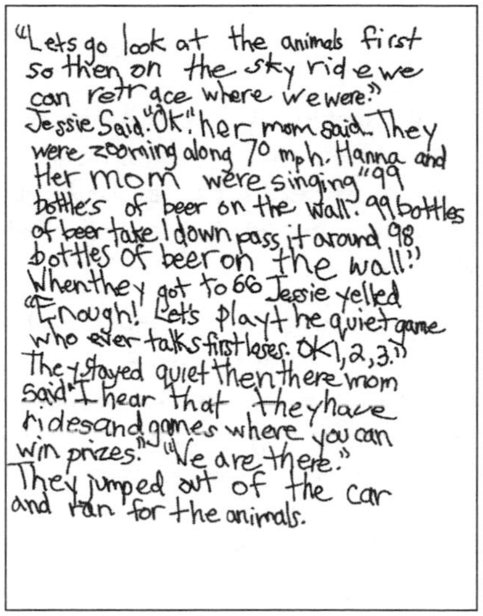
"Lets go look at the animals first so then on the sky ride we can retrace where we were." Jessie Said. "Ok". her mom said. They were zooming along 70 mph. Hanna and Her mom were singing "99 bottles of beer on the wall. 99 bottles of beer take 1 down pass it around 98 bottles of beer on the wall." When they got to 66 Jessie yelled "Enough! Let's play the quiet game who ever talks first loses. Ok 1, 2, 3." They stayed quiet then there mom said "I hear that they have rides and games where you can win prizes." "We are there." They jumped out of the car and ran for the animals.

Fig. IX-2 This time Laurel has situated her story into a few more concrete episodes.

When I conferred with Sofiya, she'd written this opening scene to her story about a gymnastics tournament. [Fig. IX-3]

> Esther could see hundreds and hundreds of seats and people trying to find good seats. Her family was going to some of the best seats. Esther had told them where the best seats were and was glad that they had listened to her.
>
> The wind was blowing from outside and she guessed that someone just walked in or out of the building. She could get a little whiff of the smell of healthy snacks cooking. Esther felt like running up to her parents—but knew that it would be better to start stretching. When she reached her stretching teammates she could taste the tension. Soon it was time for the league to begin.
>
> She sat down with her team. The judges began to introduce the teams . . .

Esther could see hundreds and hundreds of seats and people trying to find good seats. Her family was going to some of the best seats. Esther had told them where the best seats are and was glad that they had listened to her.
The wind was blowing from outside and she guessed that someone just walked in or out of the building. She could get a little whiff of the smell of healthy snacks cooking. Esther felt like running up to her parents but knew that it would be better to start stretching. When she reached her streching teammates she could taste the tension. Soon it was time for the league to begin.
She sat down with her team. The judges began

Fig. IX-3 Notice that Sofiya's draft shows her protagonist experiencing the setting.

I asked Sofiya what she had tried to do in this draft and her answer didn't surprise me. She'd tried to create a sense of place. "What really blows me away," I said, "is that even though you are only ten years old, you already realize that you can't leave the story and the character behind in order to show place. You need to have your character, have Esther, see and experience the place."

In this conference and in most of my conferences, I try to let children's work spark me to new realizations. I try not to simply admire the fact that a writer has done as instructed, but to also name what the writer has done that feels especially individual and original and new. This means, then, that conferences are one important source of new insight in my teaching.

Although I supported Sofiya's work with setting, which was her goal, this doesn't mean I didn't see some problematic aspects to her work. I noticed that Sofiya had been guided by an effort to include sensory details and was amused to see that as a result, even in the gymnasium, she had the character smelling healthy snacks (clearly Sofiya was trying to include all her senses and her repertoire of smells is a bit limited!). However, I decided that commenting on this wasn't as important as helping Sofiya understand that although she was wise to describe setting, writers need to guard against being waylaid from our main direction and message. "Your reader can't get so detoured by all the sights and sounds around the main character, that they lose hold of the main story," I said, and reminded Sofiya that her lead needs to go with her story mountain, and that she needs to remember what her story is mostly about and to highlight that in her lead. We can rephrase the question, "What's my story about?" so as to ask, "What does my character want? Struggle with?" This is a conference that is crucially important at this stage in the unit.

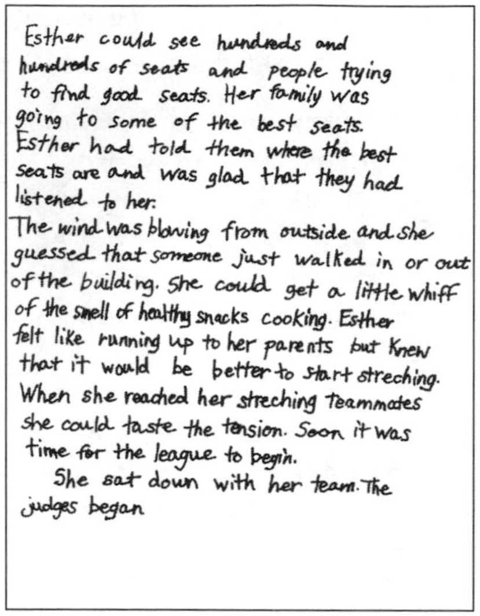

Sofiya's next lead shows that, above all, this is a story about Esther wanting desperately to do well at the contest. *[Fig. IX-4]*

> Esther walked into the building—nervous from head to toe. As soon as she walked into the building—she was able to feel the tension. "Bye mom, bye dad, by Nicole. Oh yeah! There are lots of doors to the stands, but that's the door you need. Remember, Section 20, Row 5, any seats. Although the best seats are seats 14, 15, and 16. Got it?" she asked her parents. Her family nodded, said good bye themselves and left. Esther watched them leave before she left. Esther went to the changing room and took off her warm-up suit. When she came back out she looked up at the stands. People were looking for seats, she spotted her parents, they were sitting where she told them to. Esther smiled up at them. She was glad they had listened.

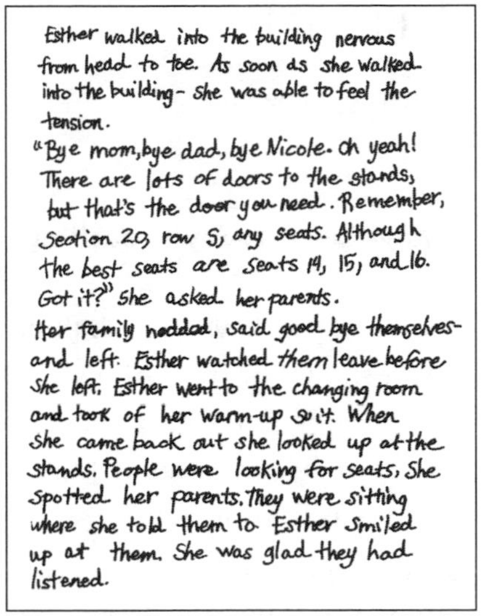
Esther walked into the building nervous from head to toe. As soon as she walked into the building- she was able to feel the tension.
"Bye mom, bye dad, bye Nicole. oh yeah! There are lots of doors to the stands, but that's the door you need. Remember, Section 20, row 5, any seats. Although the best seats are seats 14, 15, and 16. Got it?" she asked her parents.
Her family nodded, said good bye themselves and left. Esther watched them leave before she left. Esther went to the changing room and took of her warm-up suit. When she came back out she looked up at the stands. People were looking for seats, She spotted her parents. They were sitting where she told them to. Esther smiled up at them. She was glad they had listened.

Fig. IX-4 Sofiya's next lead

As she progressed, a friend reminded her that she needs to show, not tell. This too is a piece of advice you may find yourself offering at this stage of the unit. You could use the before and after samples of Sofiya's writing to help illustrate. Here is how Sofiya tried to show instead of tell. *[Fig. IX-5]*

> Esther slowly walked into the huge gymnasium with her parents and sister, Nicole. She was nervous, slightly trembling, and her teeth were gently chattering, making a quiet clicking noise.
>
> "Bye mom, bye dad, bye Nicole. I have to run if I want to be able to stretch and practice the routines," Esther told her family as she held the door to the stands open. Her family whispered good luck and nodded.
>
> They all went through the door that Esther was holding. There, they split up. Esther's parents and Nicole excitedly went to the stands that weren't even close to being thronged, while Esther ran to the changing room.
>
> When she got there Esther took off her warm-up suit in the same speed that a cheetah runs. Then she skipped to stretch. There she warmed-up, stretched, and practiced the routines over and over again. Suddenly a loud bell rang from the judges table.

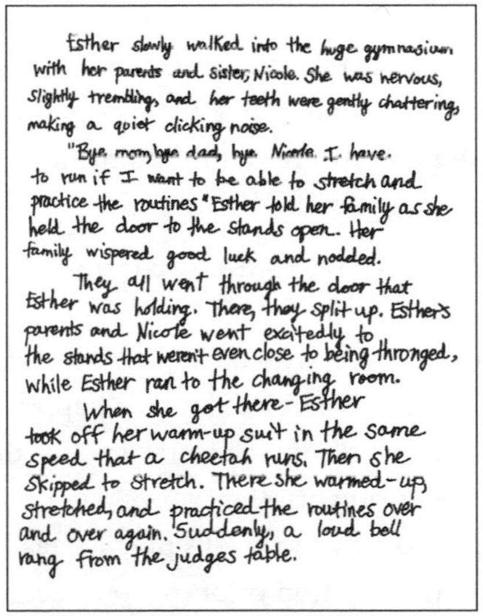
Esther slowly walked into the huge gymnasium with her parents and sister, Nicole. She was nervous, slightly trembling, and her teeth were gently chattering, making a quiet clicking noise.
"Bye mom, bye dad, bye Nicole. I have to run if I want to be able to stretch and practice the routines" Esther told her family as she held the door to the stands open. Her family wispered good luck and nodded.
They all went through the door that Esther was holding. There, they split up. Esther's parents and Nicole went excitedly to the stands that weren't even close to being thronged, while Esther ran to the changing room.
When she got there- Esther took off her warm-up suit in the same speed that a cheetah runs. Then she skipped to stretch. There she warmed-up, stretched, and practiced the routines over and over again. Suddenly, a loud bell rang from the judges table.

Fig. IX-5 Sofiya trying to show not tell

Of course, once any one child has done some significant revisions, this becomes material for a small-group strategy lesson. We could then simply pull together a small group of children, and, using the one child as an example, lead the whole group through a similar work process.

SHARE

Listening for Setting

Celebrate that children have used today's teaching point to influence their revisions and drafts.

"Today, writers, some of you have been drafting and some of you have been revising, and that is exactly how it should be in a writing workshop. And I am impressed that whether you have been drafting or revising, you have been remembering not to leave your readers in the dark. You have been sprinkling little bits of the scene and descriptions of the action into whatever happens in your story."

Ask children to share, and ask listeners to signal when they feel well-oriented to what is occurring in the story and when they feel they need more setting.

"Right now, would you find a place in your draft that you have recently written, a section of your story where you are pretty sure you've provided enough orienting information so that readers can truly make movies in their minds as they listen to your story?" I gave children a moment to find those sections. "Now would you get together with someone who is *not* your partner, someone who is a stranger to your story, and read this section aloud? And those of you who are listening, try to follow the writer's words and to dream the dream of his or her story. Show with your thumb up when you can really picture what's going on, and signal with your thumb down (as you listen) when it is harder for you to make that movie in your mind. Do this with one writer's draft, then the other writer's draft. If you have more time, look back on the drafts together and talk about revisions you might make."

Remind children they can attend to the setting of any writer's story to learn techniques for writing about setting well.

"Today you learned that writers help readers by describing what things look like in the room, the town, the place where the story is happening. The good news is that you don't need to be in a writing workshop to learn tips like this one. Whenever you read your chapter book, you can read with the eyes of a writer, thinking, 'How has this other author pulled off her story?' So right now, let's practice reading with the eyes of an insider. For now, let's look back on a section of one of our favorite read-alouds. You remember *My*

You can, of course, certainly ask students to share any part of the writing work they have been doing. You will want to angle the Share to best support whatever direction you most feel children need to take in their writing.

This share has two sections to it and of course you could select just one or the other. Always curtail your minilessons and shares if you need to do so in order to be sure that children have at least half an hour (preferably forty minutes) of actual writing time in school each day.

Name Is Maria Isabel. Listen to this bit of the story and think about what Alma Flor Ada does, in the midst of telling action and dialogue, to show the scene."

> The other kids had already taken their seats. Some were taking out their books and binders while others just seemed to be waiting for class to start. Many of them were smiling and talking to each other.
>
> Maria Isabel looked up at an enormous turkey made of construction paper on the wall behind the teacher's desk. She started to read the names that were on the tail feathers: Jonathan, Eric, Michelle, Solomon, Laurie . . .
>
> The teacher had not looked up yet. She was making notes in a large folder where Maria Isabel could see a list of names. Maria Isabel heard quiet laughter behind her. The teacher looked up only when the noise got louder.

"Okay? Thumbs up if you think you saw a technique that the author used to bring out the setting in the story."

"She told what sounds there were in the classroom," said Yasmin. "And also she described what's on the walls and what kids were doing."

"Yes! And can't you just picture that classroom in your mind's eye? Maybe it's not that different from this room we're sitting in! So from this day on, will you read whatever your chapter book is with the eyes of a writer, an insider, and notice how your author does whatever it is you are trying to do in your own story. Then use whatever the author has done to inspire you as you continue writing or rewriting your story."

Notice that we describe the techniques Alma Flor Ada has used in ways which make them accessible and replicable. It's a bit of a trick to learn to do this, but well worth learning.

HOMEWORK   ***Noticing Setting on Television***   We've done a lot of work on character and story structure in the past couple of weeks. I'm proud of all that we've done. Our stories are shaping up as we draft. But I think we need to spend a little more time thinking about the setting of a narrative.

Setting does a lot of work in a story. It can tell us something about a character's personality. If a character's bedroom is messy or it's covered in music posters, these details reveal something about the character. Setting can also tell us something about our character's mood. If the long rainy morning gives way to a bright, sunny afternoon, we might get the idea that things are getting brighter for our character. Setting also helps readers envision a story. It lets the reader really *see* what's happening and know *where* it's happening.

Tonight I'm going to ask you to do something you probably haven't ever heard me say before. I want you to spend a little time watching television. It can be a movie or a TV show, whichever your grown-ups say you can watch. I'd like you to watch a little bit with your writer's notebook in your lap. As you watch, look for the setting. Try to watch a part where the setting stays the same for a little bit. Watch, for example, a scene in a living room or in a park. While you're watching, jot a few notes about what you notice about the setting. Can you tell what the weather is? What time it is? Day or night? What colors do you see? What's high up in the setting? What's low? What does the camera show with more detail?

Once you've jotted a few notes, I'd like you to think a little bit about what parts of the setting helped you, as the viewer, understand the story more. Then make some notes on your draft, suggesting ways you can weave more setting into the draft when you come to school tomorrow.

TAILORING YOUR TEACHING

If your students have difficulty picturing the setting of their stories . . . send them back to their character development work. If you were to observe the setting of my life, you would see evidence of the kind of person I am. You would see pictures of the people I love, books strewn about the living room, dishes left unwashed far too long. My home gives clues about my personal idiosyncrasies. Anne Lamott writes that "every room is a little showcase of its occupants' values and personalities" (*Bird by Bird*, p. 74), and so it is for our fictional characters. You might tell your students, "When writers imagine the places where characters live, we must first remember what we know about our characters." Tell your students to recall their characters' interests, important relationships, and background. Then, encourage them to imagine ways to reveal these aspects of the main character through setting.

If your students develop settings that feel arbitrary . . . teach them that writers choose settings carefully to add meaning or power to our stories. You can point to many examples in books in which the setting mirrors the internal life of a character. One example is in the story "Spaghetti" by Cynthia Rylant, from *Every Living Thing*. In the beginning of the story, the main character, Gabriel, feels like a loner as he sits "on the stoop of a tall building of crumbling bricks and rotting wood" (p. 31). By the end of the story, Gabriel no longer feels lonely and the description of setting—"a room and a bed of his own in the tall building" (p. 33)—reflects the internal shift that has occurred in him.

Writers also often use the weather to create drama or interest in their stories. Some writers, like Kate DiCamillo in *Because of Winn-Dixie*, might write a scene that takes place in a violent storm to reflect the turmoil or pain that a character is experiencing. I could also imagine a writer choosing to use the weather as a foil for the character's personality, so that a scene might take place on a clear, sunny day, but no matter how warmly the sun shines, how harmoniously the birds chirp, it cannot lift a sense of gloom or sadness from the character's mood.

As adult readers and writers, we know that writers can use setting to add symbolism, metaphor, mood, and drama to our stories. Once students begin to realize what a powerful tool this is, they will make choices about setting as deliberately and carefully as they do about character and plot.

If students have worked through this unit already in previous years . . . you might teach writers that descriptions of the setting can be crafted to reflect or reveal the character's mood or situation. For example, if a character is feeling disheartened because her crush has rejected her, the school dance decorations will look different. In that case, the writer might write: "The huge overhead lights glared in her eyes, making her squint. The shiny wooden gym floor felt blinding. The bright balloons and swirling streamers all swayed with the music as if to say, 'Everyone is dancing but you!'" But, on the other hand, if the character's crush has given her some attention, the same gym will look different. In that case, the writer might write: "The overhead lights glowed like sunshine on the shiny gym floor. The balloons and streamers seemed to be winking at her and saying as they swayed, 'Come dance with us!'"

ASSESSMENT

Before long, you'll be teaching children how to write powerful endings to a story. Before you can teach this, you'll want to look at the endings your children plan to write. You'll find that many of them are planning what I call "Superman" endings. With luck, someone arrives and saves the day. Examine your students' writing to see whether the ending comes from outside the main story line. Look, also, to see if the character changes through the story. Superman endings often mean that the characters needn't experience any significant change. If a child's main character hasn't changed in some way or learned something new, you'll want to guide the child to rethink his or her ending.

Help your children learn that a story can come to a resolution without a character getting everything he or she wanted. You can draw on the mentor authors' stories to show children that often characters don't get what they want, or at least not what they start off thinking they want. For example, in *Fireflies!*, the narrator is trembling with the excitement of catching fireflies, but once he has some in his jar and sees their wings beating against the glass and their lights dim, he feels terrible. The story, which ends with the boy releasing the fireflies, is bittersweet; the narrator cries because he's losing his treasure, but smiles because he knows the fireflies will sparkle and thrive only out of captivity.

Stories can also be resolved with a change that a character can live with even if it isn't exactly what he or she wants. In *Peter's Chair*, for example, Peter is resentful of his baby sister; he doesn't like that he has to play quietly and that she's using his old furniture. But he cannot wish his sister away and by the end, Peter finds a way to live with her, filling the new role of older brother. Stories also sometimes end with a character getting something deeper (a lesson, a truth, a friend) he didn't know he was seeking. For example, in Deborah Wiles' *Freedom Summer*, the narrator thinks he wants to swim in the same pool as his friend, John Henry Waddell, but by the end he realizes what he, in fact, wants is to live in a world in which he and his friend can be treated the same way.

You'll want to be familiar with the ways in which this unit's mentor authors end their stories so you can help your students consider new ways to end their own. A child who always ends with dialogue, for example, might want to try ending her piece with internal thought or action. Encourage children to consider endings in relation to overall text structure. As with any other element of craft, endings should bring out the heart of a story and support the overall story structure.

IN THIS SESSION, YOU WILL TEACH CHILDREN THAT WRITERS OF FICTION DO THEIR BEST TO CRAFT THE ENDINGS THAT THEIR STORIES DESERVE. IN PARTICULAR, WE MAKE SURE OUR ENDINGS MESH WITH AND SERVE THE PURPOSES OF THE STORIES.

GETTING READY

- Example or anecdote to illustrate what a good ending can do for a story
- List entitled Key Questions Fiction Writers Consider in Revising Endings, prepared on chart paper
- Ending to the class story that you can use to model thinking about endings
- Display of all the read-aloud books used during the year
- Anecdote you can tell about working with titles
- See CD-ROM for resources

WRITING POWERFUL ENDINGS

A few summers ago, I was glued to the gymnastics competition at the Olympics. I watched gymnast after gymnast throw her body across the floor or pommel horse or balance beam. No matter how complicated and flawless their routines were, if they did not "stick" their landings, their performances felt ruined.

It is the same way with stories. We've all had the experience of reading and getting lost in a story. We fall in love with the characters, get swept up in the plot, and then we reach the end, and bam, it's as if a door was slammed in our face. The ending is either too sudden or unbelievable or just plain unsatisfying. We all know, too, that our students often fall into these same traps when they are writing their own endings. We've all read stories about a child who toils away at a job in order to earn enough money to buy her mother something—a valentine, a charm bracelet—and then suddenly she learns she's won the lottery. We've read about the unpopular girl who is ridiculed at the start of the story and elected class president at the end of the story.

Today, our goal is to teach children that in life, solutions don't usually fly in from outer space (nor from left field). Usually no one arrives on the scene at the final moment, solving everything. Each of us, as a person and as an author, can find small solutions in the everyday truth of our all-too-human existence. No, we do not usually win the lottery. The girl who is ostracized one day doesn't usually become class president the next day. But that girl can find a place for herself, and come to realize that there's more than one way to make dreams come true.

There is no one way to write a wonderful ending. An ending may be happy, sad, funny or thoughtful. It may contain dialogue and action, or it may be a bit of setting. What all good endings have in common is they address something essential in the story. Today's session, then, aims to show children that the writers and characters, alike, can find turning points in the details of our lives.

MINILESSON

Writing Powerful Endings

CONNECTION

Acknowledge that some children will soon draft an ending to their stories, and share author quotes which spotlight the importance of an effective ending.

"Writers, before long some of you will write your way towards the ending to your first draft. I know some of you left the mountain peak of your story mountains blank for now, and that as you've been writing, you've been rehearsing possible endings. That's smart because we all know from the television shows that end 'to be continued . . . '. that endings, like returning home from a journey, give us closure that is so important. They bring the story full circle. They are crucial. 'The opening line is a promise,' Jane Yolen has said, 'and the ending is a pay off to that promise.'"

"Rick Demarinis puts it even more strongly, 'My poetry writing teacher years ago said the ending of a poem is like a ski jump. There's the long accelerating downward glide, and then whoosh, you are thrown ballistically into space. You've been firmly fixed to earth, and now you're not.' He asks, 'Is that too much to ask of a poem or a story? Not at all,' he answers. 'That's exactly what we must ask' (*The Art and Craft of the Short Story*, p. 40).

Teach children that writers search for endings that tie up loose ends, answer questions, and bring the story's meaning home.

"Today I want to teach you that writers take our time with endings, weighing and considering, drafting and revising until we find one that fits. We know that a just-right ending will feel as if it is tailored exactly to fit our particular story. We know this ending will tie up loose ends, resolve the unresolved difficulties, and bring home the story's meaning."

TEACHING

Share something you know about how good endings go.

"When I taught very young children, I remember working with one child whose story told about a disastrous picnic but then ended with a hasty 'and we lived happily ever after.' The young writer—she was probably five—had just grown tired of her story and plopped that ending onto it. So we talked about ways she had actually appreciated the rained-out picnic after all, and I said, 'You'll definitely need to change the end of your story!'"

"I came back later and she'd crossed out 'we lived happily ever after' and was instead writing a hologram of 'the end.' Each letter of 'The End' was carefully decorated with stars and stripes. 'I'm fixing up 'the end' she said cheerfully to me.'"

"We laugh, but the truth is—many of us aren't all that different from that five-year-old. We don't have a clue how to resolve our stories. We may not slap a 'they lived happily ever after' ending onto our story booklets, but in our own way, what we do is not much better. The three girls gang up on Kayla, putting cockroaches and poop in her locker and spraying whipped cream on her face. How does that story end? The principal arrives on the scene like Superman, flying in from nowhere, and brings the three mean girls to his office where they see the light of day."

"I want to teach you one bit of advice that I think can make all the difference when you draft and revise your endings. This is it: the ending is there all along, in the problem. There is never a need for another character to zoom in from outside the story to save the day!"

Offer an example that illustrates a principle of good endings.

"Let me show you what I mean. Let's go back to that story of the three girls who gang up on Kayla. It's not a sweet story, in fact it is a tragic one, but it needs an ending nevertheless. The mean girls hide around the corner in the hall, watching when Kayla pulls open her locker door. They see her step back as the turds plop out onto the floor, reeking. The mean girls laugh at the cockroaches as one drops onto Kayla's sweater. One of the girls, to top it off, approaches with a can of whipped cream in hand, ready to spray it in Kayla's face."

"What might happen?" I said. "I've discarded the idea of the principal or the therapist or the parent arriving from outer space to teach a lesson. I'm trying to find an ending—a solution—that's right here in the midst of the problem. Hmm . . . ." I paused for a long while. "I'm trying to think what could happen in that awful moment to change things."

Then I said, "Perhaps the girl with the can of whipped cream goes to spray it, brings the nozzle close to Kayla's face, and for a moment, she looks in Kayla's eyes. She sees Kayla, the person, and she sees herself, too, and drops the can onto the floor."

"Or, then again, perhaps a cockroach drops onto this girl's arm, perhaps she is terrified, perhaps Kayla reaches out to help her, and the turning point comes in that gesture."

"In order to write an ending, it'll take lots of drafts, of course. These are just early ideas, but I wanted you to see that the solution is often in the details of the problem, and that turning points often involve a word, a gesture—on the outside. Because the real turns happen on the inside."

You might point out, "We know a lot about endings from all of the work we've done in earlier units this year. The thing is, with our personal narratives, those were stories that really happened, so while we had to decide where to end the story, we didn't have to make anything up. With fiction we need to imagine our endings, which can make it a little trickier."

You might say, "It makes me think of how Fireflies! ends. We were all sort of surprised the first time we read it, but at the same time we all thought—that ending makes sense. I can't imagine it ending any other way. Of course, that ending probably didn't come to the author on the first try. She probably revised and revised until she got it just right, just like you are going to do. In fact, I'm pretty sure she thought about a few things before she wrote the perfect ending. And you guys will be doing the same thing."

Introduce a list of a few ways writers make sure endings are of good quality.

"Here are a few key questions fiction writers consider when revising their endings and imagining how they might go." I referred to the chart I had prepared:

ACTIVE ENGAGEMENT
Ask students to think about the class text in relation to one of the considerations set up in the demonstration. In this case, ask them to consider whether the class story's purposes are fulfilled in the ending.

"So writers, let's work together and see if we can imagine some possible endings to our Luz story. You'll remember that the ending will always relate to the story's real message," I said, "So we need to remember what the story is really, really about." I flipped through drafts which we'd written on chart paper.

"Hmm. So writers, it seems to me our ending needs to somehow address Luz' fears of sleeping in the dark and also of being ostracized by the girls. Would you and your partner think about two possible endings?"

The children turned to talk, and after a bit, I asked one of them to share her idea. Sofiya said, "I think Luz can be lying there in the dark getting really scared and then another girl—maybe Marta—whispers, 'Do you have a flashlight?' and it turns out *she's* afraid of the dark too."

Turning to the whole class, I said, "Sofiya had a suggestion for an ending. We need to think, 'Does it address—even resolve—Luz' fear of the dark?' 'Does it link to her desire to be popular?' 'Does it show that she's changed internally?' I'm not sure if it does the last of these but it certainly links to her fear of the dark. And there's no Superman swooping in to save everybody!"

Then Henry said, "I want Luz to get over being afraid of the dark. I want her to realize that there's nothing to be afraid of. Maybe we can have someone make a noise, and Luz and Marta realize it's a robber and they are really brave even though it's dark and they catch him."

I said, "I know Henry's not alone in thinking that in a story, a character should change—so it makes sense that Luz conquers her fears, catches the robber and so forth. But I want to remind you that we all, as people, change and grow in small ways. This is realistic fiction and realistically, Luz isn't going to get over her fears in the blink of an eye. So Henry, can I steer you towards appreciating the much, much smaller changes that human beings actually make?"

Key Questions Fiction Writers Consider in Revising Endings

- Can the reader see evidence of the main character's evolution?
- Does my ending make sense or come out of nowhere?
- Are the loose ends tied up? Have I answered the reader's key questions?
- Have I revealed everything I need to for the story's purposes?

You could also muse, "Are the loose ends tied up? Have I answered the reader's key questions? I'm not sure about that. Is Luz still afraid of the dark? I bet people might want to know that. The story isn't only about fitting in. It's also about getting over your fears. I'm going to make a note of that right here in the margin."

At first, when Henry began talking about the robber, I was worried that his idea for the story would spin into the overdramatic. Although he ended up reining in his idea, this isn't always the case. Sometimes we need to coach students if they get off track, and sometimes we simply need to celebrate that they've tried, and save the coaching for the next time—that will depend on the student and the timing. In any case, we need to decide ahead of time how to handle suggestions that are not what we'd hoped for if we're going to call on students without having heard their comment said first to a partner.

LINK

Acknowledge that you know students will be in different stages of writing today, but if they are ready, they can move into revising their endings.

"I know you are all in different places right now. Some of you may begin to write the first draft of your ending today, and for others of you it'll be tomorrow. No matter where you are in your work, when you get to the ending, remember that writers always consider whether our ending matches our story. And we look for solutions and resolutions that come from the grit, the specificity, the truth of our story. More than this, we need to remember that endings matter. Write a few different endings. Weigh which one you like best."

Here I reiterated my point from earlier in the lesson about not rushing because the students may feel tired.

Notice that I did not explicitly teach the students how to write and experiment with different endings. I assumed that the students would hold on to that strategy from our earlier work on leads and revision. If you feel that your students need that work explicitly taught, by all means do.

WRITING AND CONFERRING

Reining in Last-Minute Additions

When you confer with children in order to help them imagine possible endings, you'll find that many of them propose endings that writers refer to as Deus ex machina. The term means "god from the machine," and it refers to an ancient Greek drama in which all the conflicts of a play are miraculously solved by an actor dressed as a Greek deity who descends from the clouds to resolve everything with a timely wave of the hand. Many children will choose a quick-fix ending because they don't want their stories to go on and on or because this gives them an easy way to resolve their story's main conflict. But students' writing becomes unrealistic because the story ends abruptly or because the student has something happen that is out of left field.

I sat down next to Joey who was quickly writing furiously down the page. I waited for him to find a stopping point and then asked, "So, Joey, it looks like you've hit upon something big. Whenever I write fast and furiously, it's usually because I've had a great idea, and I want to get every word down. What have you hit upon?"

Joey looked up with a smile across his face. "I've figured out a new way to help my character with his problem, and I wanted to get it all down before I forgot."

"That's huge! You must be so relieved," I said as I picked up Joey's paper, reminding myself of his story. It began like this:

> Gary stood in front of the store window looking at the brand new BMX bike. It was candy-apple red and had shock absorbers on the front tires. He imagined himself riding this bike, doing wheelies, jumping off ramps. He imagined himself zooming down huge hills in Central Park and zooming past people. He was like a statue standing in front of this bike. How would he be able to afford it?

"So, Gary's problem is that he wants a new bike, but he can't afford it."

Joey nodded.

MID-WORKSHOP TEACHING POINT · *Partnering in Revision* "When I was walking around, conferring with you, I was thrilled to see that many of you are sharing your ending ideas with a partner. I think that's a great idea. It makes me think that you know something that professional writers know—it helps to have fresh eyes look at a piece. After all, you've been looking at the same piece for a long time. It's hard to see all the things there are to see in it. Just like it's sometimes hard to see that your desk is messy because you look at it every day. It's only when someone else sits at your desk for a few minutes that you realize—oops—it's due for a cleaning!"

"Remember you need your partner to look not just at the ending itself, but also at your piece as a whole. If you haven't yet asked for a reader, do so soon."

"How have you decided to help Gary buy his bike?" I prepared to jot as Joey spoke so that I would have his words clear and straight in my mind.

Joey looked at his writing. "Well, I'm going to have an old lady who lives in Gary's building give him the money. The old lady hears Gary talking to his mom one day about the bike and how much he wants it, so this old lady decides to help Gary by giving him the money. Then, at the end, Gary goes and buys the bike."

I listened as Joey told his story, and jotted notes. "So let me make sure I have this straight." I looked down at my notes. "An old lady who lives in Gary's building is going to give Gary the money to buy his bike. Then, at the end, he goes to the store to buy the bike?"

"Yes, that's right."

"Well, I take my hat off to you Joey for working so hard to solve your character's problem. You know, it's not easy to solve a character's problem in a short story, because you don't have lots of time to do so."

"Yeah, I know. That's why I like my new ending, because Gary gets the money and can go buy the bike."

"Can you show me where this old lady comes into your story mountain?" I asked, flipping the pages of Joey's notebook to find his plans.

He quickly found his most recent story mountain and pointed to the top of the mountain. "She comes in at the middle of the story. Gary begs his mother to buy him the bike. Then, one day, this lady hears him and she tells him that she'll give him the money."

As Joey spoke, I thought to myself that there were a couple of ways that this conference could go. I could teach Joey to look at the events that had already happened in his story and then show him how he could use something that had already happened to lead to a solution. Or, I could teach Joey to introduce this new character earlier and think about how her story might unfold so that it doesn't feel as if she's come out of thin air. With those options in mind, I pressed on. "You know, Joey, having this new character in your story can add a whole new dynamic. It adds so many possibilities for how your story might unfold. So that was a very smart thing to do. But I want to give you a very important tip. Writers don't just add in characters at the last minute and have them fix all the problems that the character faces. When a solution zooms in from outside the story, this can throw a reader off and make your writing seem unrealistic. Instead, writers weave characters in from the beginning and then, sometimes those characters end up being heroes of the story." I paused so that Joey could take in what I'd said. "So let's look at your story mountain. Where might it make sense to have your neighbor come in? Remember, we want it to be somewhere close to the beginning. Introducing her in the middle is too late."

Joey looked at his story mountain and read out a point close to the beginning. "Well, here is the first time my character asks his mother for the money to buy the bike. So maybe, they can be in the hall or on the elevator and the woman is there and she hears it."

"That could totally happen. Absolutely! Now, you need to imagine a realistic reason for her to eventually give him the money. It feels unreal that she just gives him the money. What's her motivation for that?"

Joey thought. "Maybe she needs some chores done and she asks him to help her. He spends a couple of weeks doing chores for her and then he earns the money to buy the bike?"

"Yes, Joey, that's a realistic possibility. So, before you start writing, go back and revise your story mountain so that you are sure to weave your character through the whole of your story. And after this, try to be sure your solution grows out of the details of the story."

You will also find that some students, as they near the end of their stories, seem to feel insecure and therefore reach to add a little pizazz. Viktor did just that with his story about a boy who overslept for the ELA test (New York State's standardized language arts test). During the last phases of revision, he added pages and pages onto his draft. "I've been reading other people's stories and I realized my story was just not that exciting. So I decided to create more tension. So now, my character doesn't only miss the ELA test, but his father gets in a car crash," he explained. *[Figs. X-1 and X-2]*

I acknowledged that the car crash definitely added drama, but then continued, "You know, Viktor, a car crash is really very serious and important. In short stories, like what we've been working on, there is only room for one big event. For example, in our Luz story, we have the slumber party. We wanted to say that it was okay to be different and to be afraid of things, and the slumber party helps us show that. What important thing are you trying to say in your story?"

Viktor stopped and thought for a minute, then admitted that he was trying to talk about how stressful taking tests can be. "Maybe I should save the car crash part for another story," Viktor said, and I concurred.

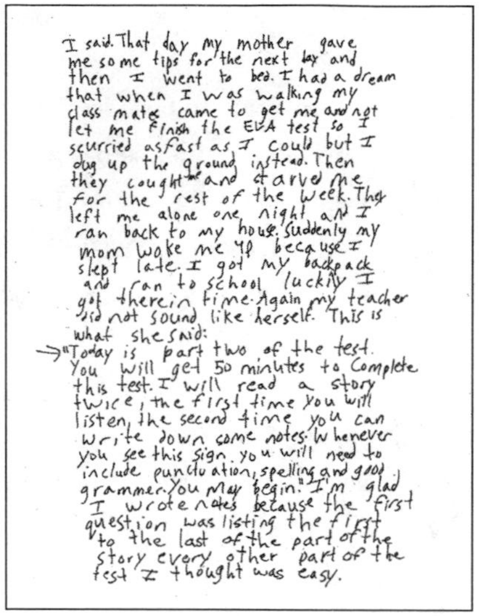

Fig. X-1 Excerpt from Viktor's original draft

Fig. X-2 Excerpt from Viktor's revised draft

SHARE

Crafting Endings

Share the story of one child's writing process that led her to write a more powerful ending.

"Writers, I want to tell you about something exciting that Deveonna realized today. Deveonna realized that she didn't need a miracle to happen at the end of her story. Let me explain. You'll remember that Deveonna's story is about a popular girl Alexa who feels as if she's been stalked by a somewhat nerdy boy, Max. In the opening scene of Deveonna's story, Alexa hides behind a tree so that Max won't find her—though of course he manages to spot her and is on her like glue. He comes close, and Alexa's friend cries, 'Run!' Later, Alexa decides she's going to confront Max and tell him she wants her privacy. She wrote": [Fig. X-3]

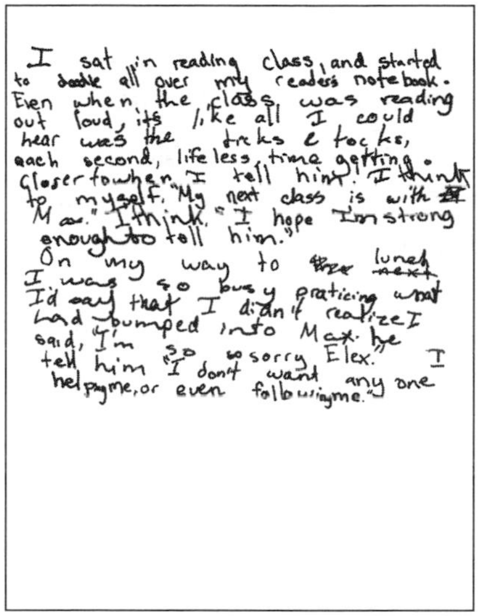

> I sat in reading class, and started to doodle all over my reader's notebook. Even when the class was reading out loud, all I could hear were the ticks and tocks of time getting closer to when I'd tell Max. I think to myself, "My next class is with Max." I think, "I hope I'm strong enough to tell him."
>
> On my way to lunch I was so busy practicing what I'd say that I didn't realize I had bumped into Max. He said, "I'm so sorry Alexa." I tell him, "I don't want any one helping me, or even following me.

"At first Deveonna wanted to write, 'He said fine, and that day after school we played chess and became best of friends.' But then she wrote in her notebook, 'I don't like that. Everything is just so peachy like an after-school special.' So she tried another ending. Will you listen to it and afterward, be prepared to list across your fingers four things that Deveonna has done in her writing that really work? This time she wrote:" [Fig. X-4]

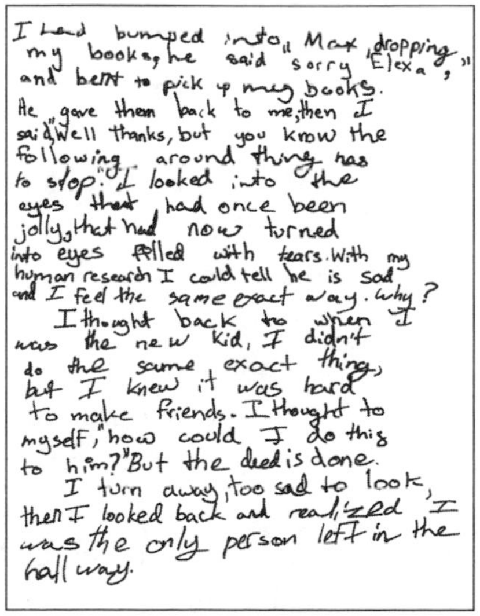

> I had bumped into Max, dropping my books. He said, "Sorry Alexa" and bent to pick up my books. He gave them back to me, then I said, "Well thanks, but you know the following around thing has to stop."
>
> I looked into the eyes that had once been jolly, that had now turned into eyes filled with tears. With my human research I could tell not only that he was sad, but I felt the exact way.

Fig. X-3 Deveonna's opening scene

Fig. X-4 Deveonna's ending

Why? I thought back to when I was the new kid. I didn't do the exact same thing, but I knew it was hard to make friends. I thought to myself, "How could I do this to him?" I thought, "But the deed is done." I turned away, too sad to look. Then I looked back and I realized I was the only person left in the hallway.

Ask children to process what they've learned from the child's process and begin considering how to improve their own endings.

"Turn and tell your partner four things Deveonna did that really worked," I said, and the room erupted into talk. After a bit, I intervened. "If you wrote an ending today, share that ending, and talk about how it works—and how it could be better still."

🔘 HOMEWORK *Using Mentor Texts to Explore Endings* Writers, remember that first and last impressions often matter whenever we come across something new. Just as we write strong leads to draw readers immediately into our stories, we need to write powerful endings so that readers finish our stories feeling that they've traveled with our main characters on their journeys. These endings need to be satisfying and strong, and there are a number of ways writers can do this.

Remember *Freedom Summer*? Deborah Wiles ended that story with action: "Then we walk through the front door together," and leaves us with the understanding that after the disappointment felt by John Henry and the narrator when they are not allowed to swim in the community pool anymore, the narrator is ready to stand by his friend's side through any other challenge that comes their way. Jacqueline Woodson's *The Other Side* ends with dialogue: "'Someday, somebody's going to come along and knock this old fence down,' Annie said. And I nodded. 'Yeah.' I said. 'Someday'" That final conversation between Clover and Annie lets us know how far they have come in their friendship and the hopes they share for a world in which a racial divide will be broken. *Chrysanthemum*, by Kevin Henkes, ends with internal dialogue: "Chrysanthemum did not *think* her name was absolutely perfect. She *knew* it!" This bit of thinking is the perfect way to end a story in which a character moves from fretting to feeling confident.

For homework tonight and whenever you are deciding how to end your stories, go ahead and try some of these different ways. If you've ended with dialogue, try to end the story with action. Then write another ending, this time ending it with internal dialogue. You might also look at another mentor text that ends in another way and try to use that kind of ending for your story. Then ask yourself which ending works better for your pieces. Which one best shows your character's journey in a clean, satisfying, and meaningful way?

TAILORING YOUR TEACHING

If your children need more help learning to write endings . . . you might say, "Finding the right ending for a story can be really hard! Many writers consider this the biggest challenge of writing. I've watched each of you look closely at your stories, imagining this way and that way to tie up loose ends. I know it's tempting to look toward the end of your story for hints about how to end it, but I wonder if you've thought about revisiting your story beginnings for hints about how to end it? In endings, characters find answers to questions they have on page one, or overcome a challenge they face at the start of the story. Sometimes a powerful image presented in the story's beginning reappears at its end."

You could go on and give examples. "*Fireflies!* both begins and ends with the narrator looking out a window, but, although the same fireflies dance before his eyes in both scenes, there's a clear shift in what he sees and feels when he looks at them. *Peter's Chair* begins with Peter making a building for himself and it ends with Peter helping his dad build something for Peter's sister. In both instances Peter builds, but his project at the end of the story shows that he has come to accept his baby sister and his role as older brother. At the start of "Spaghetti" Gabriel sits alone on the stoop outside, wishing for company. At the end, Rylant tells us Gabriel "no longer wanted to live outside." He takes Spaghetti, the kitten, and goes inside. Notice that Rylant uses inside and outside space to represent Gabriel's internal journey; with a kitten to care for, Gabriel gives up being an outsider, letting someone in. If you are struggling over how to end your stories, reread your beginning, and see if there is something in it worth revisiting. Remember that a beginning often holds a key to the end."

COLLABORATING WITH COLLEAGUES

By this point in the unit you have a good sense of the scope and shape of your students' pieces. This is a good time, then, to check in on the fiction writing you and your colleagues started a few sessions ago and push yourselves to try more. One of the most powerful ways writers support each other is to read each other's work and give feedback and critiques. Professional writers often call this "workshopping" a piece. It is such common practice that there are retreats for writers dedicated to sharing each other's work to get support as well as laser-sharp criticism.

Some argue that this regular practice of meeting and discussing each other's work is the single most important thing writers can do to enhance our writing skills. This offers us an audience for our writing and a reason to write on a regular basis. It allows us insights into how readers might interpret our work. And for our purposes, it allows us to experience something akin to what our students feel every day when we confer with them about their writing.

If you and your colleagues are interested in dabbling in the work of sharing and offering critiques for each other's fiction pieces, you'll want to decide several things up front:

- A private time and place to meet where there will be few interruptions. Depending on the size of your group, one workshop session might take anywhere from one to three hours.

- An agreed-upon maximum number of pages to bring so that the meetings don't go on too long.

- A plan for how the meeting will go. Will people read each other's pieces and prepare comments beforehand? Or will people bring copies of their pieces with them to the meeting and read them aloud so people can comment in person?

- Ground rules for the meeting. You might choose a facilitator who will start off the discussion. You might decide to start with compliments, then move on to suggestions. You might want everyone to share at every meeting. Or you might decide to take turns.

Once your group is up and running, you may wonder about ways to get the conversation going. What will you talk about? You needn't worry about what to discuss. You already have a wealth of knowledge at your disposal. You have the piece you are focused on, for starters. You also know a lot about good writing from your work with mentor texts, the strategies you've taught, and the qualities of good writing. If you still find yourself stymied, you can direct your focus to particular components of the text: structure, plot, character development, flow, word choice, characteristics of the genre, and so on. Of course, you can always turn your talk to the best parts of each other's writing and ways to teach students lessons that will help their writing become as powerful.

IN THIS SESSION, YOU WILL TEACH CHILDREN THAT WHEN REVISING, WRITERS DON'T SIMPLY REREAD, WE REREAD WITH A LENS. WRITERS VARY THEIR LENSES ACCORDING TO WHAT THE WRITER VALUES FOR HER WORK.

GETTING READY

- Latest version of the class story, on chart paper, to demonstrate revising through a lens
- Former student's draft, prepared on a transparency, for whole-class practice
- Start of a list titled Ways to Resee Our Stories on chart paper
- See CD-ROM for resources

REVISION:
REREADING WITH A LENS

In this session and the ones that follow it, you will rally children toward a serious commitment to revision. You'll pull out all stops in an effort to support revision. You'll teach revision strategies in the minilesson, confer toward revision in your conferences, and celebrate revision in your mid-workshop teaching point and your share. But above all, convey the assumption that of course children will revise.

Children generally come to us resisting revision. They often regard it as punishment for writing badly. In the series, Units of Study for Primary Writing, I introduce a unit of study on revision by telling children that when we are really proud of our work, when it is the best writing we've ever done, we revise it. Revision is a way to make our best, better. Later in that unit, I invite the youngsters to reread texts they've written, looking for whether any of them are "good enough that they deserve to be revised." My message is clear: Revision is a compliment for good writing. Lousy writing is abandoned; good writing is labored over, developed, refined, and polished.

It's important to teach and model this stance toward revision, but it is also important to equip youngsters with tools that will allow them to revise to good effect. Too many children add a clarifying phrase or insert a detail and regard that as revision!

In this session, you will teach children that revision begins as rereading, and suggest that writers can reread with any one of many lenses. This is not a new point. We can reread asking, "What is this story really about? Have I brought out that deeper story? Have I made my characters vulnerable enough to seem human?"

The larger message is that revision begins with rereading, and that writers can be deliberate and strategic, selecting a lens based on whatever we value, and rereading with that lens.

MINILESSON

Revision: Rereading with a Lens

CONNECTION

Celebrate that some of your students have finished drafts of their stories, and remind them that reaching the end allows writers to reread and revise with new perspectives.

"Hurrah! Many of you are coming to the final pages of your story booklets. And the good news is that once you reach the ending of your story, you have a chance to look over the story, and to make the whole of it fit together into a single coherent piece."

Name your teaching point. Specifically, remind children that writers revise. Writers reread, deliberately viewing their drafts through a chosen lens.

"Today, I want to remind you that even when we move heaven and earth to write our drafts really well, we will each shift from drafting to revision. And specifically, I want to teach you that revision means just what the word says—re-vision. To see again." Then Colleen leaned toward the children as if she was conveying a secret, and said, "I want to teach you that when we revise it really helps to reread with glasses." She put on a pair of glasses for effect. Then, pulling the glasses off, she said, "You don't *really* need to wear glasses to be a writer. But we do need to put on special lenses, lenses that allow us to reread our writing with one particular question or concern in mind. We sometimes call that 'reading with a lens.' We might, for example, reread looking specifically to see if our character development satisfies us, or to see if we've shown the passage of time effectively, or to study the way we've used varied sentence lengths and punctuation to create rhythm and suspense in a story."

TEACHING

Explain that, especially when writing longer texts, many writers shift often between writing and revising. Tell children that you will revise what you've written so far and ask them to notice that you start by rereading the draft through a lens.

"Let me show you what I mean when I say revision starts by rereading with a lens. Before I do, let me join you in noticing that our class story isn't finished yet—we've written three pages for our story booklet—and I want to point out that when I'm writing a long text, I usually don't wait until I'm all done before I begin to revise. I'd rather rewrite three pages than revise the whole book! Many writers do that."

COACHING

Colleen names what she hopes children learned earlier, trying to restate that teaching in a grand and inspiring way.

You will notice that here, as in most minilessons, Colleen deliberately weaves a certain amount of flexibility into the form the work of the day might take. She doesn't say, "You must look at your writing through two lenses." She says, "You might look at your writing through this lens, or this lens, or another lens that reflect something that is important to you in your writing." By doing this, she reinforces the idea that writers have to make decisions about their stories, and that the work is not the same for every writer. She entrusts these decisions to students, and they feel more invested in the process than they would if she kept a tight hold on the reins. This is one way in which we can help writers become independent.

Sometimes teachers assume that a minilesson makes literally only one teaching point, and that the one and only thing that children can learn from a minilesson is carried in that teaching point. Certainly there is one main teaching point, but there are other, subordinate points as well for those students who are ready to take them in. I worry that if our teaching isn't densely packed with interesting, helpful information, children will decide to zone out. At the same time, we have to be careful that we don't muddy our primary teaching point with the various other points we are making. Constructing a minilesson takes care.

Demonstrate rereading the draft through a lens. Explain what rereading through another lens could look like.

"So I'm going to revise the draft we've written so far. And to do so, I'm going to use a special lens—I'm going to read just a bit of it with an eye toward one issue I choose. I could choose any issue that especially mattered to me."

"Remember earlier, we said that it is really important to think, 'What am I trying to show?' and to ask, 'What is this story *really* about?' So I am going to reread our Luz story, thinking, 'Have I really brought out the idea that this isn't just a girl-has-a-sleepover story?' This is a girl-who-worries-no-one-will-like-her story, a story that revolves around Luz's worries over whether her friends will laugh that she needs a night-light."

Colleen reread the class story, underlining places that illustrated the deeper meaning. With the class' approval, she decided aloud that the class had, indeed, brought out that understory. "Did you see how I reread the draft, looking at it simply through the lens of whether I'd shown what the story is *really* about?" she asked. "As writers, we can choose any lens we want, and we usually reread and revise several times with several lenses."

Now demonstrate that you can alter the lens with which you reread your draft, thereby seeing new aspects of it.

"One revision lens that writers use is a lens that a writing friend of mine calls the 'Cardboard Character Alert.' Anne Lamott says that our stories are only as good as the characters we develop. Even if we have the most wonderful plot, we need the character to take us on the journey. We loved reading *The Great Gilly Hopkins* because Katherine Paterson created characters to take us on the journey. Writers reread to be sure that our characters, especially our main characters, look and act so real that the reader feels like the character could walk right off the pages of the book into the living room."

"Remember we talked about making sure the character had some good traits, but also some not-so-good traits? If they don't, they seem fake—they are only as real as cardboard. So when I reread our story, I'm checking that we haven't made Luz be the sweetest, most sensitive girl, the greatest artist, a straight-A student, and the perfect daughter to her parents, or else readers might go UGH! No one's like that! I find things about Luz that are not perfect—including that she is afraid of the dark. This makes her more like a flesh-and-blood person!"

"But when I put on the Cardboard Character Alert lens, I might decide we could flesh out Luz even more by giving her little traits—things only she thinks, says, and does. For instance, I might describe the way Luz eats in such a way that she'd seem unique. Maybe we

I often try to show children that when I check for whether I've done something, I sometimes find "yes," and I sometimes find "no." I do not want all my "checks" to lead to the same answer!

You'll notice that Colleen uses this form of revision to reteach a quality of writing that we emphasized very early in the unit. Early on, children thought about their characters' external and internal features, and about their characters' strengths and weaknesses. Now Colleen leads children to revisit that early work. This, again, is a rhythm you should anticipate. Plan on the fact that the qualities of good writing that you really want to highlight in a unit will need to be introduced during the first few days of the unit, and recycled later in the unit. You could, of course, harken back to this early work and even suggest that children use strategies they learned earlier to breathe life into the characters they've now settled upon.

could say she likes to eat foods that look pretty together. She is an artist after all, right? So maybe she tries to arrange food on her plate so it looks like a painting, with purple, orange, and green foods set carefully next to each other."

"So during this revision stage, a writer puts on just one lens, then another lens. We might reread asking ourselves, 'Did I show what this story is *really* about?' or 'Did I develop idiosyncratic character traits?' This rereading often prompts revisions—even before the first draft is written."

ACTIVE ENGAGEMENT
Set children up to try reading a text through the lens of a Cardboard Character Alert. Encourage them to imagine revising the draft based on what they notice when they reread it.

"Why don't we try putting on the Cardboard Character Alert lens to look at this part of a draft story by a former student? Now, really go for it! With your partner, find the places where the character feels only as real as cardboard instead of as real as your Uncle Charlie." Colleen put up a transparency with part of a draft by a former student and read it out loud to the class.

> Rex was the star quarterback of the sixth grade football team. He could kick faster and farther than anyone else on the team, and he was big too and no one could push him over. He could just catch the ball and plow through to the endline without interference. With Rex on the team, no one else ever got to play that position.
>
> "I think you should give someone else a chance to play quarterback, Rex," said his friend. (Rex had lots and lots of friends and also he was real good at school, so his teachers all liked him best too).
>
> "Okay," said Rex. Because he was really nice too.

Make sure you gather examples of student writing that will help you illustrate your teaching points. Especially keep an eye out for notebook entries and drafts in which the writer has some "typical" issue that you could teach into. For example, this piece about Rex could also be used to teach students how to add setting to their stories, how to add physical details to create a picture of their characters, or how to add a main character's internal thinking. When you find student pieces that are very flexible in this way, make copies for your colleagues. And, if you don't have any pieces from former students on hand, you can use a piece from a different classroom or a piece that you have written yourself to illustrate your teaching point.

"Do you have your Cardboard Character Alert glasses on? What do you see?" Pulling in to listen to partners, Colleen heard Caleb say, "No one is all that good at everything." He added, "I mean, who could be the star at sports *and* at schoolwork? He is too perfect."

"Yeah," Felix agreed, "and if they were, probably they wouldn't have any friends 'cuz people would hate a person who is so great. Hey! Maybe that could be Rex's big problem! He could be so super great at everything, but in his true heart, he's real lonely and just wants a good friend. So he has to change something. Break a leg or something!"

"Fantastic!" Colleen said. "You're already thinking like terrific writers and you're beginning to revise this piece of writing." Then she convened the class. "You were coming up with great ideas. Of course, it is easier to fix up someone else's stories instead of your own!"

LINK
Send children off to reread their own writing through a specially-chosen lens, and remind them to do this throughout their lives.

"Today, like professional writers, you are going to reread your writing with lenses. You might look at your own writing and ask, 'Have I brought out the real thing this story is mostly about?' You might reread asking, 'Can I make my characters seem less like cardboard cutouts?' Try other special lenses you invent to serve your purposes as well, and let your rereading lead you to revision."

"For the rest of your life, remember that writers do all we can to write great drafts, but then we return to those drafts, rereading them with different lenses in mind, expecting to revise them."

When you want to help children bring a character to life, it helps to give that character an object to hold onto. Robert Newton Peck in Fiction is Folks *writes, "Bring a thing into the scene and your audience moves an inch forward in their seats, to be close to the stage."*

WRITING AND CONFERRING

Helping Reluctant Revisers

In today's minilesson, we encouraged writers to reread drafts with a particular lens in mind. You won't be surprised when I remind you, similarly, we, as teachers, can also look over our children's work with a particular lens in mind. It is important to remember this because otherwise, we tend to believe there is something objective and universal about whatever it is we see when we look at the work being done by our writers. A researcher once pointed out, "We do not see with our eyes or hear with our ears but with our beliefs."

The good news is that we can each make ourselves aware of the lens we tend to use when viewing kids and their writing, and this allows us to make decisions. I might say, "I usually read my children's writing trying to understand the content of their pieces, but for today, I want to look mostly at the length of their writing and at whatever efforts I see them making to elaborate or to write long." There are countless lenses worth adopting for a time. Try noticing what children seem to think good writing entails. Try categorizing the scale of their revisions, or noticing what does and does not prompt them to revise.

> **MID-WORKSHOP TEACHING POINT** **Revising the Story's Sound** "Writers, you are finding so many places to flesh out your characters! The room is getting noisy with all those 'real' characters walking off the pages! Can you take off your character lenses for a moment and look at me? I want to share with you the smart revision work that Max is doing. Max has found another lens with which to view a draft. What do you call it, Max? Oh, your 'Sound Check' lens!"
>
> "Max told me he put on this lens to reread his story for how it *sounds*. That is just what professional writers do too, Max! Often they even read their stories out loud to a friend or to the mirror or into a tape recorder, just to see if they've missed words or to see if the language and the rhythm of the sentences flow and make sense. We need to read with our ears as well as our eyes!"
>
> "This lens helps us make sure our story sounds good. Consider trying Max's lens—rereading to revise the sound of your story."

For today, I suggest you deliberately focus your attention on one thing, however, and that is on the rereading your children do in the midst of writing. Ask children if you can watch them reread and hear what they are thinking as they reread. Your focus will surprise and please children; they'll expect you to be driving them directly toward revision. The secret truth is, most significant revision must begin as rereading, and children often don't realize this.

In any case, you will probably see that children need you to demonstrate and coach them before they understand what it can mean to read or reread with a lens. For example, you could reread, paying special attention to places where the dialogue seems especially lifelike and true. Then you can show children how you mull over what you find, thinking, "Why are these sections of dialogue so lifelike?"

Usually it is powerful to reread, searching for instances of a particular quality of writing, and then to ask, "What is it that I did here that worked so well?" By identifying and thinking about sections of a draft that work well, a writer gathers the strength and wisdom to tackle sections that work less well.

SHARE

Using Lenses to Reread and Revise

Ask children to share the lenses they used to reread and then revise their work. Compile a chart for future reference.

"Writers, you've come up with so many ways writers can reread and revise our work! I think we'd better record these ideas so that we can remember them forever. These are the ways we've talked about so far:"

Ways to Re-see Our Stories

- Writers use a lens to reread, asking, "What am I trying to show?" and "What is this story <u>really</u> about?"

- Writers use a Character Cardboard Alert lens to be sure that our characters, especially the main characters, look and act so real that the reader feels like the character could walk right off the pages of their stories.

- Writers use a Sound Check lens to see if we've missed words or to see if the language and the rhythm of the sentences flow and make sense in our stories.

- Writers reread our drafts, thinking, "What sections have I summarized in passing?" "What sections have I stretched out, like stories?" "Do these choices make sense?"

"Will you turn to your partner and talk about other lenses you've used to reread and think about revising your work? If you've only tried the ways on the chart, talk about ways you might try to reread and revise in the future. Then in a few minutes we'll add some more ways to the chart."

Of course, you may choose to use different questions and angles on revision than the ones we've highlighted here. The most important concept is that children do reread with a certain focus, no matter what that focus is. Rereading with a focus is a skill that will serve them for a lifetime, in both their reading and their writing.

If you notice that your students are having a hard time understanding the concept of a lens, you might want to say something like this: "Have you ever been to a movie where you got to put on those funny 3-D glasses that made everything look real, as if you could just reach out and touch it? I remember seeing a movie like that when I was a little kid. I don't remember what the movie was about at all, I just remember important things popping out in the foreground and the landscape and sky in the background. Maybe that was my first realization that what I looked at could change, depending, literally, on what pair of glasses I put on. Now I know that I can change anything if I just look at it differently. Your short story draft can be just like that movie. You can put on different eyeglasses, different lenses we might call them, and see the draft in a brand-new way in order to change it."

HOMEWORK   *Rereading with a Punctuation Lens*   Writers, I'm so pleased to see how you've found ways to revise your stories using different lenses, often with unpredictable and rich results. Tonight I'd like you to reread your stories using a new kind of lens. We'll call this the Punctuation lens.

I've noticed that when you read other authors' books aloud you read with beautiful intonation, making your listeners laugh uncontrollably, sit on the edge of their seats, gasp. But when you read your own stories, it sometimes sounds as if you're plodding along. I suspect part of the reason is that you're using the same kinds of punctuation over and over—a string of similarly placed commas or lots of short sentences ending with periods. You already know that writers vary our lenses when revising, making sure our characters aren't flat and predictable, rereading for rhythm and language fluidity, finding places to stretch out and places to summarize. What you may not know is that writers also reread for punctuation variation. Writers know that the kind of punctuation we choose and the way in which we use it can create mood or build tension or get readers to read with feeling.

Tonight I'd like you to reread bits of some stories you've read during this unit and notice how writers use punctuation to signal something to the reader. You might, for example, look at how Julie Brinckloe intersperses dashes with exclamation points and commas in *Fireflies!*, and what effect this creates. Or look at how Cynthia Rylant varies short simple sentences with longer ones, set off by commas. Then look at your own writing and find places where you can change the punctuation to enliven your stories, create mood or stir up emotion.

TAILORING YOUR TEACHING

If your students tend to write extra long leads so they can give background information on their main characters . . . remind them of what they learned about leads in the *Raising the Quality of Narrative Writing* unit. You might say something like, "When you were writing personal narratives, you learned how writers don't start far, far away from the action of the story. They start their stories right at the action. Well, writers of realistic fiction do the exact same thing. They start their stories by placing the reader right in the thick of the action." If your students know the story *Because of Winn-Dixie* by Kate DiCamillo, you might show them how the author brings the reader into the thick of the action by starting with the line, "My name is India Opal Buloni, and last summer my daddy, the preacher, sent me to the store for a box of macaroni-and-cheese, some white rice, and two tomatoes and I came back with a dog." As the story progresses, Kate DiCamillo weaves in elements of the main character's history.

It is especially difficult for students to restrain themselves from giving all the background information at once if they have done a thorough job of developing a character with vivid details. Students do not want their work to go to waste, so they tend to write pages and pages of description and background, and in the process they lose their reader's attention before they ever get to the meat of the story. Help students celebrate all the work and careful attention they spent creating a rich and interesting character. Then, teach them how to artfully reveal those details to the reader. You could say, "You already know how to balance your story by weaving together details about setting, thinking, dialogue, and actions. In just the same way, you are going to weave in details about your main character. Writers don't write everything we know about our characters all at once. Instead, we need to carefully balance our stories by weaving in a bit of detail about character here and there, along with all the other kinds of details. Imagine that your story is on a stage, and you are raising the curtain ever so slowly, so the audience sees just a tiny bit at a time. Doing this creates suspense and drama in our stories."

MECHANICS

During this unit of study, children will write a very long story, and then they'll revise and edit that one draft. Most of them will make a final, clean copy of their story, but the piece will be long enough that their energy for editing at that stage will likely run dry.

Therefore, it'll probably be important for you to have children take one of the early pages in their story booklets and help them edit as well as revise that page. Then as they proceed to revise the upcoming pages, you can encourage them to draw upon conventions they incorporated into their first page. This work will be fairly individual, but meanwhile you'll also want to teach whole-class instruction around mechanics.

You'll want to study children's writing in order to decide what to teach. If you reread their pages through the lens of mechanics, noticing what they can do and what they need help doing, you may find yourself overwhelmed. The children will produce lots of text in this unit—and this means they'll also produce lots of errors!

If you stay focused, however, you can deliberately channel yourself to also notice and admire the complexity of their work. For example, both Felix and Laurel are using complex sentences, complete with subordinate clauses. They use these to show that two activities occur simultaneously:

> He was losing, but he remembered his dad telling him to pump false turn and shoot.

> "Let's go look at the animals first, so then on the sky ride we can retrace where we were," Jessie said.

It is as if the challenge to tell a dramatic, titillating story has led both writers to stretch their grammatical skills. Not surprisingly, they also make many errors.

Often, the most helpful thing that you can teach these children is that writers use paragraphs to show either when the character takes a step forward in the action, or when the camera shifts to a different but simultaneous ring in the three-ring circus that is the story. This single bit of editing will relieve the sense that the child's words are unremitting, a torrent of language.

It might also help children to study different ways in which authors convey a character's thoughts, and to realize that sometimes authors use quotes for thoughts just as they do for spoken language. It might also help enormously to remind children that when a reader encounters a pronoun— he or she or they—the reader should instantly know exactly who is being referenced. If the reader might be unclear, then it is important to use the person's name (or a synonym for it) rather than the pronoun.

If you teach one or two of these tips in an editing conference, you'll want to give writers a chance to use the advice as they edit. Then teach another tip or two, and again invite the child to edit, putting the advice into action. When you read the resulting text, it'll be important to celebrate progress and approximation, encouraging the child to continue to do this important work in upcoming pages of the story.

IN THIS SESSION, YOU'LL TELL
WRITERS ABOUT THE INTIMATE WORK
SPACE YOU'VE CREATED FOR YOUR
WRITING AND TEACH STUDENTS THAT
THEY CAN CREATE THEIR OWN
SPACES INSIDE THEIR WRITING
NOTEBOOKS AND THEIR HOMES.

GETTING READY

- Anecdote you can tell about one writer's special work space
- Something special from your own writing life—a quote or object—whose significance you can share
- Charts of writing tips and strategies created during earlier units, for reference
- Copy of each child's published personal narrative from earlier in the year
- See CD-ROM for resources

MAKING A SPACE FOR WRITING

In this session, you'll rally children's commitment to the project before them, that of seriously, deeply revising their writing.

When I begin work on a new writing project, my first step is not to write or even to read. Instead, my first step is to clean my office! After that, I set out all the things I will need to write or, in this instance, to revise.

When I began work on this series, for example, I put the previous series, Units of Study for Primary Writing, on the far corner of my desk. Then I gathered together the books that bring my distant teachers close to me: books by Don Murray, Annie Dillard, Bill Zinsser, John Gardner, Don Graves, and others. I pinned a few letters from readers on my bulletin board; those letters and others like them have made me care desperately about this work. On my bulletin board, I tacked a calendar of deadlines, and my brilliant editor's list of tips to remember.

Children, too, need to be encouraged to build spaces in their lives that allow them to write and to revise as well as possible, and they need to be encouraged to fill those spaces with items that can inspire and cajole and guide them as writers. By physically setting up the space in which we work, we take control of our own writing processes. As we make our writing spaces, we make ourselves. And for teachers, whose ultimate goal is to help children grow to be passionately committed, zealous writers who author richly literate lives, nothing could matter more than this.

Today, by sharing with children my own tricks of the trade, I speak to them as fellow insiders in the world of writing. And by inviting them to surround themselves with items that carry reminders of their resolutions, I encourage children to review all they have already learned, and also to renew their vows to lessons that may have slipped out of view.

MINILESSON

Making a Space for Writing

CONNECTION

Tell students that you prepare for a writing project first by cleaning your office. Explain that many writers set up work spaces, putting items nearby that remind us of our resolutions.

"Writers, I think each one of you is off to a great start, revising your fiction story. So today, I thought I'd tell you that when I turn the bend in a writing project, in addition to sketching plans for that writing, I do one other very important thing. I clean my office."

"Every writer is different, and you may decide that your needs are different from mine. But many, many writers take the time to set up spaces in which we can do our best work."

Tell the story of one writer who has set up his or her writing space in ways that convey messages about writing.

"The author Annie Dillard turned a tool shed into a study, pushing a long desk against a blank wall so that she'd have nowhere to look but at the page. She says, 'Writing a first draft requires a peculiar internal state which ordinary life does not induce'." (*The Writing Life*, p. 47)

"Annie Dillard has also pinned a photograph above her desk. It's a photo of a little Amazonian boy whose face is sticking out of river rapids. White water is pounding all around his head and his dark eyes are looking up. 'That little boy is completely alone,' Dillard says. 'He's letting the mystery of existence beat on him. He's having his childhood and I think he knows it and I think he will come out of the water strong and needing to do some good.'" (*The Writing Life*, p. 58)

Debrief. Help your students see the generalizable principles in the example of one author who organized a writing space.

"Do you see how Annie Dillard has built a place for her writing, a place that reminds her of what she wants to remember as she writes? She makes sure her place whispers a message to her—and for Annie Dillard, the message is this: Wake up. Wake up to the mystery and power of your own life. Put it on the page."

COACHING

My book Living Between the Lines *opens with a chapter titled "A Place for Writing and Reading." I do believe that when we teach writing, we are also helping children author lives in which they read and write often. This series of books doesn't spotlight the importance of a writing community and writing identity as much as I'd like—it's hard to write minilessons that could be universally applicable and yet do this work. I hope this one session inspires you to create others like it!*

This minilesson doesn't require such extensive detail about Annie Dillard's writing space. I relish detail and trust that it conveys larger principles, but you may decide to abbreviate this session—it could easily be done. Obviously, you'll want to tailor all your teaching to your children.

Although the example in this minilesson is different from that in other minilessons, you should by this point be able to see the pattern of minilessons. Over and over, we explicitly articulate a point that we hope is relevant to all children on many days. We either tell or dramatize the case in point, often tucking in little subordinate tips. Then we step back to debrief, and do so by again naming generalizable ideas and strategies. In this session, I've made a new point in the Connection section of the minilesson, which is unusual.

Name your teaching point. Specifically, teach children that writers put items and words into their writing spaces that remind us of our writing goals and hopes.

"Today as you continue drafting your story, you'll want to draw on everything you've ever learned about how to write stories well in order to make your new draft as spectacular as it can be. And specifically, I want to teach you that most writers set up spaces in which we can do our best work. We can put items and words into those spaces that remind us of all we resolve to do and be as writers."

Tell students that you like to look back on ideas learned from previous writing, bringing those lessons to bear on current writing.

"What I like to do as a writer is to look back on my writing life, and to think about all I learned before today that I resolve to remember. Remember that earlier this year, we read Sandra Cisneros' essay "Eleven," and learned that when you're eleven you're also ten, and nine, and eight, and seven, and six, and so on? Because, as she wrote, the way you grow old is kind of like an onion, or like the rings inside a tree trunk, or like wooden dolls that fit one inside the other—each year fits inside the next one. Well, I really do believe that writers also grow that way. When we're working on one piece of writing, we need to bring with us all the lessons we've learned from all the pieces of writing we've ever written. Because the way we grow as writers is like trees, with one ring inside the next, or like those little wooden dolls."

You'll see that I revisit Sandra Cisneros' essay "Eleven," making a point that is not unlike one I made earlier this year. You may wonder if I forget that I've traveled this road before. I haven't! I'm convinced that children benefit from a cyclical curriculum, and I love returning to a point made earlier, to a text that's been studied earlier, each time adding to the familiar content with more experiences, more knowledge.

TEACHING
Share the dream that each child might have a writing shed (akin to Annie Dillard's) and suggest that instead, all of them can set up their notebooks and writing spaces to convey messages about writing well.

"Wouldn't it be great if instead of putting up portable classrooms outside this school, they instead put up tool sheds, one for each of us? Then the writing workshop could be like those writing colonies I read about. We could convene for a meeting, and then each of us would head to our very own writing shed to read and write all morning. In some writing colonies, a basket lunch is left outside each writer's door so as not to disturb the writer's muse!"

"It'd be great if we could each set up a writing shed for ourselves, but in this classroom, we can only set up our writing spaces, our notebooks, our folders. Still, it is important to choose the items that we will put near us as we write, items that can carry bits of advice to us."

Notice that I repeat my teaching point here, this time in a more poetic fashion. I hope that by doing so, I increase kids' energies for this work.

Although this is playful chitchat, the underlying message is that these youngsters deserve to be taken seriously as writers. Every lesson we teach is not explicitly articulated—we also teach by our assumptions, our attitudes.

Explain that before you return to the class story or your own story, you'll first set out items that remind you of advice you want to recall. Select a quote from a book or an item from your writing life and share the significance of whatever you select.

"So before I work anymore on our class story and before I work on my own fiction stories, I'm going to choose a few items to keep near me as I write, items that carry advice for me."

"First of all, I want to keep one passage of 'Eleven' near me—the bit about how the narrator pushed one hand through one sleeve of a sweater that smelled like cottage cheese. Do you remember that passage? It told how she stood there with her arms pushed back, with the sweater itchy and all full of germs that weren't even hers."

"I know I shared that passage with you to show that a writer can describe an event in passing ('she put on the sweater') or can stretch it out, telling the story bit by bit. But for me, I love this passage also because it has a ring of truth. The details feel as if they are true details, and I want to remember the power of writing the truth, even when I'm writing fiction. So I'll tape that passage inside my notebook, and remember that advice today and always as I write."

"I think I'll also tape this calendar inside the front cover of my notebook," I said. "I want to remind myself that I can't spend too long planning for writing or I won't have enough time to revise. I think it will be helpful to me in making decisions to have the calendar saying, 'Just Get on with It.'"

ACTIVE ENGAGEMENT
Help writers leaf through and revisit old charts and mentor texts, thinking, "Does any of this belong in my writing space?"

"So writers, today and tonight, would you think about ways in which you can make a space for writing both here in the classroom and at home—a space that carries messages *you* need to remember."

"Right now, I'll revisit some of the items in our classroom that *might* contain lessons for you, and as I do this, will you jot your own notes so that when I'm done, you can tell your partner whether any of these items (or others you can recall) might belong in your writing space?" I turned the pages of the chart-paper tablet back to charts from *Launching the Writing Workshop*, and read off a few items:

- Strategies for Generating Personal Narrative Writing
- Qualities of Good Personal Narrative Writing
- Monitoring My Writing Process

I deliberately selected a passage that will be familiar and memorable to children, and layered it with a somewhat new message. This is a small way to tuck another pointer about good writing into my minilesson.

I thought about whether I would also tell the class about a special stone or a rabbit's foot, just so my items would be more varied and suggest more possibilities to children for their own objects. But I couldn't come up with a brief explanation for the lessons these objects might contain. You and your colleagues might have better luck.

This lesson is reminiscent of the work in our first unit, in which we launch the writing workshop by helping students cultivate the habits of writers. Writers live with a constant, eyes-wide-open awareness, gathering ideas from the world like collecting berries in a basket. We must remind students of this often by modeling and discussing these habits. So, in addition to jotting down ideas from class writing charts during this lesson, encourage students to write or paste meaningful passages, writing advice, photographs, or other inspiring pieces into their notebooks or folders to create a rich writing space. This lesson gets to so much more than simply decorating the cover of a notebook, and it is truly the work that authors do to support their writing.

Then I turned to those from *Raising the Quality of Narrative Writing* and read off a few more:

- Lessons from Mentor Personal Narratives
- Turning Points
- When to Use Paragraphs

I continued flipping back through charts from all of our units until I reached the current one.

Ask children to talk to a partner about items they might put in their notebooks or writing spaces that can help them recall previous lessons on good writing.

After surveying these and other items, I said, "Would you turn and tell your partner if you've seen anything so far that reminds you of a message that might help you do your best writing and revision today? Because remember, writers grow like rings on a tree. When we write fiction, we still have the layers of all we've learned from earlier units of study. Which words or objects might you put into your writing space? Turn and talk."

I loved being able to come back to the passage from "Eleven" at the end of this little lesson. I think if our teaching is artful, then the teaching itself acts as a mentor text.

LINK
Put today's lesson into context by reminding writers of the many ways they can prepare themselves for writing well.

"So writers, from this day forward, remember that we can prepare ourselves for writing not only by sketching timelines, boxes and bullets, or story mountains, and not only by trying alternative leads. We can also prepare ourselves for writing by looking back over lessons we learned earlier in our writing lives and the texts that have taught us a lot. We often select passages or charts or quotations or objects to keep near us as we write, and we do this as a way of holding close the lessons we've learned."

This is sophisticated work, and it takes real self-awareness for students to identify just exactly which lessons or skills they need to keep at the forefront of their minds as they write. Think of the writing as a building. Placing the supports at random would do little to make a sound structure, and would be a wasted effort. Just as one needs architectural knowledge in order to effectively brace a building, writers need a certain amount of savvy about themselves in order to determine which words or objects will offer them the support they need.

WRITING AND CONFERRING

Learning from Our Writing Patterns

This minilesson invites each child to create an individualized work plan, one tailored to whatever particular work that child needs to do. In your conferences, you may want to help children take a larger look at themselves as narrative writers, asking, "What lessons did I learn earlier this year that really paid off for me?" and "What worked really well in my earlier stories that I'll want to remember as I revise this new story? What didn't work too well for me in my earlier stories that I could address this time, in this piece?"

To help children look back at and learn from prior work, encourage them to see the continuities between their earlier personal narrative writing and their current work with short fiction. In fact, chances are very good that a child will bring the same strengths and the same needs to both genres. Most of the problems that will show up in short fiction will also have been present in the child's personal narrative work.

The minilesson puts a spotlight on objects and texts that carry lessons—your conferences will help writers harvest insights from taking a long look at their writing over the course of the year so far. When children look across several narrative texts, you'll need to help them see commonalities. One text may be about the birth of a cousin, another about feeding a squirrel, and a third about a bully. But all three texts may be written in simple sentences, where nothing is given more emphasis than anything else nor is anything suggested, tucked in, or alluded to. In all three texts, the characters may seem indistinguishable one from the next; and all three might have strong, interesting leads. You'll want to help writers gain some ability to see patterns in how they write, patterns that show up when texts are laid alongside each other.

MID-WORKSHOP TEACHING POINT — *Using Conjunctions to Communicate Complexity* "Writers, I want to interrupt you for a moment to point out ways writers use special conjunctions—connector words—to help communicate complicated situations in writing. Here's an example—have you ever tried to explain a situation and had trouble because so many things happened at the same time? Think about the word *meanwhile*, and look how Julie Brinckloe uses it in *Fireflies!* to help us feel everything that was going on, even if it all happened at once. Remember, the narrator was eating supper, *meanwhile* fireflies flickered on and off out on the lawn? Do you see how she uses the word to help her tell what's happening inside and outside the house at the same time? There are two other *meanwhiles* in this story. "The screen door banged behind me as I ran from the house. If someone [*meanwhile*] said, 'Don't slam it,' I wasn't listening." In that example, Brinckloe doesn't write *meanwhile*, but she lets us feel it there, with two things happening at the same time. Then for a third time, at the end of the story, she helps us understand that two things happen at once: The narrator lets his fireflies go and they make circles around the moon, dipping low, soaring above the boy's head. *Meanwhile*, the boy holds the empty jar in his hands. Do you see how letting two things happen at once, with a *meanwhile* or the idea of one, can be useful in your writing? It can help with complexity or add a way to make a contrast, can't it? Look over your writing quickly, and see if you can mark a place where a *meanwhile* or another conjunction could help you explain an idea or situation. Writers use conjunctions as thoughtfully as nouns, verbs, adjectives and adverbs. It's easy to think that words like *although* and *therefore* are boring, but writers know that even apparently dry words like that can contribute to our writing in powerful ways."

SHARE

Learning from Our Best Work

Share a choice that one student made about how to set up her writer's notebook in ways that support great writing. In this case, you could share the idea that our own writing can remind us to write well.

"Writers, can I have your attention please? I want to show you the smartest thing! Celena took the story she wrote earlier this year and taped it to the inside cover of her writer's notebook. She said to me, 'When I reread it, I remember all the stuff I did in that story. Then I tell myself to do it again.'"

Ask children to set up the same kind of support in their own notebooks. In this case, ask them to mark places in their own notebooks they need to continue to learn from in future writing.

"I suspect every one of us could try Celena's idea! Right now, I'm going to pass out a copy of the personal narrative you published toward the start of this year. Would each of you read your own writing to yourself and put stars at every place in your own text where you say, 'I did something that I need to remember and do again.' After a few minutes, share what you realized with your partner."

Ask children to find, note, and share with their partners great parts of the writing they've done so far in this unit.

"After you've done this, would you look over what you've written so far in this unit, and find the part that makes you most proud. It might be a place where you made an important decision, or wrote some great dialogue, or selected an exactly true word. It might be a really catchy sentence. When you find that part, but a little smiley face next to that spot."

I watched the students as they took a few minutes to look through their drafts. I coached students who needed help finding value in their work, and set some children up as talent scouts for each other.

"Now that each of you has a spot in your piece you are especially proud of, take a minute to share that part with your partner. Don't just read that bit; tell your partner why you like that spot, and talk about how you wrote it—what strategies you used. When you're done sharing, ask your partner, 'What do you think?' Partners, start with a compliment. Something you really admire about the writing. If you have a small suggestion for how the writer could perhaps make that good work even stronger, that'd be great, because after all, the time to revise is when our writing is already really strong. That way, we can make our best work even better."

This is a great way to help children see and solidify what they've learned about writing to date, but it is far from the only helpful Share possible. Nearly any words of wisdom or meaning-laden object from one child will inspire other children to find similar bits of wisdom for their writing supports. It's like stories about pets—once a child tells one pet story aloud, many other students are suddenly bursting with animal stories!

If students become inspired by this session, you may want to spend some time creating writing spaces within your classroom. You might ask children to bring in quotes, objects, and photographs that they find inspirational. If your children have cubbies or tables or cozy writing spots, you may give students some time to create writing spaces for themselves, just like yours.

There are times in a unit when the work may get a little long, and the finish line may seem far away. Often a Share can be used as a place to catch our breath and have a small celebration. Since the drafting process may be lengthy in fiction, taking some time to do just that, while in the midst of revising, may be a welcome treat.

This session might inspire some classes to spend time creating writing spaces within the classroom. Children might bring in quotes, objects, and photographs that they find inspirational. However, if you notice students spending too much time fussing with their writing spaces, gently remind them of the writing space's purpose: writing!

HOMEWORK *Creating a Writing Space*   Writers, you won't be surprised that for homework tonight, I want you to think about the writing place (and the reading place) you've made for yourself in your house. Ask yourself, "What do I need in order to do my best work as a writer? As a reader?" Think about how you can make a place for yourself where you can do the most powerful reading and writing possible. What can you put in your reading and writing nook that will remind you of your goals?

Your special place needn't be fancy. When I was first teaching, I made a place for myself in the basement beside the furnace. I used a discarded door as a desk. That may not sound very fancy to you, but I think the first big step I ever made toward becoming a writer was creating that office for myself, down there in the basement. After that, I began a ritual of writing every evening. What big step will *you* take to further your writing? Make a sketch and write an entry about your writing space—and of course, once that place is made, press on with your story!

TAILORING YOUR TEACHING

If your students seem confused about what items to place in their notebooks to inspire their writing . . . instead of asking students to draw inspiration from a mentor text or class chart, you might suggest that students look toward their own work for powerful writing lessons as they do in the share of this session. In *The Revision Toolbox*, Georgia Heard encourages writers to reread their own writing with the purpose of finding some piece of magic. She says that as she does this, she might happen upon "the rhythm of the line that I like best, or a vivid image, or a surprising simile or metaphor" (p. 75). As students do this, they can recopy or paste that bit of their own writing into their notebooks. You might tell students to name what they did in that bit that works so well. For example, perhaps they enjoy the way they used punctuation to add meaning in a certain passage, or perhaps they used powerful language instead of ordinary words such as said, nice, and fun. Once students have named the skill they used, tell them to hold on to the idea that using punctuation to add meaning (or using powerful language, or adding dialogue, and so on) can make your story much more interesting to read. Every time they look at that bit of writing in their notebooks, they will remember to do that in their writing every single day.

When students see that they can find the qualities of spectacular writing in their own work, and not just in the work of beloved authors, they realize that they can be their own writing teachers (and, when they share these bits with their writing partners, that they can be each other's writing teachers). This rereading for their own best writing is a skill that can be added to a drafting chart and then used over and over again while gathering in the notebook, drafting, and revising.

COLLABORATING WITH COLLEAGUES

You, your colleagues, and your children can study any aspect of fiction that catches your eye. The challenges are considerable, and opportunities to learn are everywhere you look. Take, for example, the use of dialogue.

Teach children that when a character speaks, the reader needs to hear a human voice. Most writers write by ear, listening to the music of the words as we put them on the page. We choose words that fit with our characters. The phone rings, and the teenager shuffles over to pick it up. "Yeah?" he says. On the other end of the phone it's an accountant. He says, "This is Mr. Farr, with whom am I speaking?" The cadence is different, the vocabulary is different. Each character's language reflects the person, just like each child in the classroom uses language in ways which reveal that person. Each of us has a rhythm and a way of talking that's all our own. Some of us talk fast. Some of us use fancy words. Some of us say certain things all the time. And language changes based on a character's mood. A mom in a hurry sounds different than a mom sitting in a patch of sunshine and reflecting on her day.

The characters in a story need to be widely differing people. They don't walk alike, dress alike, and they surely don't talk alike. They have small individualities of speech—just as I do, and you do too. Dialogue, voice, character—they are inseparable, and worthy of study.

Once children have studied dialogue in their own drafts, they can examine books they know well. Why does Nate the Great speak in such a pompous fashion: "I, Nate the Great, am a great detective"? What makes the words spoken by Koala Lou's mother so memorable: "Koala Lou, I DO love you! I always have, and I always will!"? These jewels are precious, and writers value them.

Teach children that fiction writers use dialogue to reveal relationships more than to convey facts. We are not apt to write like this, "Ever since my friend Kay was adopted by a family from Vermont six weeks ago, I've missed her!" Instead, fiction writers find other ways to embed explanatory information into a text, reserving dialogue as a way to reveal character and relationships. For example, a fiction writer might write, "Sasha quickened her step as she neared the mailbox. Before she reached up to open the door, she whispered, 'Please, Kay, please.' But the mailbox was empty. Just to be sure, Sasha put her hand into the box, and reached all the way to the back. Nothing. No letter. No postcard. Nothing. Not today, not yesterday, not any day since that sad, awful, terrible day when Kay was adopted."

Of course, dialogue is just one of a zillion possible topics which you and your colleagues might conceivably study together. Either way, I hope that when you and your colleagues meet together in your fiction study group, you'll consider making these into potluck occasions. I love it when a group of people agree that everyone will come bearing something to share: a fruit salad, a transcript of two children in a peer conference, copies of short stories that would be perfect as exemplar texts, homemade brownies, an excerpt from a professional book. Recently I brought two items to a study group. In Patricia MacLachlan's, *Unclaimed Treasures*, two youngsters prepare for the arrival of a new baby sister, and meanwhile engage in a spirited discussion about how one goes about naming a new child (or, I infer, a character). I could imagine spinning this into a minilesson:

> "The name. What's it to be?" asked Horace at lunch.
>
> "What name?" asked Willa.
>
> "The baby," said Horace patiently. "The baby's name."
>
> Willa's father drank some water.
>
> "We have never thought about names ahead of time," he said. "We had decided that naming children was much like naming dogs or guinea pigs. You had to see them first to know."
>
> Willa's mother nodded.
>
> "Willa came first," she said, remembering. "Pushing and squalling into the world."
>
> "We almost named her Fury," said Willa's father.
>
> "You didn't!" said Willa, aghast.
>
> "No." Her father reached over to smooth her hair. "We named you after a pioneer. The writer, Willa Cather. You were, after all, our first pioneer into the world."
>
> "Nicholas we named after a horse I once knew," said Willa's mother, making them laugh. She looked at them indignantly. "I loved that horse. He was pleasant and dependable, with quirks now and then."
>
> "Such as riding too close to fences," said Willa's father, "and under low trees."

> "That's true, isn't it?" Willa's mother smiled at them all. "I suspect we'll think of a name when we see the baby. Her."
>
> "There's always Wanda," suggested Willa slyly.
>
> "I think," said Horace, leaning his elbows on the table, "that if I were to have a child I would name her Jane."
>
> "Jane?" Willa's mother looked at Horace.
>
> Horace nodded.
>
> "Jane," he said. "Straightforward and honest and calm."
>
> "Like you," said Willa's mother, something in her tone and look causing Willa to peer at Horace more closely.
>
> "Jane," said Horace, biting into a green Granny Smith.

I also brought an opening paragraph from Patricia MacLachlan's *Journey*:

> Mama named me Journey. Journey, as if somehow she wished her restlessness on me. But it was Mama who would be gone the year that I was eleven— before spring crashed onto our hillside with explosions of mountain laurel, before summer came with the soft slap of the screen door, breathless nights, and mildew on the books. I should have known, but I didn't . . .

I hope that you give yourself the gift of a study group of colleagues— and then, invent a host of topics to study together.

USING MENTOR TEXTS TO FLESH OUT CHARACTERS

GETTING READY

- Excerpt from *Pippi Goes on Board* or a text important to you that shows character through actions, copied on chart paper or transparency

- Excerpt from your own writing or the class story you can use to demonstrate applying a mentor text

- Excerpt from *Fireflies!* or other familiar mentor text, copied on transparency or chart paper

- See CD-ROM for resources

Just as I hope that over time my students learn that essays, stories, and other written genres each have a "way they usually go," so, too, do I hope that you, my colleagues, will come to sense that genre-based units of study also have a familiar pattern. Early in a unit, we help students live the kind of life that writers of this genre are apt to live, collecting the sorts of entries helpful to this kind of writing. While living the life of this sort of writer, students also read texts that resemble those they aspire to write so that a bit later in the unit, they can begin to sketch or chart or outline a plan for their own first draft. Eventually, the emphasis of our teaching and our students' work shifts toward revising texts. Now students will revisit the texts they immersed themselves in earlier, only this time they'll admire and study them, asking, "What has this mentor author done that I could try?"

When I was a little girl, I often pretended to be a character from one of the novels or short stories my parents or grandparents had read out loud to me. I explored the backs of the wardrobes in my grandparents' house, hoping to find another Narnia inside them, just like in The Lion, the Witch and the Wardrobe. *For a while, I acted just like Pippi Longstocking, producing a great deal more bravado than I actually felt inside, but I was trying her character on for size—yearning to live a life as full of adventure as Pippi's.*

Characters are the heart and soul of fiction. Without strong characters, fiction falls apart—it becomes merely a reporting of events. Readers don't care what happens in the story unless we care about the character, and what makes us care is being able to see a flesh-and-blood character who shares thoughts and emotions similar to their own.

This final revision session, then, aims to help children flesh out their characters by make reading-writing connections. The session could invite students to consider any one of a zillion different aspects of character development in particular and well-written narratives in general, and hopefully it will serve you as a template for various other minilessons. For now, I've chosen to address an especially critical quality of character development and good writing. This session aims to help children more deeply understand the adage "show, don't tell" by applying it to character portrayal.

MINILESSON

Using Mentor Texts to Flesh Out Characters

CONNECTION

Remind children of the lessons from the previous session and connect them to today's work. In this case, remind students that revision starts with rereading through a lens.

"Writers, you have learned that revision begins with literally re-visioning, reseeing our own text, and that we do so by reading through a lens, asking particular questions. We can reread our draft asking, 'What sense will a stranger make of this?' Sometimes when we do that, we realize that our story is a lot of 'he saids' and 'she saids'—that it almost seems to float, without being grounded in the specific world of the story."

Remind students that they can go to texts they love to figure out what the authors have done and then apply that to their own writing.

"Today I want to be sure you realize that there is a place that we, as writers, can go to get new glasses—new lenses—with which to view our drafts. And this is the place: We can go to stories that resemble the ones we hope to write. We can let specific parts (or aspects) of a story matter to us. We can feel the lump in our throat, or see ourselves pull in close at a favorite part, or sense ourselves getting hooked by the story. Then we can ask, 'What did this author do that seems to work so well?' And we can reread our own draft, asking, 'Are there places in my draft where I could use that same technique?' And then, reseeing can lead us to rewriting."

TEACHING

Explain that all writers read, first to be open to the power of the story, and later to learn how writing is made. Demonstrate this with a text that is important to you.

"Most writers—writers like Walter Dean Myers and Eve Bunting and Eloise Greenfield—don't have a daily schedule with time in each day set aside for instruction in writing. But authors know that they can make their own writing workshop, and to do so they read. 'I learned how to write from writers,' Cynthia Rylant says. 'I didn't know any personally, but I read.'"

"If we want to learn from another writer, we first need to open ourselves to that author's story. Then, once we let a story get through to us, we stop and say, 'Why am I crying?' or 'Why is my heart ready to burst?' and we ask, 'What has the author done that makes this part of the story so powerful for me?'"

"I've been rereading *Pippi Goes on Board*, a book that was incredibly important to me as a child; I've been remembering that Pippi was a hero to me. She had such bravado, such strength. Now, rereading this book, I find myself gasping at the power of even seemingly ordinary sections. For example, last night I read about how Pippi walked to town. That was it. Nothing great happened in the story. But for some reason, this section of the story really got to me. So I reread it, asking, 'What has Astrid Lindgren done in her story that makes it so powerful?' Listen to it and see what *you* think."

> A few minutes later they were marching down the road to town—Tommy, Annika, and Pippi with Mr. Nilsson on her shoulder. The sun was shining so gloriously, the sky was so blue, and the children were so happy! And in the gutter along the roadside the water flowed merrily by. It was a very deep gutter with a great deal of water in it.
>
> "I love gutters," said Pippi and, without giving much thought to the matter, stepped into the water. It reached way over her knees, and as she skipped along briskly it splattered Tommy and Annika.
>
> "I'm making believe I'm a boat," she said, plowing through the water. Just as she spoke she stumbled and went down under.
>
> "Or, to be more exact, a submarine," she continued calmly when she got her nose in the air again.
>
> "Oh, Pippi, you're absolutely soaked," said Annika anxiously.
>
> "And what's wrong with that?" asked Pippi. "Is there a law that children should always be dry? I've heard it said that cold showers are very good for the health."

"I realized that Astrid Lindgren didn't just *say* what Pippi did—that Pippi walked down the street en route to town. She *showed* Pippi doing this, and did so in a way that put a Pippi-like imprint on the experience. Pippi didn't walk to town in the same way that you and I might. She walked in her own uniquely adventurous way."

Demonstrate applying the technique you've noted from the mentor text to your own writing. Debrief.

"So class, after I notice something that an author I admire has done, I think to myself, 'Are there places in my draft where I could use the same technique?' So let me reread our Luz story and see if I can not only tell what Luz does, but show how she does that thing— and in so doing, convey what she's like as a person."

Notice that we do not approach a text looking for examples of literary devices. We read with receptivity, letting ourselves be blown away by the story. Only later, after weeping, gasping, laughing, do we pause to think, "What did the author do to create such an effect?"

Jane Burroway reminds us, "Your fiction can only be as successful as the characters who move it and move within it . . . we must find them interesting, we must find them believable, and we must care about what happens to them." (Writing Fiction, p. 100)

Lots of people grow up believing that they don't have what it takes to be a writer. "Writers," they think, "have very special talents." In a writing workshop, we try to help children realize that in fact, the skills and talents writers draw upon are available to all of us. In this minilesson, I essentially say that we can learn how to be great from the books around us. I intend this to be a powerful, lifelong lesson. In this way, I try to lure all the children into believing that becoming a great writer is possible for them.

I quickly reread the story and circled a section that described Luz trying to fall asleep at the slumber party. "I think I could write this in more detail, and this time really show Luz's fears—and show her, too," I said. I wrote:

> I pulled my sleeping bag as high as it would go without covering my nose. I heard a strange noise by the window and imagined big hairy beasts slamming though the front door, grabbing us up in our sleeping bags and carrying us away. I squeezed my eyes shut, so tightly I could see stars. "Don't think about those things," I said to myself.

"Do you see how I used some actions by Luz to show more about what she's like? That's what Astrid did with her character Pippi, and so that's what I tried to do."

ACTIVE ENGAGEMENT

Ask children to use the text you offer as a mentor text, studying an excerpt for what they might try. Ask them to discuss with their partner ways to apply what they discover to the class story.

"Now let's try to do this whole process together. We've talked about how you love this section of *Fireflies!* when the narrator traipses off to bed, his jar of fireflies in hand. Tell your partner what Brinckloe has done here that works so well that you could, conceivably, try doing in your writing."

> Daddy called from the hallway,
>
> "See you later, alligator."
>
> "After a while, crocodile," I called back.
>
> "I caught hundreds of fireflies—"

I listened as children talked to teach other, and then convened the class.

Henry said, "The author uses the real words that kids say, so the story sounds true."

"So let's look back at this section of our Luz story, and could you and your partner think together about whether *Fireflies!* gives you ideas for how you could revise our story:

> The doorbell rang. "Welcome, come in," Luz said. Soon the room was filled with girls.

Before long, this section had been revised:

> The doorbell rang. "Hey!" Luz said jumping aside in a gesture that said, "Come in!" Then Luz added, "Pizzas comin', lots of them."

My apprenticeship in this instance is very open-ended, and you may decide to be much more explicit about the way in which a writer can emulate another text. For example, you may decide to teach children to copy sentences they love from the mentor text, to name what specifically they love about a particular sentence and then to emulate that quality.

If you feel it's likely your students can't yet follow this process easily, you might lengthen the active engagement section of this minilesson to include charting together the steps writers need to take to learn from mentor authors. The chart would end up something like this:

Studying Mentor Texts for Our Own Writing
- *Select a part of the story that works for you.*
- *Name specifically what the author did on the page.*
- *Suppose why the author did this particular thing.*
- *Look at your own writing and find places where it would help the text to try something similar.*
- *Try it!*

LINK

Remind the children of all their options for revision today and anytime they revise. Remind them they can always turn to mentor texts to discover ways to revise.

"So writers, you already know that for the next few days, you'll shift between writing scenes of your story and revising scenes. If you want to revise, you can definitely reread with the lens of 'Does my story make sense?' You may notice, as we discussed yesterday, that some scenes seem to float—in which case, be sure to detail who is talking, where the person is, and what the person does. And you may decide to find another lens for revisioning your draft. You can learn ways to resee your draft if you find a text you admire, notice a section of the text that seems to work especially well, and then ask yourself, 'What did this author do that I could try?'"

WRITING AND CONFERRING

Helping Struggling Readers

When you confer today, you'll probably check in with your struggling writers first to be sure that each one has a mentor text in hand that he or she can read. You may feel tempted to leave the child with a text that the student "knows by heart" but the truth is that you're asking children to reread and examine the wording an author has used, and this is challenging enough when we can read the text.

Mel Levine says: "Writing is the largest orchestra a kid's mind has to conduct" (*The Myth of Laziness,* p. 7). There are enough things for a struggling student to contend with when writing—reading should not be one of them.

Once you've made sure that each of your strugglers has a mentor text he or she can read, you'll want to coach the child to notice something admirable in the mentor text. Help the child do so by taking any paragraph at all, and then thinking, "What do I like in this passage?" It doesn't help to scan the whole text, over and over, looking for a noteworthy feature. Zooming in early on makes it more likely the child will notice craftsmanship. Help the child to talk about what the author has done. Then show the child that he or she could take that same technique and apply it to his or her own writing. You'll probably want to demonstrate this, saying, "I could imagine your story might go like this . . . " You may want to give two or three examples of the way the child could use that one technique in a variety of ways.

Of course, you'll also want to confer with your stronger writers. Resist the urge to only go to the students who need us the most and leave the more sophisticated writers alone, rationalizing that they know about writing. The truth is, even professional writers rely on the advice and suggestions of their editors to help them develop their work. It is crucial that we offer our strong writers opportunities to develop their skills as individuals.

We can offset the concern that we'll have nothing to teach our skilled writers by taking time to plan some possible teaching points.

MID-WORKSHOP TEACHING POINT   *Naming an Author's Techniques*   "Writers, today we reminded ourselves that we can take courses from any writer, living or dead, as long as we are willing to really study what that author has done. We studied the way the father and son in *Fireflies*! said good night to each other—'See you later, alligator. After a while, crocodile.' But we didn't say, 'We liked the way Brinckloe's characters said good night to each other' and we didn't have Luz turn off the light and say to her friends, 'See you later, alligator.' Instead, we named our observations, saying, 'The author uses words that people actually say to make the story sound true.'"

"But some of you have been telling me that you didn't really get how to do this. Let me try to help you. First I explain to myself what an author has done. Let's use Brinckloe's description of the dying fireflies in the jar."

And the light grew dimmer, green, like moonlight under water.

"Then I try to talk about what I notice she actually did. (I don't say how it worked: 'I can picture it.') I say what she has done."

continued on next page

Colleen pulled up a seat next to Hannah, curious to know how Hannah was doing with her character who was only five years old—the same age as Hannah's little brother.

Hannah explained that she had changed the character to a little girl, "Angelina," so her story would be fiction. "Now I won't be tempted to copy my little brother," she said.

"Hannah, it's brave of you to choose a character who is five years old, and I'm glad you are drawing on what you know from your brother. And that you are taking the risk of writing about a character who is a bit different from you. Good writers are risk-takers—but then, you knew that right?"

Hannah nodded, clearly pleased by her teacher's support.

"I want to let you in on something. Lots of fiction writers say that every character in a story contains a bit of the writer. Even though I'm not like Luz, because I'm grown-up and I'm not having slumber parties anymore, I still know

> continued from previous page
>
> "She wrote one sentence that has three parts to it. The first part tells what the light did (it grew dimmer), then the next phrase describes it (green), and the final phrase compares it to something else (like moonlight under water)."
>
> "Then, I try to figure out why she wrote like that. I think Brinckloe probably wanted to tell what happened, then to show how it happened. Now, having spelled out what the author did, I can try it in my own draft. So right now, reread a mentor text that matters to you, and follow these same steps. For me, I'd tell what something did, then I'd describe it, then I'd compare it to something else. Do this with your own text now, with your partner's help."

what it's like to want to fit in with other people. And I also know what it's like to be afraid. I can take those parts of myself and let them help me as I work on my character so that she becomes even more believable—more real—because she has bits of me inside her. Do you think there's a way you can do some of that work?"

Hannah's whole face lit up, "Well yeah. I'm already thinking of my brother to get ideas of what a five-year-old does and thinks. And my brother is kind of a part of me. But I can also think about what *I* was like when I was five. Like, I loved art and sometimes I would get in trouble for getting into things I shouldn't have gotten into, and I could never figure out what the big deal was. I could make Angelina a little like that too." Hannah started to jot some things down right away.

SHARE

Highlighting Revision

Share examples of actions revealing emotions. Remind writers they can do this in their own writing.

"Writers, this morning, as I was waiting for you to line up in the yard, I took a few minutes to watch the kindergartners lining up. I noticed they line up differently than you. First of all, most of them weren't talking. Yet I could still sort of tell how they were feeling. One little girl fell on the ground, then started rubbing her knee. At first she didn't cry, but then all of a sudden her lip started to tremble and a big fat tear rolled down her cheek. I could tell she was kind of surprised that her knee hurt. Then I noticed a little boy who was clutching a teddy bear to his chest. He couldn't stand still. He kept smiling and hopping up and down. I could tell he was really excited. I didn't need to hear their words to guess how they were feeling. Just by watching their actions and gestures, I could tell their feelings."

"I'm telling you this because it is really important, when you write, to use actions to show your character's feelings. Let me share with you some smart work I saw Leo do today. He studied *Fireflies!* and he noticed this section of it:"

> I tried to swallow,
> but something in my throat would not go down.
> I shut my eyes tight and put the pillow over my head.
> They were my fireflies.

"He decided that Brinckloe used actions to show feelings: the character tried to swallow, he put a pillow over his head. So, Leo made a little tiny scene at the start of his own story, and had his character do an action that showed her feeling of loneliness. You can do this too! Listen:" [Fig. XIII-1]

> Alicia was a nobody. She had no friends and always sat in the corner. She was always seen walking home from school alone. None of the kids in her fourth grade class cared if she was there or not.
>
> Each night Alicia thought about friends. She dreamed about them too. One night Alicia looked out the window and saw a beautiful starry sky. She had been thinking about Tatiana, Alicia's dream friend. Alicia looked up and saw a star shoot across the night sky.
>
> Alicia made a wish, "I wish I had a friend."

> Alicia was a nobody. She had no friends and always sat in the corner. She was always seen walking home from school alone. None of the kids in her fourth grade class cared if she was there or not.
>
> Each night Alicia thought about friends. She dreamed about them too. One night Alicia looked out the window and saw a beautiful starry sky. She had been thinking about Tatiana, Alicia's dream friend. Alicia looked up and saw a star shoot across the night sky.
>
> Alicia made a wish, "I wish I had a friend."

Fig. XIII-1 Leo's notebook entry

HOMEWORK *Naming Our Stories* "Writers, have you ever named someone? A brother or sister? A pet? It is an amazing responsibility. Tonight, it is time for you to consider names for your story. List ten titles, considering the significance of each. Your title, like *Charlotte's Web,* might have a double meaning. *Charlotte's Web* is a book about a spider who weaves a web, but we know that webs are also seen as things that are very craftily made—like the way that Charlotte craftily saves Wilbur's life. And *Because of Winn-Dixie* has one of the main character's names in it, but it also tells us something about the book. Things happen to Opal because Winn-Dixie is in her life.

Tonight, I want you to spend some time thinking about your favorite titles for books, then try to figure out why you think the authors chose them. After you've done that, don't just slap the first title that comes to mind on your story. Jot down a list of titles, then choose the one that you think really connects to some big ideas you have in your story, one that will really catch a reader's interest.

TAILORING YOUR TEACHING

If your students characters simply aren't fleshed out much yet . . . you might try simply letting them have more time to focus on their characters. You might start a minilesson with the purposes of allowing students more time to focus on their characters something like this: "The other day, I told you about a story—*Pippi Longstocking*—that really mattered to me when I was a child. And the reason the story mattered was that the character Pippi mattered. You and I can listen to the news and hear about all sorts of bad things happening to people, and we don't usually find ourselves reduced to tears. But in the stories we really love, when bad things happen to the character, we find ourselves totally devastated—almost as if these things were happening to us. When we know a lot about a person or character, even if we've never met him or her, they matter to us. Have you let your readers know enough about your characters so that the reader can really care about them? Writers do that. Today, would you reread your story, and find ways to let your character shine through even more? If your character walks down the street, ask yourself, 'How can she—or he—so this in a way that shows who she is as a person?' Then try some revisions."

Naming characters is no small project for some writers! Colleen once wrote a list seventy-five titles long to find the perfect name for her own book. You might find, as Colleen did, that students will still need input from other writers to help narrow down the options and commit to a final title.

COLLABORATING WITH COLLEAGUES

As you and your colleagues help children find ways to create memorable characters, you might want to consider some of the less obvious or direct ways in which this can be done. For example, you might think about how writers reveal things through characters' observations of other characters, or of places or things.

You'll notice that many of the stories you've read with your students include animals, and that the animals often have profound effects on the characters. In "Spaghetti," for example, the kitten Gabriel finds brings Gabriel out of his isolation and loneliness. Gabriel feels an immediate connection with the kitten. His observations of it tell us a great deal about who Gabriel is and how his experiences have shaped him.

When Gabriel sees the kitten, he notices its "skinny stick-legs, wobbling to and fro." Gabriel doesn't see an infected animal, or think the kitten is pathetic or ugly or something to avoid. He sees an animal that is small, weak, and underfed. We know that Gabriel lives in a run-down building and that he doesn't have much to eat himself (recall that he thinks about his "butter sandwich"), so we can surmise he is poor. It's not surprising, then, that he would notice the kitten's thin legs and its wobbly state. Gabriel is someone who notices other creatures' needs and can empathize. It's telling, too, that Gabriel thinks the kitten smells like noodles—a pleasant, comforting smell. Later Rylant writes that "Gabriel was amazed. He had never imagined he would be lucky enough one day to find a kitten." Gabriel can't imagine his good fortune. How could he have been so lucky? Someone who has had more in life than Gabriel might not consider this kitten such an extraordinary find. Gabriel's amazement reveals

how much he wants to be needed, to have something to love, to find a friend. Gabriel isn't used to having much of anything at all.

As we see the kitten through Gabriel's eyes, we learn volumes about Gabriel himself. We see not only how Gabriel's life and experiences have shaped him, but also what he longs for and how he comes out of his shell. It would be interesting to have students think about how they would describe a kitten they saw in the middle of the road. They also might think about how Cynthia Rylant might have added to Gabriel's observations of the kitten—how the kitten might have triggered memories that would reveal details about Gabriel's backstory, or his dreams. Have kids imagine things authors can show about characters through their observations.

To help children understand how description reveals character, you might find it useful to have them do exercises in which they observe a place or an object through different eyes. For example, one teacher I know tells her students to imagine a barn and then to describe the barn as if they're one person (someone from the city) and then as if they're someone else (a person seeking shelter) and then someone altogether different. She says to children, "Look at the barn. Imagine you're an angry farmer. What do you see? What do you notice?" You could also try an exercise that focuses on objects. Picture the same people who were looking at the barn now holding something in their hands instead. What are they holding and how does this object reflect who they are? Or what thoughts do they have about the object? How do the objects bring these characters to life? You'll want children to imagine all sorts of ways they might reveal their characters without directly describing them.

EDITING WITH VARIOUS LENSES

In this session, as in other editing sessions, you will remind your children of all the editing skills you have already taught including paragraphing, use of end punctuation and capital letters, use of quotation marks, use of tenses, use of high frequency words, use of common irregular verbs and so forth. Now you will add onto that list, with the new skills joining the others on a cumulative editing chart that remains posted in your classroom year-round. As the list grows, so do your children's abilities to effectively and independently edit their work.

Fiction stories pose special editing challenges. The stories tend to be long, which means that editing and recopying will take more than a day. The children will be chomping at the bit to share these stories, and the fact that their author celebration can't occur until they've edited and recopied will frustrate some of them. For you, the trick will be to show children that just as you earlier taught them revision is a way to honor their best efforts, so, too, editing is also a way to celebrate a text.

The second major challenge that children usually face when editing these stories is that the excitement of writing fiction will have inspired them to use more sophisticated vocabulary than they might normally use, and their stories will be chock full of invented spellings. Fixing every misspelled word can feel like an impossible task. You will need to remind students of all the resources they already have in their "spelling toolboxes" as well as teaching them some strategies they can use to figure out correct spellings on their own. You might have already taught your class some of these strategies in your Word Study curriculum. If this is the case, all the better!

In this session, you will teach students how to edit their work by rereading with great care and thinking about everything they know about grammar and punctuation. You will ask them to think especially carefully about spelling, and you will teach them how to use the wealth of strategies and resources available to them.

IN THIS SESSION, YOU WILL EXPLAIN THAT JUST AS FICTION WRITERS REVISE WITH "LENSES," THEY EDIT WITH THEM AS WELL, REREADING THEIR WRITING SEVERAL TIMES FOR SEVERAL REASONS, MAKING EDITS AS THEY GO.

GETTING READY

- Passage from the class story you can use to demonstrate rethinking word choice
- See CD-ROM for resources

MINILESSON

Editing with Various Lenses

CONNECTION

Remind children that editing involves bringing all that the writer knows and is able to do to the draft. Tell students they will be rereading carefully, and relying on class editing lists, on resources such as dictionaries, and on each other as they seek to correct and clean up their drafts.

"You've all worked hard and should be so proud of yourselves. I know you are as excited as I am to share your stories with the rest of our community. But, before we do that, there is important work ahead. We still need to edit these stories so that not only the ideas and craft of the stories, but also the spelling, punctuation, and grammar of them will all reflect the best that you can do."

"Remember, as you prepare to edit your stories, that a writer calls to mind everything that he or she knows about spelling, punctuation, and grammar—you can recall those tools and mentally lay them out for yourself even before you reread, rather like a carpenter lays out the necessary tools as a way to prepare for his work. Keep these tools in mind as you reread your story. While you reread, be especially on the lookout for misspelled words because I know that many of you pushed yourselves to reach for the precisely right word as you wrote and that this led you to write with words you haven't tackled before. You were inventive spellers in this unit of study and that's been great to see—but you will want to be sure you spell conventionally before you bring your stories to the world."

"Remember that when we want to fix up our spelling, we rely not only on the strategies we have for effective spelling but also on resources that are outside ourselves in order to be sure our spellings are accurate. In specific, we rely on distant teachers—the authors of written materials—and on nearby teachers—the writers in our community—to help us go beyond what we can do on our own."

COACHING

As you teach this minilesson, you will want to have the cumulative chart of all that the class has learned thus far in the year close by you as you teach. That chart will contain skills you have taught during word study time as well as the writing workshop, and of course it will be a very different chart for third graders than for fifth graders, and for more inexperienced writers than for children who have grown up in a writing workshop.

Name your teaching point, Specifically, tell children that when rereading their drafts, if they find misspelled words they should circle these, and then try them again. Teach them strategies for progressing from a spelling that is invented to a spelling that is conventional.

"Today I am going to teach you, (actually, I will be reminding rather than teaching you), that before or after you edit your draft for other concerns—paragraphing, punctuation and so forth—you will want to read your draft, checking on your spellings. Usually this means eyeing each word and thinking, 'Does this look right?' It also means rereading the letters in each word to double-check that those letters actually do spell the word you have in mind. When a writer is uncertain whether a word is correctly spelled, we generally mark that word (in this class, circle it) and then we try spelling the word again and again, drawing on all we know and on all the help we can locate to assist us with those spellings. I will show you how to go through this progression of work."

TEACHING

Referring to the good work one child has just done, emphasize that writers reread a draft many times, checking for first one sort of editing concern, then for another. Include in your summary of the work one child has already done an overview of how you hope children go about checking for punctuation and tense and consistency.

"Deveonna finished drafting and revising her story yesterday and without my saying anything to her at all, she began editing it. She did something really smart that I want to remind all of you to do. She reread her draft, looking first for one 'kind of thing,' and then she reread it, looking for another 'kind of thing.' Each writer will proceed in a different sequence, but none of us can simply reread our draft once, fixing everything we want to fix! We all need to do as Deveonna did, and reread it multiple times."

"Deveonna read her draft first for punctuation and capital letters. She read it aloud to herself, adding in any periods that she'd missed. Like the rest of you, she didn't have a lot of trouble with end punctuation—she mostly adds periods when she drafts. But because Deveonna had tried to write this story in a way which built up tension and created suspense, she'd written with some sentences that required pretty complicated punctuation, so in this draft, she included ellipses, parentheses, and lots of sentences that used commas in complicated ways. If Deveonna *had* noticed that she hadn't used a variety of punctuation, she might have regarded that as a clue that she could use editing as a time to

It would have been very easy to simply say, "Today I will teach you how to edit your draft." The reason that this teaching point is long and clunky is that I try to do more than name the subject of the minilesson. I try to actually tell children the answer to the question—in this case, I try to tell them how to edit their drafts—so that this section of the minilesson crystallizes the most important message of the session.

When the children write fiction, we teach them that after they come up with a gigantic sequence of events, they need to decide which of those events will be backstory. Which will happen before the opening scene actually plays out? So in Because of Winn-Dixie, for example, while Opal shops for tomatoes at the local grocery store, the reader learns that she has already suffered the loss of her mother, and she has already moved to this new Florida town. Similarly, when teaching a minilesson, we need to think of the entire sequence of work that we want to support and then we, too, can decide which part of that sequence of work will have happened off stage, and which part of it will be emphasized because it actually unfolds on stage in the minilesson. In this minilesson, I summarize what Deveonna has already done, hoping as I do so to lightly support children in doing similar work. The "story" actually begins with me demonstrating how Deveonna does the one thing I want to highlight now, which is checking for tenses and misspellings.

really listen to her sentences, combining some or tweaking others so they built up the drama of the story."

"After Deveonna checked for punctuation and capital letters, she decided to reread using a different lens. This time, she paid attention to her tenses. And again, she found that especially in the sections of her story where she really reached to write beautifully and well, she'd sometimes written in ways that shifted between past tense and present tense. Deveonna thought to herself, "I better be clear. Am I writing about something that is happening now, or about something that happened a while ago, like last year?" She decided she wanted the story to be in past tense, so watch and join me as I show you how she doubled-checked for tense consistency. Let's look at this section of her story. It tells that the protagonist, Elexa, hides behind a tree with her best friend, Lexi, hoping to hide from her stalker."[Fig. XIV-1]

> When I reach her, she puts her hand on her face, and shakes her head, then points behind me. I turn, and there was the most unwanted person ever . . . "Sir Stocker Max." On the inside, I could have made my head exploaded. I hide behind Lexie, as if I were a baby and she was mom that has to protect me.

"Deveonna reread the first sentence. 'This sounds like it is happening now: "When I reach her, she puts . . ." that is now. If I want this to be past tense, I better change it.'"

> When I reached her, Lexi put her hand on her face, and shakes her head . . . .

"Hmm . . . that sounds wrong. Did I just switch back out of past tense? Let me look . . . I did. I can fix that."

> When I reached her, Lexi put her hand on my face and shook her head, then pointed behind me . . . "Sir Stocker Max."

Describe and then demonstrate how the child reread, checking spellings. Highlight the fact that the writer tried the word in question several times, seeking outside resources after she'd drawn on her own resources.

"After rereading first for punctuation, then for tenses (checking that the action was either consistently in the past or consistently in the present tense), Deveonna paid special attention to spelling. She inched her way through the text, checking each and every word. When she came across a misspelled word that she knew, that was easy! She simply corrected it right then and there."

It is crucial for you to notice that I don't go through this student's entire draft. Why do so? I can make my point much more succinctly by focusing on just a tiny chunk of the text. Notice this is not the lead of the story: the lead didn't pose as many editing issues as did this excerpt. Notice also that in the summary of how Deveonna dealt with tenses, I taught briskly and incompletely. I can't go back and teach an entire hour-long session in which I define tenses, go through the fact that action words can be called verbs, show children that verbs change in past and present and future tenses and so forth. In order to write, children need to orchestrate a vast number of skills and strategies. There is absolutely no way to teach any one of those in enormous detail at one time in a minilesson. In order to maintain the full orchestration that comprises writing, we often teach incompletely, over-simplifying. Even if we decided to teach a subject fully and completely, children can only learn one or two increments at a time, so I think it is wise to resign oneself to the fact that we will revisit all that we teach over and over, month after month and certainly year after year, and each time our teaching can become a bit more complex.

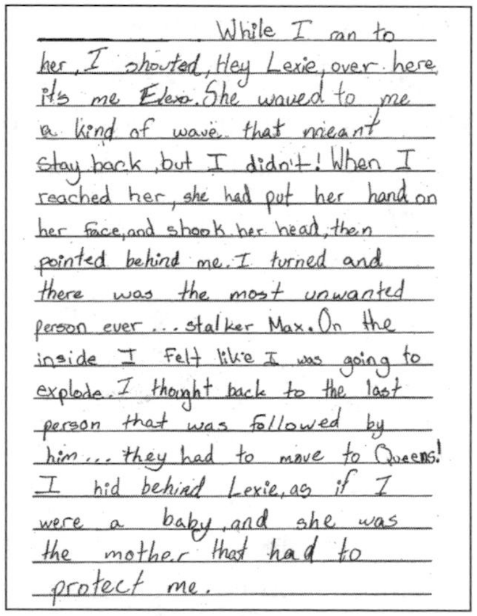

> While I ran to her, I shouted, Hey Lexie, over here it's me Elexa. She waved to me a kind of wave. that meant stay back, but I didn't! When I reached her, she had put her hand on her face, and shook her head, then pointed behind me. I turned and there was the most unwanted person ever . . . stalker Max. On the inside I felt like I was going to explode. I thought back to the last person that was followed by him . . . they had to move to Queens! I hid behind Lexie, as if I were a baby, and she was the mother that had to protect me.

Fig. XIV-1 Deveonna edits her tenses in the midst of her draft.

"But, since Deveonna is the kind of writer who pushes herself to use sophisticated language in her work, she also found words that she was not sure how to spell. For example, in this paragraph, she used some very specific, colorful words—'explode' and 'protect'—and she wasn't sure how to spell those. This is what she did, watch." I said and then circled those words. Then, I showed that Deveonna pulled out a sticky note tag and put one beside each of the troublesome words. Before having a second "go", with *protet*, I showed that Deveonna reread her first try at the word, thinking aloud to herself, "Is *part* of this right?" She copied the first syllable as she'd written it. Then I showed her saying the word again, hearing the sound she'd deleted (the *c* sound) and adding that into her new version of the word. "Does this look right now?" Deveonna asked herself, and when she thought yes, she copied the new spelling into her draft.

"After going through a similar sequence with the word, "explode," Deveonna was still not able to correct her misspelled version: *exploaded*. At that point, Deveonna asked herself whether she might be able to find that word written somewhere close at hand: perhaps on a chart in the classroom, a word list, in a story in her writing folder, or a reference book such as an atlas. Deveonna decided that she would be better off in this case asking her writing partner, who she knew was a strong speller, to help her fix up her spelling. With the help of her partner, she picked the version of the word that looked correct and made the change in her story."

Debrief, highlighting the replicable process one child demonstrated that you hope others follow.

"Did you see that first Deveonna reread for punctuation, then for keeping the action in her story consistently in the past tense or in the present tense. Then she reread for spelling and marked words that looked wrong, trying them again on the side. In order to try them again, she examined her initial spelling to ask, 'Is part of this right?' and copied that part. Then she tried the puzzling part first by listening again to be sure she'd represented all the sounds, then by thinking if there were class resourses that could easily help her, and finally by recruiting her partner to help. This is the sort of work each of you will want to do today and whenever you edit your writing."

Of course, this minilesson must be revised so that it teaches your kids whatever is most essential for them to know. It may be that if you teach third graders who struggle with spellings, you may decide to emphasize simply the fact that writers say words really slowly and try to listen to be sure they have recorded each of the major sounds they hear when articulating the word. A version of this could also teach that writers don't simply sound out the missing sections, they ask, "Do I know of other words which include that sound?" That is, you could tuck lessons in using what you know in order to spell what you do not know how to spell.

You may decide to ask your children to pull out their drafts and reread the first paragraph to check for punctuation, perhaps talking with each other about what they notice. Then they can reread for tenses, and again they could (or could not) talk about what they notice. You'd need to decide how to work your time so this process doesn't extend the length of the minilesson. Sometimes when teachers ask children to get started on the work of the day while they are still sitting in the meeting area, the teachers decides to bypass the link and to simply gesture to one child, then another, to move to his or her seat, continuing the work in that place.

ACTIVE ENGAGEMENT

Set students up to follow the model you have given them, editing the next paragraph of the child's story.

"Now, you're going to assume the role of editor. With your partner, could you read the next section of Deveonna's story?" I said, passing out copies of just the next paragraph. Read it once, checking for and fixing punctuation. Then read it again, checking for and fixing tenses, then put on your 'check-for-spelling' lenses. If you find a misspelled word that you can't fix immediately, have a go on the side of the page, spelling the word several possible ways. Remember that you can use resources outside yourselves, such as other writers in our community:"

> He comes even closer. Lexie whispers "oh, no." then I shout "RUN!" That's when we heard the bell, "dinnnggg." We tried to run as fast as we can, but being so populur we don't run a lot but we try. We rush for the door, trying to slip into class without being noticed by a hall monitor or a teacher.

"Writers, as I talked to some of you about your editing work on this section, I heard many of you say that you had found places where you could fix punctuation and grammar, such as changing the verbs to past tense and capitalizing the *t* in *then*. Many of you are also thinking especially hard about spelling."

LINK

Recall what you have taught and send children off to edit their own work.

"Writers, as you edit your fiction stories or any other piece of writing, remember that all of us, as writers, take editing very seriously. We generally reread our writing once, twice, three times, and often we make a decision, saying, 'This time I will read with this lens,' or 'This time I will rereads with that lens.' I have emphasized rereading for punctuation, tenses and spelling, but you may know that you need to reread and think about characters, or about being sure your draft makes sense. You are in charge of your own writing, and the real goal is to make sure that every word, every dot, is the best that it can be."

I hope you notice Deveonna's understanding of the ways being popular constrains the behavior of her protagonist. Elexa and Lexie are popular. "We tried to run as fast as we could, but being popular, we don't run a lot . . . ." You will need to decide when you want to open up some of the social issues that these stories will bring to light. I don't suggest you use this minilesson as a time to embark on a big discussion of Deveonna's understanding of what popular kids need to do in order to maintain their status. But you may well want to make an aside at some point, saying something like, "How sad that this character lives in a community of kids where kids feel that being liked by other kids is such a fragile thing that by merely running, a person jeopardizes her social status!"

> He came closer! Lexie whispered, "OH, NO," then I shouted, "RUN!" We tryed to run as fast as we could, but we knew that wasn't fast. We rush for the door, trying to slip into class without being noticed by a teacher or just a hall monater.

Fig. XIV-2 Deveonna edited her story based on input from her peers.

WRITING AND CONFERRING

Making Editing Choices

"Writers, I gathered this group because I think that as you reread your story, you will find that you are not using a variety of punctuation marks. If almost every sentence of yours ends with a period and if you do not use parentheses, ellipses, colons or semi-colons, these are signs that your sentences plod along a bit. This is also a sign that there is one, fairly easy thing you can do to make your writing a whole lot better! Right now, I can show you how you can become writers who use a variety of punctuation marks, and the important thing about this is that writers who use a variety of punctuation marks are also writers with a more elastic sense for how sentences and paragraphs of print can create mood, tone, rhythm, and feelings."

"So take just a minute, and make a list of the punctuation you have already used in your story. See if I'm right when I said that I think that you've used mostly two or three forms of punctuation." The children did this, and concurred. "This means your writing can get better really easily. Writing with only a few kinds of punctuation is a bit like writing with half the alphabet!"

"Try revising your sentences—not toward the goal of using more punctuation because I don't think any writer on earth has ever sat down with the goal of writing with three semi-colons and an ellipsis! But try revising your sentence so that when people read your sentences, they'll be swept along in the feelings you want them to experience." Then, to demonstrate what I mean by this sort of sentence, I deliberately used one, gesturing with my hand at the places in my very long, oral sentence where the commas might go. "Try writing with a more elastic sense for how sentences can go, so that some of your sentences are long ones, with parts that pile up, one on top of the next, phrase after phrase, as you hear in this sentence of mine."

MID-WORKSHOP
TEACHING POINT

Editing with Attentiveness ""Writers, can I stop you? I really, really need your attention. All eyes up here, all minds up here."

I waited an extra-long time. "Writers, right now, I have your attention. You are listening keenly, attentively, with your minds turned onto high. What I want to tell you is this: this is the sort of keen attentiveness you need to bring to the job of editing. I know this will sound unbelievable to you, but I have actually seen some people leaning back in their chairs, editing like this", I said, and role played a lackadaisical, sloppy editor. The word editing should bring to mind a person who is sitting up, pencils sharpened, with extra-keen eyesight, eager to catch each and every little item."

"In order to edit well, then, you need to have checklists at your side to remind you of details that deserve your attention. But you need your own personalized checklist for the ways of acting that can help you shift from playing the part of writer to playing the part of editor. Usually people use a special pen to edit. Usually people sit at a desk to edit. Often people read aloud (either actually, or in our minds) in order to edit. This can force us to really see and register each and every word. You need to devise your own personalized checklist for what you need to do in order to remake yourself from being the passionate writer who writes with great fervor toward being the meticulous, attentive editor who doesn't let anything go by, unchecked."

At this point my voice abruptly switched so I could demonstrate the opposite kind of sentences. "Try the opposite. Try making curt, brief points. Say what you mean. Be blunt. But then, turn a corner in your thinking, and suddenly let your sentences be large rambling ones once again, with ideas that link together, building off each other, expanding on earlier bits."

"Just to practice writing with sentences that convey your mood, would you right now imagine that you are running, running, through the school. Partner 2 [I reappointed people into these roles] say a long, rambling sentence to your partner, showing what you pass by as you run, how your body is feeling as you get more tired. Start, 'I ran out the door' . . . (keep going)."

"Now, just to practice writing in abrupt sentences, partner 1, would you be the principal who catches the runner. Tell the runner to stop. Order the runner to do one thing. Then order the runner to do another thing. Show your anger. But do so in very short, abrupt sentences. Partner 1, start by saying, "Stop . . . ."

After the writers did that, I said, "Right now would you look at your draft of a story and see if there is one place where the sentences should push readers to read faster and faster, in a piling up, expansive, warm (or frantic) kind of way. Mark that section with a marginal note: long sentences with commas and parenthesis. Then read your draft over and see if there is one place where the sentence structure should signal that this section is abrupt. Brief. Cold. Mark that section with a marginal note: Short sentences. Perhaps ellipses. Perhaps colons before a list."

"Once you have marked sections of your draft where you could revise your sentence structure, would you go back and write in the air with your partner, each of you taking a turn writing an oral version of each person's draft. Then see if you can get a small sheet of paper, rewrite the section on it, and tape it right on top of the original draft. Make sure the flap can lift up so I can later admire this important editing work."

"If you'd like a mentor test, use a copy of this draft of Ari's. In her editing she's made use of every conceivable punctuation mark—to strong effect! Listen to this:"*[Fig. XIV-3]*

> The next day, I was ready. Of course it was 5:07; the family had just sat down to dinner. I looked at them, both of them, squarely in the eyes. My palms sweat; my hand bounced; my pulse kicked into turbo drive.
>
> "Dear," my mom started, looking guiltily at me.
>
> "Yeah?" I said, looking up from the takeout Chinese food. "We . . . have to tell you something," said Dad, exchanging glances with Mom. I propped my head on my hand.

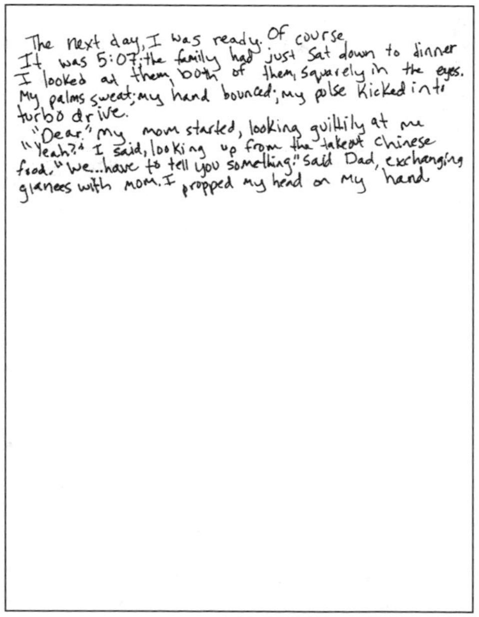
The next day, I was ready. Of course
It was 5:07; the family had just Sat down to dinner
I looked at them, both of them, squarely in the eyes.
My palms sweat; my hand bounced; my pulse kicked into
turbo drive.
"Dear," my mom started, looking guiltily at me
"Yeah?" I said, looking up from the takeout Chinese
food. "We...have to tell you something," said Dad, exchanging
glances with mom. I propped my head on my hand.

Fig. XIV-3 Ari uses a variety of punctuation to strong effect.

SHARE

Working with a Partner

Ask children to share their work with a partner, asking for particular editing feedback, as writers do.

"We writers know that even after we've done our most careful editing, there can still be some mistakes in our stories. Sometimes we miss mistakes because we ourselves don't know exactly how to spell or punctuate properly and sometimes we miss mistakes because we just get so used to reading our own writing that we have a hard time seeing our errors. Every piece of writing needs fresh eyes. Remember that your writing partners can provide those fresh eyes for your story. In addition to helping you with accurate spelling, your partners can help you effectively edit your story for sense, punctuation, and grammar. So, let your partner provide you with a fresh pair of eyes. Partner 2, will you reread and edit partner 1's writing? As you do this, remember that the writer is the ultimate decision maker, and if someone else writes on our drafts, they do so lightly and respectfully, in pencil not pen!"

HOMEWORK *Creating an "About the Author" Paragraph*   Since we're almost done with our stories, I realized that we can start thinking a little about how we want our pieces to be published. I know one thing many published stories have is an "About the Author" paragraph. It's the place readers can learn more information about the writer. There's usually a picture of the writer and a few facts about the writer's life—where she lives, whom she lives with, any hobbies she has. That sort of thing.

Tonight, I'd like you to work on your "About the Author." Find a picture of yourself. Maybe a grown-up will let you have one. Or, better yet, you can draw one. Then write a small paragraph about you, including the things you think your readers will want to know. If you're not sure what to include, read a few examples and see what those authors say and how they say it. One thing you're going to notice right away is that almost all of the "About the Authors" are written in third person.

If your children get caught up in the story every time they read and have a hard time reading with an eye toward editing . . . you might decide to teach them that writers at the editing stage of their writing process often go through their daily life thinking hard about grammatical structure choices, word choices, punctuation choices and paragraph choices. You might ask children to try living their daily life thinking about editing, and collecting ways they might make their own work stronger.

One way to help children learn about editing from their daily life is to direct them to replay a conversation they've had or heard that embodies the tone they are trying to create in their writing, in a particular place. Where were (and how long were) the pauses in that conversation? How could we recreate those kind of pauses in punctuation? What particular kinds of words did the speakers use? How could we find that kind of word to fit with our topics to help give us that same feel? How could we help create the tenor and urgency of that conversation with our own written words?

Of course, this same kind of thinking could be applied to any bit of text that holds the right tone, not just an overheard conversation. Does the marketing copy of a catalog hold just the right slick, overbearing tone your character uses to convince her mother to buy her an over priced tea set? Does the lead paragraph of the day's news story have just the right flat, unemotional tone the character in your story uses to tell her friend she doesn't care about her any more? What is it about each of these kinds of texts we encounter throughout the day that we can use for our own writing? Children might write in the margins of their drafts the tones they are aiming for, think of some common texts that might carry these tones, and then study them, seeing what from those texts could be imported into their own work to help create the same tone, then trying it.

COLLABORATING WITH COLLEAGUES

While the children are working on editing their stories, you and your colleagues will, no doubt, be busily preparing for your upcoming units of study. I hope that you have allowed yourselves time enough to teach a unit of study on poetry and another one or two on topics of your own choosing. You will want to reread the chapter I wrote on "Creating Your Own Units of Study" in *A Guide to the Writing Workshop.*

If your upcoming unit of study is on poetry, which I suspect will be your decision, I suggest you start by talking together about some of the over-arching decisions you need to make. First of all, you will want to decide whether you will put a different spin on poetry in third grade, in fourth grade, and in fifth grade. That's what I'd recommend. The children will absolutely benefit from having opportunities to revisit a genre year after year, but you will want them to feel as if there are lots of ways in which each year's unit of study opens new horizons.

You may decide, for example, that in third grade your unit of study on poetry will emphasize revision and reading-writing connections. Then in fourth grade, the unit could incorporate revision and reading-writing connections, but perhaps this time, children will especially attend to the contribution literary devices can make to a poem. And finally, in fifth grade, perhaps the unit will spotlight the importance of metaphoric thinking, with children learning that even their use of white space, can, in a sense, be regarded as metaphoric. Of course, the list I just made is fairly arbitrary (though I did try to build in rising complexity.) You and your colleagues will want to think about poetry across the years.

Then, too, you will want to think about the fact that I haven't written a book in which I share the minilessons we give to children when we teach

poetry. This was a deliberate choice. I know that you and your colleagues will need to develop lots of units of study in order to support your children's learning journey across all the years of upper-elementary school, and it makes lots of sense for you to do this first with poetry because there are so many wonderful resources available to help you. If your children didn't study during the K-2 grades with teachers who were relying on the primary set of Units of Study books, then they will never have had the chance to experience the poetry unit that Stephanie Parsons and I laid out for them. That book was the final one in our series, and the most sophisticated. As I wrote it, I was pretty clear that I could rely on that book to guide my teaching of college students as well as first graders, so I know it can be a resource to you.

Then, too, there are all the wonderful books that Georgia Heard has written. Georgia was one of the very first members of the Teachers College Reading and Writing Project's initial team, and she has continued to work closely with the Project ever since. So you will find that her ideas are closely aligned with ours. She's written lots of books that are spectacular—don't miss the chance to teach with either *For the Good of the Earth and the Sun* or *Awakening the Heart* at your side.

Although I definitely hope you give yourselves shoulders on which to stand, I also hope that you regard this gap in our Units of Study as an invitation for you and your colleagues to invent lots and lots of your own ideas. By now, you know that the way to do that is to bring a couple of poetry books and set them in the middle of your table, and bring, also, some sharpened pencils.

PUBLISHING ANTHOLOGIES:
A CELEBRATION

IN THIS SESSION, WRITERS WILL HAVE AN OPPORTUNITY TO SEE THEIR WORK "PUBLISHED" IN BOOK FORM, AND TO EXPERIENCE THE THRILL OF RECEIVING "REVIEWS" ON THEIR CONTRIBUTION TO THE CLASS SHORT-STORY ANTHOLOGY.

GETTING READY

- Children need to have been assigned roles for leading the day
- Small group of children need to have prepared a choral reading of a poem
- Bound (stapled or otherwise) anthologies of the students' short stories, including "about the author" paragraphs for each child
- Gift box or bag to hold all the anthologies
- Class of peers needs to join the celebration
- Sheets for reader feedback for each author, headed "Critics Agree"
- Refreshments
- Decorations—streamers, balloons, or just a few carnations in a cup—to create a festive atmosphere
- See CD-ROM for resources

When a novelist or short-story writer's book is released, it is common practice to have a book party. First the author reads a bit of the book, and then copies of the book are available. The author autographs copies of the book. Friends and fans attend the party, and sometimes reporters come too.

Today you'll want to give your young authors a taste of what it feels like to be a famous author at a book party. The guests this time will be other children, rather than parents. The stories to be shared are longer than children's other published texts have been, and it will probably be important for the writer to have a chance to read whole stories. This means that instead of convening the entire group to hear a few shared texts before dispersing people into small reading circles, you may want to start the small circles from the start—and you may have more of these circles, each containing fewer readers, to keep the pace up.

Writers always long to hear a response to our writing. One writer said that writing can feel like dropping rose petals into a well and waiting to hear the splash. So today, be sure that each child has a page titled "Critics agree . . . " (as in advertisements for novels which feature acclaim for the text) and be sure you create time for children to write on each other's "Critics agree . . . " pages.

Finally, remember that although children want responses from each other, probably you will be the reader who matters most to them. How will you let each and every child know that you have thought carefully about his work? I urge you, if you possibly can, to select a book that you believe in some way matches each writer in your class, and inscribe a message inside the front cover. If you can't afford books— give each child a poem!

> "Dear Author Claudia, When I read this book, Baylor's I'm in Charge of Celebrations, I thought of you because you have the gift of seeing and celebrating the small miracles that are everywhere in our lives. Cherish this talent of yours, because it makes you an extraordinary writer . . . and friend." or "Dear Lakeya. I've chosen . . . "

CELEBRATION

CELEBRATION

Create a drum roll leading to the event by recruiting the class to help make class anthologies of short stories and by inviting children to help ready the classroom for a book party.

Before the appointed time arrives, you will want the room to be dressed up for the festivities. Earlier, in Collaborating with Colleagues, I described the way in which children could work together to create carefully planned anthologies of stories, and to practice reading aloud and prepare for signing autographs. On the day of the event, children can help you roll butcher paper over the tables to keep soda and crumbs from spilling everywhere, and they can decorate that paper to turn it into festive tablecloths. They can also put a carnation in a paper cup at the center of each table and drape a roll of crepe paper wherever they think best.

Ask children to perform different roles in today's celebration. Two can greet visitors at the door, four can escort visitors to their assigned small circle, one can explain how the

COACHING

This celebration will have a different feel than the other events. Those celebrations probably felt to the kids as if they were engineered by you, and given in their honor. This occasion will feel to the kids as if it is by and for kids. They'll probably enjoy it all the more (you may enjoy it less!), but in any case, this allows for the occasion to feel new, not like a replica of all the other author celebrations in your classroom.

Mirror Magic By Hannah

Angelina felt as though the devil started controlling the neighborhood children and made them not want to play with her during this beautiful weather. She felt as though a gate separated her from happiness and led her to misery. She felt as though she was captured in a paper bag that led her to boredom, nothing going on in her mind except for terribly horrid thoughts about the children playing outside without her – thoughts that are too horrible to tell you. So guess what she did? She dreamt her day away.

The dream wasn't that nice either but it wasn't as bad as her thoughts. She dreamt of one day sprouting out of her small five-year old self and blooming way up into the fluffy white clouds that tickled her nose. Then she stepped on all the children who didn't welcome her into their games. If they ran away she would reach out her longs arms and grab them, shaking them up and down, throwing them up into the air and catching them just before they hit the hard sidewalk.

Her dream ended when she heard her mother call from the kitchen to brush her hair. Angelina tossed and turned, moaned and groaned and finally rolled off her comfortable couch. Her knotted golden hair lay spread out on the white carpet. She felt as tired as a baby cuddled up in their mother's arms in the middle of the night, and she felt as heavy as an elephant sinking in sixty feet of deep water. So she pushed and pulled herself to roll over again and again towards the wooden stairs to get to the bathroom.

Yawning heavily, she pulled herself up the stairs. At the top she lay down and rested, practically falling asleep again until she felt a wet

Fig. XV-1 Hannah's final story

---

glob drop onto her face, which could only mean an Emimay alert! Emimay was Angelina's pet lab. She was as brown as a chocolate bar, and as friendly as when your best friend in the whole world smiles and waves at you.

Angelina quickly wiped the glob from her face away with her palm, and now with some energy she shooed Emimay off and walked into the bathroom. Her bathroom had tiled walls that were turquoise with white stripes and her bathtub had little paws to hold it up that always made her laugh when she was younger.

Angelina looked at herself in the mirror for a few seconds. She not only saw herself but the reflection of the kids that were playing outside. That was enough for her, she practically bounced off the walls. She jumped up and down again and again and then ran to the sink and banged her head on the white porcelain.

"What are you doing up there?" screamed her mother, who was confused and worried about Angelina. She lifted her face from the sink. Her head was a little red but otherwise no harm was done. "Nothing mother" she said, "I'm fine." Then she looked down to see if the sink was okay and to her surprise instead of the white porcelain, she saw something that looked like whipped cream! She dipped her finger into the soft cream and put that finger into her mouth. In that second her face turned pea green and she spit it out of her mouth onto the mirror. She looked as the slimy white cream that had trickled down and thought that it tasted like something she had eaten before when she was younger, not knowing what it was.

"That's it!" she cried out loudly. "It tastes like my father's shaving cream, he must have left it out!" Her face looked even greener as she

Fig. XV-2 Hannah's final story, page 2

---

remembered. Staring at the cream intently, she realized the it looked like an eyeball and made another eyeball next to it.

Her grandmother was visiting and she had put all of her make-up neatly around the sink. Angelina dipped her finger into one of her tanning creams that had bumpy lumps in it and she flung it at the mirror to make a messy nose. Now she needed a mouth. She used a red make-up pencil to trace her mouth onto the mirror. This delighted Angelina so that she also traced her eyebrows with the pencil even though they weren't red. The make-up that really caught her eye was a glittering gold body spray bottle that was the exact color of her gold shimmering hair. She gripped the bottle nice and tight and sprayed all around the eyes, nose and mouth. Now all she needed was to color in the eyeballs. She found a bluish bottle that glistened on the shaving cream. The best part of it was that it smelled like blueberries.

There staring back at Angelina was her masterpiece of all masterpieces that enchanted her heart. It had changed her boring day into a fabulous day. "Angelina" she heard he mother call. "Dinnertime, hurry, the landlord will be coming soon." Angelina glanced one last time at the picture in the mirror before she needed to go down to dinner and then gleefully skipped down the stairs.

She smiled throughout dinner eating all her veggies and slowly savoring her dessert. But her smile turned around when the doorbell rang and the landlord walked in. He hated them. He thought they were slobs and didn't like their sense of humor. Angelina and her family didn't care for him either.

His tie was purple, resting on his green shirt. His thick eyebrows were neatly combed but Angelina couldn't be 100% sure because the hair on

Fig. XV-3 Hannah's final story, page 3

---

his head was resting down on them, just about covering his green as grass eyes. He had a habit of fiddling his fat fingers, which bothered Angelina.

"So how's my baby doing?" he said as he patted a table to his left. "Fine" said Angelina's father, Tony. "Was I talking to you?" questioned the landlord as Tony turned around and grumbled under his breath. That basically kept happening between the two as they walked throughout the first floor.

Walking up to the second floor, Angelina felt as bored as she had in the morning but then she remembered her masterpiece in the bathroom. They were all heading in that direction when she stopped and decided to wait in case she was going to be in trouble. She heard her mother gasp and the landlord exclaim, "wonderful!" Her dad never liked anything the landlord liked, so as he was about to say "ugh" instead he said, "It *is* wonderful." They looked at each other, slapped each other's backs with a loud "thud" and chuckled, as they walked down the steps to have dessert together.

Angelina sat down at the table looking at her half eaten dessert of cherry pie and whipped cream listening to her father and the landlord chatter away gleefully.

"I guess my artwork brings people together", she said proudly. Then she frowned and said "Now I need to make something for my mother and the neighbors." She quickly gulped down her dessert and took out some paper, glue, string and a few markers.

Angelina's day had definitely changed.

Fig. XV-4 Hannah's final story, page 4

sharing will proceed, and several can be sitting in the small groups to welcome the visitors to those groups.

When the actual appointed time arrived, Colleen and I assumed our posts, and the children assumed theirs. Two were at the door, ready to say, "Welcome to our fiction celebration." Others escorted the visitors to the appropriate group, based on preplanned rosters for each group. Still other authors sat in the small groups, holding their stories, ready to welcome the newcomers to the small group.

Welcome the guests. Mark the occasion, and unveil the anthologies.

"Writers," Colleen said, waiting for the room to grow silent and for an aura of significance to grow. "Today we will have a book party which exactly resembles the book parties that are held for many writers across the world." Then she said, "In this class, we mark many of our biggest occasions by the sharing of a poem," and on cue, four children stood, gathered, and did a choral reading of a poem they'd chosen.

"Now's the big moment," Colleen said, and I brought a large box to her, setting it on the table. The children craned their necks to see what was happening. Colleen stood and bit by bit, unwrapped the beautiful paper from the box. Finally, she opened the box, peered in, and then back up as if to say, "Wow. You won't believe it." Reaching ever so gingerly into the box, she produced a stack of published anthologies—one for each writer and one for each visitor.

The books are delivered to each sharing circle, and one child after another read his or her story aloud. Afterward the class had a party, and during this time, children signed each others Critics agree sheets.

After the readings are complete, celebrate! During this time, children write responses on critics claim sheets.

You'll want to decide how to make the party a happy one for children. Do you want it to be the prelude to a special outdoor play time? Do you want the class to take a field trip after the party to the local library, which may have agreed to showcase the children's writing in a giant display case? Do you want to gather the class for some reflection about how the unit went for them and what they learned?

You can open the box in a manner which creates rising action—all the components of a story are components of an occasion as well!

If you decide to give your writers the gift of a story or a poem, at the end of the day, as children leave to go home, you'll want to give these out. Be sure that you also send a copy of the child's publication home with an accompanying letter to parents, asking them to give the writer very specific, detailed responses.

Superficial

Niki and Chloe walked into school. Kids were slamming lockers and papers were thrown everywhere. Suddenly, there was a smell so great it could make the flowers pop up. The smell traveled through the halls, past the lockers and over the garbage that was everywhere. It was fruity passion Herbal Essence. Niki looked. Soft blonde hair was swaying in the distance. There was only one thing it could be . . . Samantha Stillman.

Niki pulled on Chloe's arm. "C'mon, Chloe." They moved behind the lockers.

"What?" Chloe asked, still looking down the hall at Samantha.

"I don't want her to see me. She's probably going to make fun of my clothes again." Niki lifted her backpack shaking with fear. "I hate her!" Niki glared.

"She's not that—" Chloe stopped herself mid-sentence and looked at Niki.

"Don't tell me you were going to say that she's not that bad. She's terrible!" Niki wanted to scream out, but she didn't want anyone to see her behind the lockers.

"Hey!" a voice said. Niki's heart beat out of her chest. She looked up to see Samantha Stillman standing in front of her.

Niki opened her eyes wide and looked straight up at Samantha. "What do you want?" she asked shaking. It seemed like the walls were closing in on her. She wanted to walk behind the lockers, turn and run the other way, but she didn't.

"I just wanted to see your new, I mean, your clothes from the back of the closet," Samantha said laughing. Niki stared at her hard. Chloe looked at the floor. "C'mon, Chloe. We have class," Niki said. But Chloe just stood there. Niki wanted pull Chloe away and run down the hall. But she did nothing.

"I have a question for you, Chloe," Samantha said gritting her teeth at Niki. "Why are you friends with her?" Samantha motioned with her chin in Niki's direction.

"Because," Chloe said proudly. Niki gave her a nudge. Samantha stared. Chloe's face turned red. "She, um, well, I don't know. I mean—" Niki wanted to crawl away.

"I mean, like she has the worst taste in clothes, right?" Samantha said cutting Chloe off.

"Yes. I mean no. I mean I don't know!" Chloe whined. Niki turned away. She didn't get it. She and Chloe had made a pact—Best Friends Forever.

Sorry, Niki," Chloe whispered.

"Chloe," Niki said, turning around and wiping the tears from her face. But it was too late.

"Let's go," Samantha said. They all stood in the hallway looking at each other. Doors were opening and closing as kids went to class. Samantha pulled Chloe by the shirt and together they followed the rush of other kids.

The doors shut behind them as they walked off to class. Niki stood alone and wondered if it was worth being class president. I should have known after beating her last year in the election. If you mess with Samantha Stillman, she'll mess with you.

Niki started to walk to class, not sure which way to turn now that she was all alone.

Fig. XV-5 Beccah's final story

Fig. XV-6 Beccah's final story, page 2

Jane's First Sleep Over

One spring, sunny day Jane and Abby's families all went for a picnic in Central Park. They played baseball, tag, duck-duck-goose, and other fun games. Abby's brother Jack and Jane's brother Rob thought the baseball game was the most fun because they both scored runs. Jane's sister Anna and Abby's sister Robin thought the picnic was fun and they should plan another one again soon. The parents—Mary, Chris, Mel, and Kevin—thought it was a great idea to have another picnic in Central Park because it was big and there were great places to play.

Later in the day when the sun was setting over the carrousel and they were about to leave Abby asked, "Hey Jane, do you want to sleep over at my house tonight?" Jane's face froze for a second she didn't say anything; then Jane said, "I can't sleep over."

"Why not?" questioned Abby. Before Jane was able to say anything Abby added, "You aren't scared, are you?"

"No way, of course not," said Jane. "I just can't."

All of a sudden Robin and Anna started to chant, "Jane is scared. Jane is scared."

"At least I'm smarter than you guys!" Jane said as she huffed off. But Jane thought about how Robin and Anna were right about her being scared. She felt like a baby which made her feel bad inside. Why couldn't she sleep over at Abby's house? She'd played there a million times but she'd never slept anywhere but at her own house with her parents right across the hall.

Coincidentally, two weeks later, Jane and Abby's families had tickets to "Typo" at the

New Victory Theater. After the show, Abby asked again, "Jane do you want to sleep over at my house?"

"Why don't you sleep over at my house?" said Jane.

"But I always sleep over at your house and you never sleep over at my house. I think Robin and Anna are right when they say you're scared to," said Abby.

"Well I'm not . . . it's just . . . I don't want to," said Jane.

"You don't want to! That hurts my feelings! Anyway, I think you're scared and you're lying to me. Maybe if you tried to sleep over at my house you might like it," said Abby.

"Fine," said Jane. "I'll do it just to show you I can. See you Friday night after school."

When Jane walked away she thought "I hope I won't embarrass myself and start crying like a baby for my Mom and Dad or worse wake up in the middle of the night and want to go home. Yikes! I can't believe I just said 'Yes'," thought Jane. "But I have to because Abby looked so excited and I did say I would."

Friday came along quickly and Jane was pretty nervous and excited at the same time to sleep over at Abby's house. At first the girls were having a blast. Jane and Abby watched their favorite movie "Elf" and said the lines they knew by heart. They played Candy Land and watched the Disney Channel. They painted each other's nails and put on make-up. They ordered Chinese food and ate until their stomachs ached. Abby's Mom came in the room and told the

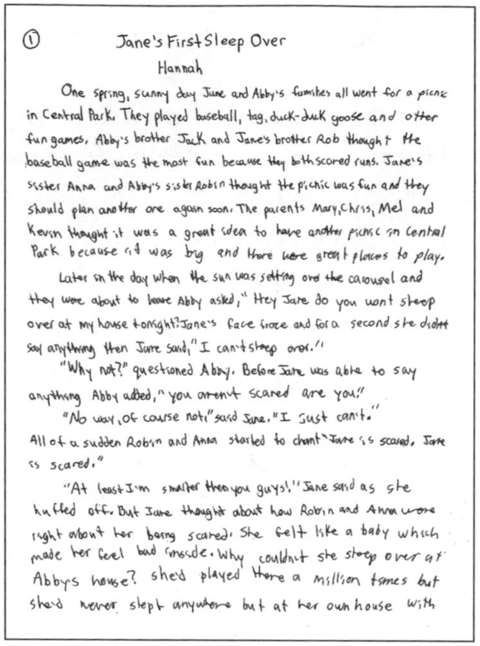

Fig. XV-7 Hannah's final story

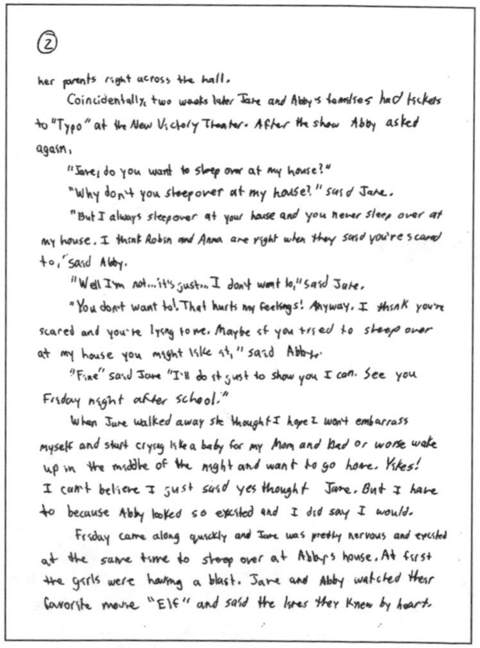

Fig. XV-8 Hannah's final story, page 2

girls it was time for bed. As Jane got into the bed next to Abby she started thinking about her mom and dad. She got quiet and her eyes filled with tears. Abby noticed and said, "Let's play one more game in the dark with a flashlight so my parents won't see the light on." The girls played game after game of War until Jane and Abby fell asleep.

Jane woke up the next morning when she heard Abby in the bathroom brushing her teeth. As she laid in bed she smiled thinking about all the fun she had and how proud she was that she made it through the night without her parents. She couldn't wait to tell her family how much fun she had and how she wanted to to do it again soon.

Spencer Bellhorn is not a Wimp by Caleb

Fifteen minutes had past and I was tired of watching the charcoal-black squirrel run up and down the big oak tree that shaded Kolben St. from the bright morning sun.

Where was Sarah? Had she forgotten? No, Kolben St. had been our meeting spot for the past three years. She's probably sick, I reassured myself. "Yeah," I mumbled, "sick." and set off to school.

"How's it going?" yelled Mr. Crabapple from his porch.

"Great!" I lied.

Then Mr. C smiled a smile I wish I could smile. But I couldn't. I could only manage a frail grin, like the one you see from a sick grandmother. I bit my lip until I couldn't feel it anymore. My eyes twitched side to side like a nervous squirrel. I closed my eyes and repetitively muttered, "Sarah's with me, Sarah's with me, Sarah's with me." trying to convince myself she really was . I walked past every house like in it was a man with a knife.

That day elm trees leading to the playground of the Mario Gabinetto School seemed bigger, but then again, so did everything.

"Auggghhh!" screamed a voice as something

Fig. XV-10 Caleb's final story

---

collided with my chest. Then all I felt was the hard playground concrete against my cheek.

"Sorry." I apologized as I stood up and brushed myself off.

Watch where you're goin'!" growled a voice that I thought I had heard before. All at once I realized I what I had bumped into.It was Humphrey Dugbill, the meanest bully in the history of Butts, Missouri.

I absent-mindedly tried to walk away so that the oversized predator wouldn't prey on me. My puny frame is no match for his bulgingm one. I wanted to shrink and shrink till he couldn't see me anymore. Well, well, well if it isn't Spencer Bellhorn! About to get beat up and without your girlfriend to protect you!" he emphasized the word girl a lot.

"Any last words?"he asked smugly. What was I going to do? Where was Sarah when I needed her?

Right on time the 'Bading-A Dinga-Ding' of the 9:00 bell filled the air. "Saved by the bell, Bellhorn I'll see you after school!" Humphrey yelled over the crowd of screaming kids.

I couldn't pay attention to Mr. Jimenz in math class because I was thinking of a plan, a plan to defend myself against Humphrey. Could I run away like all the other kids had done? No, I would have to stick

Fig. XV-11 Caleb's final story, page 2

---

③

They played Candy Land and watched the Disney Channel. They painted eachother's nails and put on make-up. They ordered chinese food and ate until their stomachs ached. Abby's Mom came in the room and told the girls it was time for bed. As Jane got into the bed next to Abby she started thinking about her Mom and Dad. She got quiet and her eyes filled with tears. Abby noticed and said, "let's play one more game in the dark with a flashlight so my parents wont see the light on." The girls played game after game of War until Jane and Abby fell asleep.

Jane woke up the next morning when she heard Abby in the bathroom brushing her teeth. As she layed in bed she smiled thinking about all the fun she had and how proud she was that she made it through the night without her parents. She couldn't wait to tell her family how much fun she had and how she wanted to do it again soon.

Fig. XV-9 Hannah's final story, page 3

---

up to him. Then I a thought crossed my mind. Humphrey had never actually punched someone, he had just threatened to! So why should I be afraid? It was a risk, But also, it was the only way.

I stood in the playground of the Mario Gabinetto School to await my fate. If my plan worked, I would never need Sarah to defend me again. If it didn't, I would.

"Spencer?!!" growled a voice behind me, "I thought you would run away like all the other wimps. Oh well, all the better for me!" I didn't have to turn around to know who it was.

"Whatever, Humphrey." I said calmly. Kids of all shapes and sizes gathered to watch. I could hear a "Yeah Humphrey" chant starting in the crowd.

Humphrey braced himself. With his fist up and the grimace on his face he looked like a heavy weight boxer. I didn't pose like him. I just stood there, arms folded, and a grin on my face. He picked up his fist and pointed his elbow towards the clouds behind him.

Sarah's definitely not my girlfriend!!!!!!! This is gonna work!" I thought and grinned.

His fist shot forward. The grin faded from my face. I felt like Roger Clemens had thrown a fastball at

Fig. XV-12 Caleb's final story, page 3

---

my face. My head hit the ground. I lowered my hand to my upper-lip. I lifted it back up. I saw red.

Humphrey and the other kids smirked. Their smirk turned into a giggle and they started to walk away like I wasn't really there. I needed help, couldn't they see that. They just left me, in the dirt, like I wasn't there.

I wanted to cry, I really did.

Then I remembered Humphrey's words; 'I thought you would run away like all the other wimps' I didn't run away! I wasn't a wimp. Even though I was standing there with a bloody nose, I felt like I had won. It was then that I realized that everyone at one point in his or her lives needs to be protected. Even the mighty Roger Clemens has bodyguards, and he isn't a wimp, I'm not a wimp.

Spencer Bellhorn is not a wimp.

Fig. XV-13 Caleb's final story, page 4